Regression Healing II: Joe & Marilyn

Wendy Rose Williams

REGRESSION HEALING II: JOE & MARILYN
COPYRIGHT © 2024 WENDY ROSE WILLIAMS

PUBLISHED BY WENDY ROSE WILLIAMS
KIRKLAND, WASHINGTON, USA

REINCARNATION/ BODY, MIND & SPIRIT/ SELF-HELP
FIRST EDITION 2024
PRINTED IN THE UNITED STATES OF AMERICA

10 9 8 7 6 5 4 3 2 1

ISBN 979-8-9853497-3-3

EDITED BY SIAN PHILLIPS, HTTPS://SIANPHILLIPS.IE/

COVER DESIGN BY CUSTOMCOVERPRO.COM
COVER IMAGE BY LEILANI DOORNBOSCH

Dedication

I'd like to express my warmest gratitude to the talented hypnotherapists who facilitated my sessions shared in this book, and to the Marilyn client who allowed me to serve as her Past-Life Regressionist.

Thank you Angie, Carole, Deborah, Faith, Lynn, Marcella, Starfeather, Simon and Travis. I appreciate your help to let go of 'what will other people think'; to establish pristine boundaries; and to master forgiveness.

Table of Contents

"You Are Not a Human Being Having a Spiritual Experience. You Are a Spiritual Being Having a Human Experience."

– Pierre Teilhard de Chardin

Prologue

I was introduced to the concept of past-life regression in 2010 when I read Dr. Michael Newton's best-selling "Journey of Souls." I had my own initial therapeutic past-life regression in 2011. A lifetime of anxiety was resolved in a mere two hours, awakening a hunger to further understand and utilize this incredible healing modality.

I began to have countless spiritually transformative experiences during my own rapid and profound spiritual awakening. I yearned to know who I was as a soul, and to understand my life purpose. What was the nature of consciousness, vibration, and frequency?

My metaphysical deep dive included not only the most well-researched books and studies I could find in reincarnation and past lives, but NDE (Near-Death Experience) accounts, afterlife research, psychical studies and more. In addition to Dr. Michael Newton's case studies, I was fascinated by Dr. Brian Weiss' ground-breaking work with regression clients; Dr. Helen Wambach's pioneering research in group past-life regression therapy; Dolores Cannon's Quantum Healing Hypnotherapy Technique (QHHT) results and Dick Sutphen's soul mate experiences.

My belief system was challenged and changing so profoundly - and so frequently - that I felt uncomfortable much of the time. Wonderful, exciting things were beginning to happen, yet there was a lot of contrast in my life.

I was laid off as a single mother from a wonderful job that supported not only me but my two college-age daughters. My car was totaled when three airbags deployed during a collision that symbolically spun me around almost

1

three hundred and sixty degrees.

I recognized I needed to "step to the plate" energetically but did not know what that meant. I sensed a tall, lanky man with short dark hair near me with increasing frequency. It looked like he was wearing an old-fashioned New York Yankees uniform.

My family did not know what to make of my unexpected spiritual awakening. They were not having similar experiences and could not relate to mine. Multiple friends left my life in ways that at first left me reeling.

As I worked to make sense of my new world – my own "New Earth" – I concluded that our souls are eternal and that we have free will to choose to reincarnate where and when we want, and with whom. I believe the purpose is to learn carefully chosen lessons. I feel the soul craves experiences, above all else, to have an opportunity to progress.

I began to see that emotions are timeless and are stored at the soul level. I was now observing that trapped emotions could present physically or emotionally as pain, anxiety, depression, or disease. I embraced the techniques that allow us to heal and release these emotions.

You had to "feel it to heal it" as denying, projecting, or attempting to stuff one's emotions was a spiritual bypass that does not serve us well. I had a plethora of challenging experiences that showed me the importance of balancing the ego and the need to release fear to live a peaceful, loving, and joyous life.

To my surprise, I felt driven to train in my fifties as a past life energy healer. I studied with Dr. Brian Weiss, among other leaders in the field, to become a hypnotherapist specializing in past-life regression. I became a Reiki Master energy healer, a Certified Spiritual Teacher, and a channel. My goal was to help others lead a happy, healthy life, to unstick their creativity, and to discover their life path.

I began to fully embrace the power of forgiveness as a gift for myself, and to ground and clear my energy daily as well as to raise my vibration and frequency.

My friend in the blue and white striped jersey continued to make his presence known. I could sense, feel, hear, and see him in my mind's eye. I knew he was an old friend dating back to early childhood.

I felt conflicted about exploring who he was as I suspected he was famous, as was his wife. I did not want to work through those complicated implications. I questioned whether these experiences were an ego trick.

I was struggling to complete my life lesson "to let go of what will other people think!" That lesson clearly included resolving potential historic, biblical, and famous past lives of my own so that I could help others in this arena. I had learned exploring possible past lives of this type often required special support.

I needed a fresh perspective from a neutral party. I'd been working beautifully with my first spiritual teacher but felt she might be too close to the issue. Two talented psychics independently looked at a side-by-side photo comparison. They compared photos of my potential famous past life persona with photos of me in my current life at approximately the same ages.

Both confirmed the past life based on reading the energy, as did a numerologist. One of the psychics confirmed who my daughter had been in the past life in question, without my even inquiring.

I appreciated these validations greatly but needed to be confident of my own deepest truth. I contacted a friend who was not only insightful and level-headed but a talented Quantum Healing Hypnotherapy practitioner. I did not think she was a sports fan.

That felt important for neutrality as what I most needed to know was who was the man in the Yankees uniform? And why did I sense his gentle, wise presence around me so often? Was he truly offering me assistance? And if so, should I accept it?

It was time to put my fears aside and to have my own past-life regression to gain clarity. As a practitioner myself and based on my own previous regressions, I knew it was critical to have an open mind and to have my session without expectations.

I knew from my own training and experience that "famous past lives" can have many explanations. They can be an archetype, a fantasy, a case of mistaken identity where the person simply knew the famous person, or an imprinted memory from the Collective Consciousness. Famous, historic, or biblical past lives can be a delusion or attention-seeking on the part of the client – or even the therapist – if there are mental health issues or the ego is not balanced.

I considered fictionalizing this non-fiction account. But I knew if I did, I would not be in full integrity. I would not have let go of "what will other people think," which is an important part of my Life Path 33 journey. I would not have fully embraced who I am. It was time to step to the plate, and to spiritually surrender the outcome.

The past-life regression transcripts in this non-fiction account have been smoothed in places for readability and for teaching purposes. More information came to me during the sessions that I did not speak aloud but clearly recalled as I listened to my audio files while writing this

3

book.

Here's to discovering your own deepest truths.

—Wendy Rose Williams

November 25, 2021

Chapter One – The Sandlot

A simple text message in October of 2016 changed my life.

My spiritual teacher had texted me, "Joe wants to speak with you. Are you ready?"

I gulped as this was rife with implications. No, I was not ready! But it was time. I had sensed Joe's energy around me strongly for more than a year. I left the kitchen and meditated for a half-hour in my bedroom before texting a reply to my teacher Birdie.

"Joe told me who I was in his timeline. It's a lot to accept. But I feel relieved. I needed this clarity."

She texted back quickly, "You've got your identity straight now. You know who you are and were. I'm here for you however you decide to proceed."

←→

I needed assistance to process the implications. I chose to have a past-life regression session with a friend a few weeks later. She had trained with Dolores Cannon for the Quantum Healing Hypnotherapy Technique (QHHT).

We spent about an hour reviewing the questions I had for my own Higher Self and Guides. My hypnotherapist helped me attain a wonderfully relaxed state, lying comfortably in my own bedroom with my eyes closed. She would be my skilled tour guide to help me access the wisdom of my own subconscious.

A past-life regression is a gentle way of accessing the client's own sacred knowledge that they cannot typically retrieve. It is not a psychic past-life reading with the hypnotherapist suggesting or telling the client who they might have been.

I chose not to share my memories and experiences with the man in the Yankees uniform to not influence my Past-Life Regressionist. She appropriately asked me open-ended questions as you will see from our conversation.

←→

(session in progress)

Hypnotherapist: "You're drifting down to the surface from your beautiful cloud - what is the very first thing you see or your first impressions as you arrive at the most appropriate time and place to stop and look at and examine?"

Wendy: *(slowly, sounding half-asleep)* "I see a – a - corner sandlot – like where kids play in the neighborhood?"

Hypnotherapist: "Okay. What else do you notice around you?"

Wendy: *(still speaking slowly – getting oriented to another time and place)* "It's a quiet neighborhood. I see some cars parked here and there – some big trees. The houses are far apart. It's a nice neighborhood. It's working class, but it's still nice."

←→

Hypnotherapist: "So what are you doing right now?"

Wendy: "We're gathering. The kids are coming around - we're putting together things to be able to play a ball game."

Hypnotherapist: "So you're going to play a baseball game?"

Wendy: "Well, it's really stickball. We don't have any bases. We don't have much equipment. We don't have a real bat. It depends on who shows up with what how we're able to play."

Hypnotherapist: "Okay, so it's impromptu. What sort of surface are you standing on?"

Wendy: "It's grassy where I am. There's some long grass. This lot isn't used much is why we pick it. It's sandy toward the middle. It's a sandlot."

←→

Hypnotherapist: "Great, so what kind of shoes are you wearing?"

Wendy: *(sounding surprised as she looks down)* "Oh, they're kind of beat up! They're cleats but they're so old. They're my older brother's cleats but they still have a good grip, so I decided to wear these."

Hypnotherapist: "So they're comfortable?"

Wendy: "Yes, they are, even though they're too big."

Hypnotherapist: "And they're good for running in the grass?"

Wendy: "Yes, they're good for running in the grass and in the sand because we have both."

6

Hypnotherapist: "Okay, that's great. And what kind of clothing are you wearing? You can look at your body from your feet on up."

Wendy: "I'm wearing shorts and a t-shirt. It's summer."

Hypnotherapist: "So it's summer. That's great. Approximately what age are you? Teens?"

Wendy: *(laughing)* "No, I'm nine or ten! I'm just a kid."

Hypnotherapist: "Does your body feel male or female?"

Wendy: "I'm a boy."

Hypnotherapist: "Can you describe the others around you?"

Wendy: "I see several of my brothers and some other neighborhood boys. There are maybe two girls watching, but only boys playing. It's just neighborhood kids. It's very impromptu. You just go ring some doorbells until you get enough kids to play a game."

Hypnotherapist: "That's great."

Wendy: "Plus you can hear when there's a game being played, so then more kids come out to play most of the time."

←→

Hypnotherapist: "Oh, that's great. How many brothers do you have?"

Wendy: *(casually)* "Oh, I have a whole bunch. Could there be at least six or seven of us? Or more."

Hypnotherapist: "So you have a large family?"

Wendy: "Yes, we have a large family."

Hypnotherapist: "Are you wearing anything on your head?"

Wendy: "Nope, there's nothing on my head."

Hypnotherapist: "Are you holding or carrying anything in your hands or on your back?"

Wendy: "I have one of the – the - oh, I see – it's like an old flour sack? It is an old flour sack. That's what we're using for bases. We fill them with sand and dirt from the lot to make the bases."

←→

Hypnotherapist: "Oh, great, that sounds like fun. And are you wearing any kind of watch or jewelry on the body?"

Wendy: *(snickering)* "Nah, I'm just a kid!"

Hypnotherapist: *(smiling)* "Okay. Does your body feel healthy?"

Wendy: "Yes, but I wish I was bigger. I'm one of the littler, youngest kids. I'm little, but I'm scrappy."

Hypnotherapist: *(smiling)* "Okay, and do you know what your hair looks like? Is it long or short and how about the color?"

Wendy: "My hair is short and dark. I think my mother

cuts it?"

Hypnotherapist: "Is it straight or wavy?"

Wendy: "It's straight."

Hypnotherapist: "Okay, great, it's straight. And do you know where you live in relation to where you are right now for the game?"

←→

Wendy: "Sure, I live just up the block – I'm like three houses away. That's why we could hear when a game was being played because the windows are open in summer."

Hypnotherapist: "Fabulous. Before the game starts can we go to your house? Do you walk or run home when you check in?"

Wendy: "I walk home."

Hypnotherapist: "As you approach the front of your house, can you tell me what it looks like?"

Wendy: "It's older – kind of sprawling - it's not in the best shape. I think we're hard on it because we're a big family."

Hypnotherapist: "That makes sense. What else can you see to tell me about your house?"

Wendy: 'I'd call it hacienda style maybe? It's one story – it's more narrow on the street on the front from the road but then it goes back – it's pretty big, but it's really full as there's so many of us."

Hypnotherapist: "Do you know what it's made from?"

Wendy: "It's stucco – like a pale peach – it has some white shutters on the front."

Hypnotherapist: "What else do you notice about your house?"

Wendy: "I see a white door."

←→

Hypnotherapist: "A white door. So let's go ahead and enter your home and tell me what you see – what's the layout?"

Wendy: "The living room's on the left, the dining room is on the right."

Hypnotherapist: "Did you enter straight into one of the rooms or is there some sort of foyer or entryway?"

Wendy: "I was immediately in a little entry."

Hypnotherapist: "And how are the rooms arranged?"

Wendy: "You connect through the dining room to the kitchen – then there are bedrooms in the back.

←→

Hypnotherapist: "How many rooms do you think there might be?"

Wendy: "We have four or five rooms but you have to share – there are bunk beds squeezed in everywhere."

Hypnotherapist: "Who do you share a room with?"

Wendy: "My younger brother? The younger one, I think – the others are older? There's so many of us kids."

Hypnotherapist: "Do you know your younger brother's name? Does it pop into your mind?"

Wendy: *(long pause)* "It might be Jimmy. Or Donny, maybe? I'm not sure. There's a lot of us here."

←→

Hypnotherapist: "That's okay. Are your parents home?"

Wendy: "Yes, Mom's in the kitchen. She's cooking. Oh, I see – I was supposed to come home, she called us for dinner! Dad will be home from work soon. That's why we came home, to wash up and to help carry things to the table."

Hypnotherapist: "Oh, that sounds nice. How do you feel about that?"

Wendy: "It's happy, it's busy, everybody's talking at once – it's good."

Hypnotherapist: "As you look around the kitchen is there anything valuable or important to you? Are there any family dishes or anything you really like?"

Wendy: "I like the kitchen nook built in. You can't fit many of us in it – you can squeeze maybe four or five. We use it only at breakfast or lunch in shifts. We usually eat at least dinner together at the bigger table in the dining room, but I like the kitchen nook."

Hypnotherapist: "That sounds cozy. Where is it located?"

Wendy: "It's in the corner by the two windows – there's one window on each side."

Hypnotherapist: "Good. Let's move forward in time when you're sitting down for the meal. How many people are at the table? Look around carefully - you can see this very clearly."

←→

Wendy: *(slowly, counting people aloud)* "Wow – there's eleven of us – I see eleven in my family!"

Hypnotherapist: "How is everyone sitting?"

Wendy: "My father is at the head of the table where you come in the door from the outside - from the front door. My mother at the foot by the kitchen."

Hypnotherapist: "So it really is a big family."

Wendy: "Yes, it's loud and chaotic at times. There's a lot of us. We're really squeezed in elbow-to-elbow to get all of us at this one table."

Hypnotherapist: "Do you ever have people over for dinner?"

Wendy: *(laughing)* "Are you kidding? Where would we fit them. It's very small in here. The table is practically touching the walls with the chairs around it. When we were smaller, we'd sit two to a chair."

9

Hypnotherapist: "Oh, I see."

Wendy: "Sometimes we might have one friend, but not one each."

Hypnotherapist: "I understand."

←→

Wendy: "We're overrunning this small place. It's much smaller than I thought when I first described it to you today. Maybe I was describing the entire building and we live in an attached unit? I'm not sure."

Hypnotherapist: "That's okay. Just focus on what you can see now."

Wendy: "Luckily the weather is nice here much of the time, so you can be outside a lot. We have a big table outside in the back yard – it's under a roof thing – what is that called?"

(long pause)

Wendy: "I know – it's an awning!"

Hypnotherapist: "What does the backyard look like?"

Wendy: "It has a patio, and we use it a lot, too. That's all that's back here. It's quite small."

←→

Hypnotherapist: "Okay, let's go back inside to the family meal at the big table. Can you look down on your plate and at the table and tell me what you're having for dinner?"

Wendy: "I see roast chicken and green beans and some mashed potatoes."

Hypnotherapist: "Is this something you like?"

Wendy: *(enthusiastically)* "Yes, this is one of my favorites. My mother is a great cook!"

Hypnotherapist: *(smiling)* "Oh, that's great. Will you be going out to play ball after dinner or tomorrow, do you know?"

Wendy: "Tomorrow is church. Today is Saturday. I think that's why we're having roast chicken dinner? We'll go to church in the morning and then we can have play time, free time in the afternoon, but we need to visit Grandma first."

Hypnotherapist: "Oh, very good. Well, let's move forward to the next day. After your commitments are fulfilled – you go to church, you visit your grandmother – what do you do then?"

←→

Wendy: *(enthusiastically)* "We want to play ball! We can't wait to get out of our church clothes. Oh – wait – we can't play until we hang up our church clothes and put them away right away."

Hypnotherapist: "Very good. What do you wear to play baseball?"

Wendy: "Let me look. It's cooler today, so we're wearing

10

jeans if there are jeans in our size, or pants like chinos? Whatever we have that we're allowed to play in."

(pause)

Wendy: "We don't have a lot of clothes – there's so many of us. There's only one bureau for the boys and the clothes are sorted by size in different drawers. The smallest ones are in the bottom drawer, and you work your way up by size. We don't really have our own clothes except for special occasions like church."

Hypnotherapist: "I see. What happens next?"

Wendy: "Some of my brothers put shorts on, or pants. T-shirts."

Hypnotherapist: "Where are you now?"

Wendy: "We're ready to play."

Hypnotherapist: "Ok, move forward in time. Place yourself ready to play stickball – back at the sandlot."

← →

Hypnotherapist: "What's happening there? What's the feel of the game – does everyone get along?"

Wendy: "There were few conflicts – they're good-natured. We always worked it out. You knew these were people you were going to continue to know and play with – your family, your neighbors – there aren't many people moving in and out of the neighborhood."

(pause)

Wendy: "Everyone was smart enough to know you needed to get along. This was an important lifelong skill for me to learn. It served me well."

Hypnotherapist: "Good. And what position do you usually play?"

Wendy: "Umm – I was playing a lot of second base at first, but now that I'm getting older I'm playing center field more."

← →

Hypnotherapist: "Let's say there's somebody that just made a fantastic hit – it's coming toward you and you're not paying attention – what do your teammates call you to get your attention?"

Wendy: *(no hesitation)* "Joe. They'd say 'Heads up, Joe! Pay attention, Joe.' "

Hypnotherapist: "How old is Joe now?"

(Wendy continues speaking as Joe)

Joe: "I'm thirteen. I was thinking about a girl."

(pause)

Joe: *(laughing)* "I got distracted."

Hypnotherapist: "Let's move forward to an important event – something that feels important to you and tell me where you are now."

← →

REGRESSION HEALING II: JOE & MARILYN

Joe: "I'm still going to school – I'm in high school now. A couple of my brothers finished with school. They're out of the house. There's more room at home. Mom and Dad are looking a little older."

Hypnotherapist: "Do you have a girlfriend yet?"

Joe: *(sighing)* "It's hard to understand this whole girl thing. There's this girl I like – she's so pretty, but I don't know how to talk to her or relate to her well. So mostly I just admire her."

Hypnotherapist: *(smiling)* "Okay."

Joe: *(ruefully)* "I can't figure out my approach. So much for growing up with all those sisters!"

Hypnotherapist: *(laughing)* "Let's move forward in time to Joe's early twenties. Where do you find yourself now?"

←→

Joe: "I was able to work my way into professional ball. One of my older brothers was fortunate to get drafted to the minors. A player on his team got injured, so my brother talked the manager into calling me up from where I was playing ball."

(pause)

Joe: "I'm going to get to play for the big team over time!"

Hypnotherapist: "Was there a certain team you played for as Joe?"

Joe: *(smiling happily)* "Yes – for my whole career."

Hypnotherapist: "So as things unfolded, did he play professional baseball?"

Higher Self: "Yes, he did!"

Note: Joe begins referring to himself in the third person. He is now speaking as his Higher Self. The soul level consciousness is also referred to as the Super Consciousness. Some think of it as the subconscious.

←→

Hypnotherapist: "Who did Joe play for?"

Higher Self: *(sounding coy)* "Why, his favorite team!"

Hypnotherapist: "Who was his favorite team?"

Higher Self: *(laughing)* "The Yankees, of course."

Hypnotherapist: "You played for the New York Yankees?"

(Joe takes over for the Higher Self and speaks in first-person)

←→

Joe: *(with great joy and gratitude)* "Yes! My entire professional career was with the Yankees once I was called up from the minors."

Hypnotherapist: "How does that feel as you remember being Joe?"

Joe: 'It was so rewarding to play with my older brothers first for the Seals, and then to move all the way across the country to New York City and to play for the big team."

(pause)

12

Joe: "It was a big deal to move to New York from a more rural part of California. We drove all the way across the country to get to New York City. I was so excited! I was only in my early twenties."

Hypnotherapist: "I can see why. What else are you feeling as you go through these major changes?"

←→

Joe: "I just feel truly fortunate. This is the American dream!"

Hypnotherapist: "Is this profession fulfilling to you, would you say?"

Joe: "Yes, absolutely. It's the most important thing in my life."

Hypnotherapist: "So it's fulfilling you and making you happy?"

Joe: "It sure does for now. You can't do this for more than ten to fifteen years if you're lucky – but I'm giving it my all."

←→

Hypnotherapist: "Okay, that's great. Let's switch gears and look toward a significant partner. Do you meet one?"

Joe: "I meet a nice girl and it's time to settle down. We date, we laugh together, we get married."

Hypnotherapist: "Great. Does that change or influence your career?"

Joe: "No, I can't allow it to. Professional sports are a very short window. I'm still playing – she doesn't love it when I travel, but sometimes she can see a game if it's not too far away."

(pause)

Joe: "Baseball is a long season. They work us hard eight or nine months of the year, but she understands this life and it's not forever. She knows I'm true to her, so that's not a problem."

Hypnotherapist: "Do you feel comfortable being faithful?"

Joe: "My wife knows I keep my nose clean and that's easy to do. She knows I come from a family with good old-fashioned values. We saw Dad very faithful with Mom and..."

(Joe interrupts himself; sounding thrilled)

←→

Joe: "Oh, wow – look at that! We have a child now – we have a son. I have a son! Man, oh man – I have a son!"

Hypnotherapist: "Oh, good, I was just going to ask you that. As you look further ahead – do you have more children together?"

Joe: "Things are changing – a lot of things are changing."

(pause)

Joe: "I need to sort this out to see the best way to explain it to you. I need a minute of silence."

13

REGRESSION HEALING II: JOE & MARILYN

Hypnotherapist: "Okay, just take your time."

(long pause)

Joe: "She's not as happy with the lifestyle."

Hypnotherapist: "Do you know why?"

Joe: "Let me try and understand this from my wife's perspective."

(pause)

Joe: *(speaking more and more rapidly)* "I see, it's harder for Dorothy once we have a child. It's a lot of lonely nights for her because she's home alone with our son, and I need to be away playing ball. There's not really anything I can do about it. I'm doing what I'm supposed to be doing and I'm quite fortunate to have this career."

(pause)

Joe: "She knows it, but there's resentment building. Wait a minute – something is happening..."

(pause)

Joe: "There's also a lot of unrest not just in the country but in the world. Oh, this is bad – oh, this is unbelievably bad – oh no, this is a World War. Oh my God, this is World War II coming!"

(sound of Joe's ragged breathing)

←→

Hypnotherapist: "World War II is starting?"

Joe: "Yes. But there's more. Oh no, we're getting divorced. This is a big issue – I'm a Catholic."

(pause)

Joe: "This was not done lightly, but we're not happy. Neither of us is happy. We're fighting all the time now – this isn't good for our son. This isn't good for us. We can't work it out."

(long pause)

Hypnotherapist: "What happens?"

Joe: *(sadly)* "We get divorced."

Hypnotherapist: "Okay – do you continue to play baseball?"

←→

Joe: "No, I volunteer."

Hypnotherapist: *(sounding surprised)* "You volunteer for what – the military?"

Joe: "Yes, I volunteer to serve in World War II. I really feel I need to help. I've been so fortunate with my life playing ball, and with my family."

Hypnotherapist: "What will that mean for your career?"

Joe: "It's a huge risk – it's a big sacrifice, honestly, to lose what may be some of my best playing years. I don't know if I'll be able to get back into pro ball, but this is the right thing to do. I've already had so much – this is a way to give back a little. It's the right thing to do."

14

Hypnotherapist: "Where do you serve?"

Joe: *(flatly, sounding embarrassed)* "They're not going to let me anywhere near the front lines. They call it something like – ummm – Public Relations?"

(pause)

Joe: "Let me sort this out. Oh, I see – they want me to help with morale for the troops. The brass is touring me different places to help keep morale up for the enlisted men."

Hypnotherapist: "How old are you, approximately?"

Joe: "I'm in my early thirties. No, I think I'm just thirty, so I can still relate to most of the men. As I look around there are too many young faces here."

(pause)

Joe: "There are so many eighteen to twenty-year old boys. This is terrible. So many will die. My gut is just churning. Feels like an ulcer starting."

(pause)

Joe: "I'm young enough I can still relate to them and more importantly, them to me. I'm not like a fifty-year-old has-been. These young men can still relate to me."

Hypnotherapist: "That's great – is there anything significant during the war that influences you in a profound way? Let's move forward in time to that moment."

←→

Joe: "Yes. I meet my second wife. She's in a similar role – she's entertaining the troops – she is so loved. She is incredibly popular!"

Hypnotherapist: "You meet her as you move around during your military Public Relations work?"

Joe: "Umm – I think so?" *(Speaking slowly, feeling confused by the timeline as to when he met his second wife – did she entertain the troops in a different war? A later war? The therapist moves on before he can sort it out.)*

←→

Hypnotherapist: "Let's move forward in time – what happens then in your relationship with your second wife?"

Joe: "We become friends. We go slowly for a couple of reasons. I've been married before and there's an age difference. I'm more than ten years older than her. I'm quite protective of her."

(pause)

Joe: "Also, she's really launching her career. She needs to focus on her career. The question is are we meant to be friends or to marry? We're sorting that out."

Hypnotherapist: "Let's move forward to when that decision is made. What happens next?"

←→

REGRESSION HEALING II: JOE & MARILYN

Joe: "I was truly fortunate I was able to play for a few more years after the military. My second wife's film career is now really starting to launch."

Hypnotherapist: "What about your first wife and your son?"

Joe: "My former wife is on better terms with me now. My son is around ten. Things are stable enough that I'm ready to make a commitment."

(pause)

Joe: *(beaming)* "We get married! I marry for the second time."

Hypnotherapist: "Are you still playing baseball?"

Joe: "No, I had retired before we got married. I was starting to have some significant pain – foot pain, back pain, other issues. Baseball was so good to me, but my body has had enough."

←→

Joe: "Wendy is still carrying a lot of that pain. She needs to let it go now that she's remembered this life. It was a link she has so many of my same injuries though she never played sports. She can let it go now. It doesn't serve her."

(pause)

Joe: "The past life bleed-through pain has been a push for her to be willing to admit she was me. She doesn't want to step to the plate and let go of other people's opinions."

(pause)

Joe: "Do those really matter? No, they don't. You just need to be true to yourself – to know who you are at the core - deep in your own heart."

(pause)

Joe: "She needs to let go of the outcome of what others think knowing that's not a true reflection of her. It's a reflection of them. She'll then be able to release the physical and emotional pain from my lifetime."

Hypnotherapist: "I was just going to ask you if any of those injuries were still impacting her now. That's quite helpful to know. Let's release that pain."

(pause)

Joe: "Yes."

Hypnotherapist: "Let's look forward to overview the rest of that life – was the rest of that life satisfactory to you? Let's move forward in time."

(long pause)

←→

Joe: "I retired in my late thirties I think. No, my mid-to-late thirties. Your question covers a lot of ground because I lived to be an old man. I didn't die until I was in my late seventies, maybe?"

(pause)

16

Joe: "No, I was in my eighties. I'm well into my eighties. I'm mid-eighties at the end of my life.'

(pause)

Joe: "It's too broad a question for me to answer for fifty years. Parts of it were very satisfying – parts of it no, they were not."

Hypnotherapist: "Okay, so let's move forward to you being in your eighties. Let's go to the last day of your life in this lifetime. You may watch this as an observer – do whatever is most natural to you. Where are you on the last day of your life?"

←→

Joe: "I'm in Florida. I live in Hollywood, Florida now."

Hypnotherapist: "What are your surroundings like?"

Joe: "It's a wonderfully comfortable home. I'm back in my own home now. I can afford medical care to come to my home."

(pause)

Joe: "I have friends and loved ones around me, visiting with me – their presence is deeply appreciated."

Hypnotherapist: "Have you suffered with an illness?"

Joe: "I have lung cancer. I'm okay with that. I'm ready to drop my body and move on. I'm ready to go Home."

Hypnotherapist: "Did the doctors do anything for you?"

Joe: "There wasn't much they could do. I was in the hospital for a long time. I'm happy to be back in my house now. It was around six months or so from the diagnosis to when I die."

←→

Hypnotherapist: "Do people know your time is near?"

Joe: "Yes, it's why I'm enjoying some visits from people I care about. It's surprisingly pleasurable. We reminisce and have some good laughs."

Hypnotherapist: "Do you feel peaceful? What thoughts flow through your mind if you realize you'll be leaving your body soon?"

Joe: "It was a life well-lived, in many ways. I have a few regrets that I'm trying to work through."

←→

Hypnotherapist: "What do you regret?'

Joe: "The divorce with my first wife and then another divorce with my second wife Marilyn."

Hypnotherapist: "Oh?"

Joe: "And my son became estranged. Wendy's daughter is mirroring that same energy. Same soul – same energy. Her daughter was my son when I was Joe."

Hypnotherapist: "What happened with your son?"

Joe: *(slowly)* "He couldn't handle my fame. We couldn't work out our relationship. I certainly wanted to reconcile.

17

He stayed close with his mother, at least. He was also surprisingly close with his stepmother Marilyn while she was still alive."

(draws in a long shaky breath)

Joe: "My biggest regret was I couldn't keep my second wife safe – she predeceased me by many years. Decades."

Hypnotherapist: "What really happened to Marilyn? We're talking about Marilyn Monroe, correct? How did she die? She was quite young."

← →

Joe: *(flatly)* "Yes, I'm talking about my wife Marilyn Monroe. She was murdered. I couldn't keep her safe, despite my influence."

(begins sobbing loudly)

Hypnotherapist: "You have some grief around not being able to protect her?"

Joe: "Hell, yes!"

Hypnotherapist: "Could you forgive yourself and the events that happened?"

(long pause)

Joe: "That's a struggle."

(continues to be wracked by sobs)

← →

Hypnotherapist: "What are you holding onto? What's hard to forgive? This was a long time ago."

Joe: "It's hard to forgive myself for not being there. We had reconciled after our divorce. We were planning to remarry, but she was killed a few days before our wedding."

(pause)

Joe: "That was so bitter – so traumatizing – I feel bitter now still. This is part of the pain Wendy is carrying."

Hypnotherapist: "Could you reconnect with your wife now before you leave your body?"

Joe: "I do all the time – I feel very connected to her. I feel Marilyn's energy frequently."

Hypnotherapist: "Do you feel any relief you'll see her after you die?"

Joe: "Absolutely. It's part of why I'm ready to go."

← →

Hypnotherapist: "Did you every remarry or have another significant partner?"

Joe: *(flatly)* "No. I didn't remarry. There was no want for someone new as there was no way to top her. I shut down in a lot of ways after she was taken from me – taken from all of us."

Hypnotherapist: "Let's offer this pain and remorse up to Spirit – let's forgive and release that energy. Let's leave it behind now. Is that a possibility, Joe?"

Joe: *(slowly – soberly)* "Well, I can forgive myself – I would

18

have prevented her death if it was humanly possible. I would have done anything to help save her."

(pause)

Hypnotherapist: *(quietly)* "Yes, I'm sure you would. What else is troubling you?"

←→

Joe: "I am having trouble forgiving those who took her out. I still feel some anger. That's not good for my future incarnation's body and our shared soul."

Hypnotherapist: "You're right. Let's find the best way to let the anger go. Are those your last thoughts as you exit that body?"

Joe: "Yes, it's hard to let go of those thoughts."

Hypnotherapist: "Can you take me up to when you leave the body – can you describe it for me?"

Joe: "It's very hard to breathe – it's so hard to breathe. I'm so very tired. I can't move the water out of my lungs any longer. I'm okay with that. I'm ready to go. I've been blessed with an amazing life in countless ways."

←→

Hypnotherapist: "What happens after you decide it's time to go?"

Joe: "I go to the Light quickly and easily – I just go up above the trees, I feel the pull – it's very easy."

Hypnotherapist: "Is there anyone with you?"

Joe: "No, I'm traveling swiftly by myself to get Home, to cross over. I've got these long legs, you see – I can move fast! It's part of why Wendy is so annoyed at times to be short – she remembers being tall."

(laughs)

←→

Hypnotherapist: "Tell me what happens when you cross over, Joe."

Joe: "I'm anxious to reunite with my loved ones, but I know I need to heal first. So, I go to a garden."

Hypnotherapist: "Do you stay there long? What's it like?"

Joe: "You stay there until you feel centered again. I need to drop the angst regarding my wife's death and not being able to resolve things with my son."

Hypnotherapist: "Is that son now Wendy's daughter?"

Joe: "Yes. The younger one."

←→

Hypnotherapist: "What happened with your son, Joe?"

Joe: "I tried to help him many times, but he was pretty – ummm – what's the word when you don't take care of yourself? He was self-destructive – drugs and alcohol and accidents – so reckless."

(pause)

19

Joe: "He struggled to keep on task and to keep it together. Life was hard for him."

Hypnotherapist: "Now that you're on the other side, does it make more sense what his life was about?"

Joe: ""Yes, I'm sure he learned a lot – his soul progressed. He learned what doesn't work. Some people are experiential learners. Wendy has one of those types of children – the one that was my son."

(pause)

Joe: "He did better in his first thirty years. He only lived into his fifties; I think. I lived much longer than he did."

Hypnotherapist: "Can you meet with him later here at Home?"

Joe: "Sure if I need to. Let me sort this out some more."

(pause)

←→

Joe: "Oh, gosh, did he predecease me? That's not natural – that's not good. That's sad when any child dies before you. It feels like we died around the same time, but he was already gone from my life by his choice. Sadly, it was like he was dead to me before I died. It feels like he died in the physical soon after me."

Hypnotherapist: "So you had two major losses – your son and your second wife."

Joe: "Yes. As I've been saying one of Wendy's children is the same soul as my son Joe. Also largely estranged from her now. Wendy had four pregnancies but only two live births – one of those pregnancies is my son Joe."

(pause)

Joe: "The pattern continues of the child being estranged. Wendy should heal this now to the best of her ability, knowing she needs to release the outcome. She can only do her part."

(pause)

Joe: "That other soul needs to do their part, too, regardless if they're on the planet or not. Despite whether the estrangement is due to being one of the births that didn't make it full-term or a child – a young adult – choosing to not speak to their father or mother."

←→

Hypnotherapist: "Yes, they do. Can you comment if there is much impact between your life and Wendy's? Are you possibly parallel lives meaning the same soul incarnated into two different bodies at the same time?"

(pause)

Hypnotherapist: "I'm not sure what years you were born and died as compared to when Wendy was born."

Joe: "Yes, we were parallel lives. We were both alive at the same time for about forty years. There shouldn't be this much bleed-over between parallel lives. Parallel or simultaneous lives are meant to be quite different to offer varied experiences for the shared soul to have the opportunity to progress more quickly, but she and I have some bleed-over between our lives. We need to straighten this out."

(pause)

Joe: "She is quite psychic. She had some sense of our relatedness even as a child when she would see me advertising Mr. Coffee on TV or would catch a news clip about me."

(pause)

Joe: "She would catch herself critiquing how I did the commercial or radio or TV appearance. It was like she had a deep knowing of how the commercial or appearance would go before she even saw it or heard about it because she was tuning into my energy."

←→

Hypnotherapist: "So what should she do about the bleed-over, if anything? Is it still affecting her now although you're on the other side? We talked about her having some pain now that seems related to your life."

Joe: "She should heal our parallel life imprint right now – the physical and the emotional bleed-through. It's impacting her physical health and her relationship with her child and with her future partner in a negative way."

Hypnotherapist: "Okay. We'd like to request any more feelings – any cords we can release, be released now to clean up the past and to get you to a neutral state. If that's possible, that would be fantastic. Can you do that for me?"

(long pause)

←→

There was a long silence, with the sense of everything in Wendy's life hanging in the balance...

Chapter Two – Marilyn's Mysterious Death

Joe finally replied to the therapist's question. Could he release his old feelings and emotions at the soul level?

Joe: "I'm trying. That's very hard to do."

Hypnotherapist: *(gently)* "Why is it hard to do?"

Joe: "I'm still angry regarding my wife's murder. That energy is still running rampant in this country in a lot of ways."

Hypnotherapist: "Can you tell me more what you mean?"

Joe: "Hmmm – I'm looking for the right words. It's what was going wrong with our country in the early 1960s. We got off our path as a country."

(pause)

Joe: "It's a murderous energy – it's a loss of innocence. It's like 'The End of the Innocence' – Don Henley's song."

(pause)

← →

Joe: "We have a lot of karma as a country – there's so much war energy. It's part of why Wendy incarnated at this specific point in time. She's meant to help restore the Divine Feminine in balance with the Divine Masculine, and to reinstate sustainable peace on the planet."

Hypnotherapist: "That sounds important."

Joe: "It is. Don Henley from the Eagles Band gets it. He had a hit solo studio album called 'The End of the Innocence.' He won a Grammy for it."

(pause)

Joe: "Wendy loves Don Henley and Glenn Frey's music not only because it's her high school music but because she recognizes them from their previous life together. Her current father was in that life, too. Oh, and her ex-husband.

They were Transcendentalists in Concord, Massachusetts in the 1800s."

Hypnotherapist: "Can we get back to what you were saying about our country getting off track in the 1960s – back when your wife Marilyn died? Let's focus on releasing that energy."

←→

Joe: "Sure. Those assassinations were really a corrupting of the White House and what the country was meant to be."

Hypnotherapist: "Which assassinations?"

Joe: "Marilyn's murder – President John F. Kennedy's – Attorney General Robert Kennedy's and Martin Luther King, Junior's assassinations."

(sound of Joe sucking in a deep breath)

Joe: "Dark days – dark energy. Bobby Kennedy stirred the pot too hard, and it took Marilyn down. That's why I publicly refused to shake his hand at Yankee Stadium."

Hypnotherapist: "Let's focus on cleaning up that energy as it pertains to you specifically, Joe. You're in the Healing Garden for this reason to heal at a soul-level. This helps all your future chosen incarnations, including Wendy. Is some of that energy retriggering in our country now?"

Joe: "Yes – it's showing up again in our politics now. We're hitting the lowest of the low to clean out the old energy for good. That's the path being taken."

(pause)

Joe: "It's like an infected wound – it's so deeply infected. You need to cauterize it, cut it out and clean it out for it to heal right – do you understand?"

Hypnotherapist: "Yes, I do. That's a good analogy. What else can you now see from the higher plane perspective?"

←→

Joe: "Oh, I see better now what was happening. Before it was just cover-ups, cover-ups, and more cover-ups. That reached its apex with Nixon and the Watergate scandal."

(pause)

Joe: "What we're doing now – with the candidates for the American President we have now – that's why they are so not wanted."

(Note: This past-life regression session took place in October 2016, a few weeks before the American Presidential election.)

←→

Hypnotherapist: "Are you referring to the pattern of their behavior?"

Joe: "Yes. It's being exaggerated for effect – Trump is like a character. This is to clean out the old energy by bubbling up the very worst of the worst, you see."

(pause)

Joe: "The reprehensible behavior – the total lack of class.

23

It's a sort of caricature. He's playing his part well and shouldn't be blamed for the part he agreed to play. That part is needed in the theater we're currently undergoing in the United States. It's happening elsewhere, too, including in Great Britain."

←→

Hypnotherapist: "So spiritually did the country need something that dramatic to get its attention?"

Joe: "Yes, exactly, you understand. It was to lift it up – to lift the country up, though most people don't understand this."

Hypnotherapist: "Can you tell us more?"

Joe: "I'll give you another recent example. It's just like President Barack Obama and his graceful, strong family – they came in a bit early in a landslide. They were a bit ahead of their time."

(pause)

Joe: "I want to be careful with generalizations – very careful, having suffered the sting of racial bias myself especially early on in my life and career. And let's look at how my parents were treated during World War II as enemy aliens because they were Italian immigrants."

(sucks in a deep breath)

←→

Joe: "This is a country with many citizens who are still racially and ethnically biased. They were not ready for a bi-racial President – a black President."

(pause)

Joe: "We now have a strong female candidate for President. Are people ready for that, even though Hillary Clinton's the likely win? She was a senator and Secretary of State as well as First Lady. She's arguably the most qualified candidate this country has ever seen."

(pause)

Joe: "But we have major purging going on. Is this country ready for a female President after a black President? Or are they going to go for Trump as an outsider to clean it all up in a not-so-fun way?"

Hypnotherapist: "You're exploring this quite well. Tell me more."

←→

Joe: "This leads back to the Kennedys being assassinated. Two Kennedy brothers, as well as Marilyn Monroe and the Reverend Martin Luther King, Junior. It's all related."

(pause)

Joe: *(sighing heavily)* "All these amazing bright lights were extinguished. It weighs on me heavily still now."

Hypnotherapist: "Do you think that may happen again – does it appear like it may happen again?"

24

←→

Joe: *(brusquely)* "I will not conjecture about that. That would not be wise. We're not here to fortune-tell. We're here to heal."

(pause)

Joe: "I will not poke at this energy – this is a place where angels fear to tread. They're telling me to pull back and mind my own business."

(sound of Joe breathing heavily)

Joe: "My parallel self has already suffered severe psychic attacks for having done work on behalf of mankind where angels fear to tread."

(pause)

Joe: "We'll have no more of that while she's in a body. It's not good for her. Some contracts needed to be changed on her behalf. The future is what we make it – we need to choose wisely for the generations to come."

←→

Hypnotherapist: "Yes, let's focus on healing. But is it similar with the public anger with the government? This is happening in many countries, not just in the U.S."

Joe: "Yes – that's what Donald Trump is specializing in stirring up. He is doing what he was born to do. He is doing what he is meant to do."

(pause)

Joe: "I'm not going to compare him to the man from Germany in World War II where the comparisons keep getting made. This is nothing to do with Hitler other than to show the darkness – to expose the darkness. Let's thank Trump for doing his job in such short order. It's been an ugly campaign, but one that was needed."

←→

Joe: "We need to be here in force to hold up the mirrors. The Lightworkers need to stand strong and to hold up the mirrors to bring in the Light to balance up these energies. The mirrors allow the Light to really come in and shine."

(pause)

Joe: "We need to embrace and heal the wounded dark places within ourselves first, like I'm doing today."

Hypnotherapist: "That sounds perfect. Do you need a break now or can we move forward?"

Joe: "No, I don't need a break. I'm less angry now that I remember and recognize we all play the roles we're supposed to play. My parallel soul-self can be less angry and heartbroken now, too."

(pause)

←→

Joe: "She's still releasing today. She still sleeps with a baseball bat under her bed like I did. She laid down her sword when

25

she restored her trust in the Divine. That was not easy to do, after witnessing the crucifixion."

(pause)

Joe: "Now she needs to allegorically lay down my bat and to not war but to instead continue to raise her vibration. She's safe – she's protected at the highest levels."

Hypnotherapist: "So she's processing it all okay – all this incredible past life energy she's consciously aware of, as well as a large life purpose?"

←→

Joe. "Yes, she is. She's strong mentally and as a soul. There's a price to having conscious recall of so many lives. Most could not handle it, frankly. It would lead to a psychotic break of some type."

(pause)

Joe: "It's why that information is normally stored in the Akashic Records and only retrieved when needed, but she fully opened her records herself in a most unusual way."

Hypnotherapist: "Why did she do that?"

Joe: "It was necessary to fulfill her soul mission. She's had to master healing and releasing past life energy at the highest level. It's one reason she's so good at helping people from around the world release past life energy."

(pause)

←→

Joe: "Wendy has developed exceptional clairaudience. She can speak with her Guides at any time and can hear them accurately."

(pause)

Joe: "She initially lost significant hearing in her left ear. The ear ringing was severe when all the Guides, Angels and off-planet beings came in to talk with her when she first woke up."

(pause)

Joe: "She can hear her Guides perfectly well now at the same time as she walks and talks among people in her daily life, whether it's informally or in a client session."

(pause)

Joe: "We have her ego balanced. We got her grounded in her body and on the planet, which was crucial."

←→

Hypnotherapist: "Does she translate from symbols like many psychics do?"

Joe: "No. She doesn't have to translate from symbols like a clairvoyant would or even from other galactic languages. She can hear one hundred or more unique guides, Ascended Masters and Archangels as well as many ancestors and animals."

(pause)

Joe: "She can speak so quickly and naturally for the Beings of Light most don't realize she's channeling the Divine at times. It sounds like natural present-day speech."
(pause)
Joe: "There are no long pauses or repetition, or backtracking like with many mediums and channels. Plus, she's channeled eyes open from the start."

Hypnotherapist: "That's unusual, isn't it? It's wonderful she can release this energy and serve as a channel. We also need to remember there was a plan before we came to Earth – let's relax into that."

Joe: *(sighing heavily again – releasing old energy)* "Yes. There's a cost to living – but so much to gain!"

←→

Hypnotherapist: "You were in the healing garden. Let's go back to your afterlife – where do you go next?"

Joe: "I reunite with my loved ones and my guide. I have my life review."

Hypnotherapist: "What is that process? Do you meet with a guide, or specialists? The Council of Elders?"

Joe: "Yes, it turns out well. In general, it goes well. They're joking with me. They're saying, 'You hit it out of the park, Joe!'"
(pause)
Joe: *(laughing)* "It was impossible to hit a fair ball out of Yankee Stadium – it was just too damned big!'"

Hypnotherapist: "That sounds wonderful. Is there anything else to learn?"

Joe: "They're complimentary in general, but they want me to work more on the healing to forgive myself and to forgive the others..."
(There was a long moment filled by the sounds of harsh sobbing)

←→

Hypnotherapist: *(gently)* "You can do this, Joe. Let it go."

Joe: "This is one of the hardest life lessons and skills. This is what Wendy is wrapping up this life. She's here to finish what I couldn't complete."
(pause)
Joe: "That's why we asked her to write her first book. And her second. Both are about forgiveness."
(pause)
Joe: "This is why she and the soul mate in 'Regression Healing I' had such challenging lessons around forgiveness, including forgiving oneself."

Hypnotherapist: "Is the book based on the importance of forgiveness?"

Joe: "Yes – it's the theme. And the consequences if people don't forgive. Not forgiving can lead to a lot of repeating energy cycles."

(pause)

Joe: "People can get stuck. There's a lot of ghost energy if people don't forgive themselves or don't feel worthy of going Home to the Light. They get stuck on the Earth plane as ghosts. Earth-bound energy."

Hypnotherapist: "What do you mean when you say ghost energy? Tell us more, please."

Joe: "Low vibration energy can take on a life of its own. It can create dark pits – vortexes – false holograms – stuck souls – ghosts. Not forgiving creates opportunities for lower vibration energy to get on-board – to spread itself around."

(pause)

Joe: "That's her second book – the ghosting from Plimoth Plantation in Colonial American times. She's cleaning up the ghosting karmic pattern."

← →

Hypnotherapist: "So what's the solution? Is there one?"

Joe: "It's very simple – just lift the stuck souls up to the Light! I don't know why we make it so complicated."

(sighing with exasperation)

Joe: "You don't need an exorcist very often, for Pete's sake, not that most of them knew what they were doing."

Hypnotherapist: "What was the problem?"

Joe: "Most of the church exorcists didn't know to clear the ghost or other low vibration energy up to the Light or down to Mother Earth. They ended up taking the ghosts into their own field. Not good. Not good at all."

(pause)

Joe: "Not understanding energy may be one reason we have such corruption in the priesthood at times. Yet there are exceptionally good men and women serving, too. I don't like generalizations as I mentioned earlier."

← →

Hypnotherapist: "So tell me more why ghosts are created and why they get stuck? What would be better?"

Joe: "We get stuck in the human experience too often. We're looking in the rear-view mirror back at our old life and feeling regrets, or anger, or not sufficiently mastering forgiveness or self-forgiveness."

Hypnotherapist: "Anything else?"

Joe: "In other cases we don't take long enough to heal at Home. We come back too quickly and re-open old wounds that weren't sufficiently healed."

← →

Hypnotherapist: "So looking back over your lifetime as Joe, was the main lesson forgiveness – was that the life purpose?"

Joe: "It was about many things. What you said is correct, but there's more. It was about service, and strong family

28

values. When you are given so many opportunities and are a public figure whether it's as an athlete, an actress or a musician, I believe service is key."

(pause)

Joe: "I feel strongly you owe some of your kindness, caring and time back to your fans and your public to help lift them up. It's your most important job. It's your moral imperative. It's likely your life purpose via a soul contract."

← →

Hypnotherapist: "So were you in that role as Joe?"

Joe: "Yes, I was. It was much easier in that era – the 1940s and 1950s. It was much easier back then."

(pause)

Joe: "It's so different now given the social media. It's so much harder to have the positive role models in Hollywood, in the sports arena and to shine that light into the public domain as was intended."

(pause)

Joe: "There's this little niche of country music that seems to get it right. There are some nice wholesome, humble, giving entertainers. Dolly Parton's child literacy program comes to mind."

(pause)

Joe: "Old-fashioned family values can really help with the headiness of what it's now like to live in the public eye. Having strong roots."

(pause)

Joe: "Few can handle it well."

← →

Hypnotherapist: "Are there any skills or knowledge from that life as Joe to bring to the current life as Wendy now?"

Joe: "Well, we're going to (meaning her whole spiritual team) make it obvious to Wendy why she was asked to help clear that White House energy although she is extremely apolitical. She does not like anything to do with politics."

Hypnotherapist: "Is there a particular reason she feels this way?"

Joe: "Yes, her strong aversion to politics and to the news is largely because she – I – our soul – was sucked into that political quagmire at that critical juncture in the late 1950s and early 1960s."

(pause)

Joe: "She – I – we – lost someone to that energy. It's why she was asked to help clean up that energy now in the Fall of 2016."

Hypnotherapist: "So has that been accomplished for her to understand this consciously?"

(Vibration rises as the Higher Self begins speaking about Joe and Wendy in the third person)

← →

Higher Self: "Yes, she'll get it when she listens to the recording from today. Let me make this crystal clear – Joe DiMaggio's wife Marilyn was a war casualty. She metaphorically got taken out by the same bomb that took out the Kennedys."

(pause)

Higher Self: "That made Joe and therefore Wendy a casualty, too, as they're the same soul. It is one source of Wendy's PTSD. She has been healing it by leaps and bounds. She's cleared about 98% of it."

Hypnotherapist: "Thank you for explaining that so clearly. Is there more?"

Higher Self: "Yes. Marilyn being Joe's friend – Joe's wife, Joe's former wife and Joe's future wife – she was so many things to Joe – and her being killed – murdered – had a big imprint on this soul having this session with you today. Thank you for helping her – for helping Wendy."

Hypnotherapist: "It's my pleasure. What else can you share with us in this vein? How can mankind best progress?"

← →

Higher Self: "We'd like people to look up to the Light and to trust it and to tune into it more. To realize politician and/ or famous lives need to be handled with a lot of maturity."

(pause)

Higher Self: "These roles are only chosen if they can be managed well. They are role-played before incarnating like a dress rehearsal before a play."

(pause)

Higher Self: "This is high-stakes – the planet is at risk."

Hypnotherapist: "Are others able to help? We plan complex goals together as groups at times."

Higher Self: "Yes. There's a lot of support for these big public lives from the other side and from soul group members, in most cases, depending if they can remove the veil of amnesia."

(pause)

(Joe took over narrating for the Higher Self)

← →

Joe: "Playing these big roles can be done and done well. I feel fortunate I was able to do that."

Hypnotherapist: "Okay. This is excellent. Regarding the lifetime as Joe, can we drift and float away from it, leaving those personalities there? We thank them and ask them to recede back to their own life where they belong. Would it be helpful to dissolve any past issues that are ready to release?"

Joe: "Yes, it would. But I stay nearer to Wendy than most past life personas do. We were parallel lives for almost forty years. I'm helping her and she wants my help at this point. I know to honor her free will."

(pause)

Joe: "She has the body now – she's in charge. When and if she asks me to step back, I do, and let her hit her own home runs. Yet I'm able to coach her in a uniquely powerful way."

Hypnotherapist: "That's good. It sounds like you're nearby much of the time?"

Joe: "Yes. It's why clairvoyants and psychics sometimes see me, if we allow it. Several psychics have asked her about the tall man in the baseball uniform standing behind her or next to her."

(pause)

Joe: "I can also easily step out of her field, or she can jokingly tell me to take a hike – I'm not stuck in her field. I'm not a ghost. I've healed at Home, and we took that healing deeper today."

← →

Hypnotherapist: "Okay, I think I understand. Let's focus on her – what else does she need that may relate to the life as you?"

Joe: "She needs to finish healing my injuries as quickly as possible as they're showing up in her body too much."

Hypnotherapist: "Where specifically? Can we heal them now?"

Joe: "My right foot – I mean her right foot – her left knee and below – her back and shoulders and neck. Possibly her elbows, her hands, her wrists."

(pause)

Joe: "She tore out both her wrists delivering her eldest daughter. She needed surgery on both wrists. She's had multiple surgeries on her right foot – major surgery on her back."

(pause)

Joe: "It's all past life energy that's been difficult to release. Playing professional sports took a toll on me like it does on any athlete."

Hypnotherapist: "So how do we best help her? She's in pain at times?"

← →

Joe: "Yes, though she's made great progress it's been a rough go as she's healing so many things from so many lives."

(pause)

Joe: "She also heals mankind, not just specific clients, or groups of people. I'm talking all of mankind. She's doing her galactic work, too. It's a lot."

(pause)

31

Joe: "She needs expert healers for a bit longer to help her heal her body and emotions. I don't want her to blame herself for it. It's a sign of strength for her to ask for help and to accept it."

(pause)

Joe: "She needs to practice receiving, and to be discerning which healers and people to allow in her field or even near her energy as it's rather unique."

Hypnotherapist: "Can she find the right people?"

Joe: "It's a bit isolating for her, but she can manage this. I had the same loneliness due to my fame, especially compounded with Marilyn's."

(pause)

Joe: "I'll help her handle her upcoming fame well. I'm good at it, and she's fully grounded now. She has balanced her ego well though that work must continue for a lifetime while one is in a human body."

←→

Hypnotherapist: "Thank you, that's quite specific. Now we would like to bring all the consciousness of Wendy back to the forefront – to fully return – to fully integrate to heal the physical body and to answer the questions she posed before this session for her Higher Self and Guides. May I speak with Wendy's Super Consciousness and her Higher Self, her soul?"

Higher Self: "Yes."

Hypnotherapist: "May I ask you Wendy's questions to help her in the best way possible?"

Higher Self: "Yes, you may."

Hypnotherapist: "The Super Consciousness could have brought forward any experience – why the lifetime as Joe?"

←→

Higher Self: "For many reasons – to master forgiveness. For her to master self-forgiveness. For her to remove the block to her incoming new life partner. He was involved in the murder of Joe's wife Marilyn."

(pause)

Higher Self: "There was some grinding – some angst on her part around their match as she hasn't been consciously aware of it. Think about consciously knowing your partner was involved in the murder of your previous beloved?"

(pause)

Higher Self: "It could be a great match. It would require her to fully master forgiveness, but it's still a question mark."

Hypnotherapist: "Has Wendy met him already?"

Higher Self: "No. They communicate telepathically and know they could choose to move forward as life partners."

←→

Hypnotherapist: "Thank you. Was there any other purpose

32

to show the life of Joe DiMaggio today?"

Higher Self: "Yes. For her to heal her discomfort around public speaking. To be willing to speak on the radio – possibly on TV or film."

(pause)

Higher Self: "To be willing to host in-person workshops – to become a published author and more. She needs to step out as a Past-Life Regressionist, to create a website, and to learn some social media basics."

Hypnotherapist: "So can she do it? This sounds like an important piece of her life purpose."

Higher Self: "Yes, it is. It will take time. Due to the scope of the role she's meant to play being so large, it kicks off fear."

(pause)

Higher Self: "Realize she's handling this all alone without a partner; with a family that can't comprehend her life purpose; with friends who keep disappearing or who don't understand these dramatic changes in her life as few can keep to her pace spiritually."

←→

Hypnotherapist: "That sounds hard. Is it supposed to be like this? What types of clients or business partners is she meant to work with, if any?"

Higher Self: "She doesn't need to accept every prospective client who is interested in working with her. She can refer out – she is not to take all comers."

(pause)

Higher Self: "She needs to become highly discerning. She requires bullet-proof boundaries to fully serve as she's meant to."

(pause)

Higher Self: "She so wants her partner to come in and help her hold the line. That's a reasonable request and true need."

←→

Hypnotherapist: "Should she open her home to clients? Would that be appropriate?"

Higher Self: "No, her one-on-one sessions are meant to be done remotely with her safe in her sacred temple of her home. We've cloaked her home and property for a reason."

(pause)

Higher Self: "We want her to do Skype/ Zoom type sessions with clients. She can then serve the best matched clients from all over the world while at her highest vibration."

(pause)

Higher Self: "She needs to keep her home private – a sanctuary – a temple. She needs to keep it beautiful and clean and to not have to clear other people's energy from it so regularly."

(pause)

Higher Self: "The vibration of her home is becoming so high some will be uncomfortable in it. It's filled with Archangels and Ascended Masters."

(pause)

Higher Self: "The high vibration of her home became an issue for her daughter. It's why she moved out so suddenly as a teen, without a word to her mother."

Hypnotherapist: "So she needs to keep work and home separate? Should she have an office location for her clients?"

Higher Self: "She's not meant to serve clients from an office location. That's why when she looked, she did not find anything suitable. We told her to perfect working via teleconference call and via Zoom."

←→

Hypnotherapist: "So it's best for her to do remote client sessions when she is alone in her home."

Higher Self: "Yes. We take her up and out of her body high up to the Light at times during sessions. It's best for her to not drive on those client session days and to be able to immediately meditate, sleep, shower or eat after a session – whatever we ask her to do to complete the energy release for the client."

(pause)

Higher Self: "She sometimes works with serious cases of child abuse or those who were tortured on-planet or off. She can help them heal in a profound way."

(pause)

Higher Self: "This is not a typical hypnotherapy service. She can well-serve the public if we send select yoga instructors or others to her to help. But they'd need to be firmly on the path and to have a specific need for her expertise."

(pause)

Higher Self: "I repeat, she is not to take all comers. Discernment is key. This is not being elitist – there simply needs to be a vibrational match."

←→

Hypnotherapist: "Thank you. How can she best heal her physical challenges? Can we do a body scan?"

Higher Self: "She needs to love her body exactly as it is for it to get better, and to link healing to a spiritual practice."

Hypnotherapist: "What else do you see with the body scan?"

Higher Self: "The root chakra is now strong. She's extremely well-balanced and grounded."

(pause)

Higher Self: "The healing work she did with the Native American Shaman was incredibly powerful. He was right to

34

call out her sacral chakra was the issue, not the root. The sacral is now the weakest of her seven chakras but resolving rapidly."

(pause)

Higher Self: "She's now strong energetically and the body is catching up thanks in part to today. Thank you for helping her."

←→

Hypnotherapist: "It's my pleasure. Is there anything else the body needs to thrive?"

Higher Self: "She needs more sleep. She's been sleep-deprived for years – no, decades. Most adults need a minimum of seven-and-a-half to eight hours sleep a night."

(pause)

Higher Self: "Sufficient sleep assists with weight loss because the body can heal. When she shorts herself in sleep, it makes her gain weight. It's a proven fact she's not accepting – many find it counter-intuitive."

←→

Hypnotherapist: "Thank you. Can we check in on the body – how is any chakra clearing going?"

Higher Self: "She feels a band across the sacral strengthening – it's doing very well. The Shaman we spoke of earlier replaced her sacral chakra with her agreement a few months ago."

(pause)

Higher Self: "It's like a baby trying to catch up to the adults. Today was quite helpful. It was a teen when we started today – the sacral chakra is now a young adult and will continue to progress well after this session."

←→

Hypnotherapist: "Good. She has lots of loud left ear-ringing to the point it damaged her hearing. May we follow this back in time? When did it start? May we go back to the original event that set this off?"

Higher Self: "Your protocol is good, but she needs something different than finding the lifetime of origin. That was already dealt with by the Shaman healer."

Hypnotherapist: "So what does she need?"

Higher Self: "A recent past life exacerbated the original cause. Old World War II energy is the issue. Specifically, the World War II nuclear explosion over Japan is stuck in her auric field. We need to release it. That's causing the ear-ringing."

Hypnotherapist: "How do we heal it?"

←→

Higher Self: "Call in Mother Mary. It's an old imprint from before her first life on Earth. It's been reinjured many times including the nuclear explosion. It's like an energy divet. Water keeps going back into it in the physical and it's reinjured again."

Hypnotherapist: "So can we heal it now?"

Higher Self: "I'm requesting Dr. Lorphan heal this for her. This ear ringing no longer serves her. She can hear Spirit at the highest levels with precise accuracy without it frightening her or making her question what she's hearing and what's happening in her life"

(pause)

Higher Self: "Her ear-ringing began before her Earth lives. It began galactically – cosmically. It made it harder to heal on Earth now as it's such an old injury – reinjure pattern. Many highly adept healers have tried to help her heal this challenge."

Hypnotherapist: "So how does it look now?"

Higher Self: "She needs to appreciate Mother Mary and Dr. Lorphan healing the ear ringing completely now as it's no longer needed. She can now understand what happened, how many times this occurred and let it go."

(pause)

Higher Self: "As Albert Einstein famously said, 'There are only two ways to live your life: as though nothing is a miracle, or as though everything is a miracle.' "

Hypnotherapist: "Yes?"

Higher Self: "She's choosing the miracle of returning to full health."

Hypnotherapist: "That's fantastic. Is Dr. Lorphan an astral plane doctor?"

Higher Self: "Yes, that's one way to describe him. He's an off-planet surgeon."

←→

Hypnotherapist: "Does she need to see an ENT physician?"

Higher Self: "She did that several times – we told her to stop. She doesn't need a brain MRI - she refused it. She knows she doesn't have a brain tumor."

(pause)

Higher Self: "She had several hearing tests with an audiologist. She knows she doesn't need hearing aids and other things she was told to prepare for. There is nothing Western medicine can do for her."

(pause)

Higher Self: "The Native American Shaman removed the implant in her left ear, but she couldn't immediately catch up to the healing. It was the only healing she couldn't master in the moment as the session with him was so all-encompassing."

(pause)

Higher Self: "With her permission, he facilitated major brain surgery for her with the Divine. He removed a tremendous number of old implants and mind-control programming from her brain."

← →

Hypnotherapist: "So are we continuing that work?"

Higher Self: "We're healing the residual. That Shaman-facilitated healing was profound. Picture agreeing to major psychic surgery on your brain. It was intense. She agreed and fully participated."

(pause)

Higher Self: "It was extremely positive for her and very well done, but it was only done in late July or was it early August?"

(pause)

Higher Self: "She didn't realize she's post-op. She was meant to be taking it easy in post-op recovery for three months. It's only October now, but he didn't mention the concept of post-op to her which is why I'm bringing it up. Knowing this will help."

← →

Hypnotherapist: "How can she keep opening and developing her five clair centers – particularly her clairvoyance?"

Higher Self: "Her clairvoyance will be extremely strong. It will come in fine. You can only take on so much at a time."

(pause)

Higher Self: "There's the concept of titration which she doesn't yet understand. Picture a medicine dropper – you only want so many drops to come out at one time."

Hypnotherapist: "So what does she need to do in the area of clairvoyance, if anything?"

Higher Self: "She's highly active in her spiritual work as meant to be. We're blocking her full clairvoyance purposefully right now as it would be too much for her."

(pause)

Higher Self: "Her clairvoyance will come fully on-line after the ear-ringing is resolved. We'll find a vehicle to do so, or she may notice it during meditation. She's correct we're blocking it from her right now as she sensed. It will come naturally soon and be quite full scope."

Hypnotherapist: "Is she prepared for that?"

Higher Self: "That's an astute question. Yes, there is wisdom in 'be careful what you ask for in life.' Make sure you're divinely guided and not reacting to the caprices of the ego."

(pause)

Higher Self: "We'll open her clairvoyance in a controlled way so she can function well in all aspects of her life. It won't be overwhelming. It won't be the trauma of the third eye fully opening and not knowing what's happening."

(pause)

Higher Self: "She's been asking why it felt blocked – it's been purposeful. The block will soon be removed."

←→

Hypnotherapist: "Thank you. May I ask one question for myself Wendy agreed to?"

Higher Self: "Certainly. You may proceed."

Hypnotherapist: "Why is my switch feeling turned off – my connection to the Divine? My need to write?"

Higher Self: "It's a new stage of life for you. You're balancing up – recalibrating."

(pause)

Higher Self: "You both can have it all. Just realize you should not have it all at the same time. It would be overwhelming. There are many energetic building blocks available to you both."

(pause)

←→

Higher Self: "Here's an example. Let's say your capacity for juggling is fifteen balls. The balls represent your energetic areas of interest. You now want that bright new shiny red ball and the glittery green ball. Please put two balls down first before you grab the new ones."

(pause)

Higher Self: "It's a capacity issue. Neither of you need to constantly increase your consciousness all the time. This is unusual – most people do benefit from that practice."

(pause)

Higher Self: "You're both here to practice being human and to have some limits while you're in a body. You're highly experienced souls who are used to being limitless."

Hypnotherapist: "Thank you. That's very helpful. Is there anything else I should know before we turn our focus back to Wendy?"

Higher Self: "Yes. Please understand your light didn't go out in any way – you refocused it. You deserve it. Just enjoy your marriage - kudos! Your connection with the Divine will be at a higher level when it's time to reconnect. All is as it should be."

←→

Hypnotherapist: "Thank you. That's wonderful to have confirmed. Let's talk about her finances now. I'd like to call in the best light and good energy for her to experience positive flow in this arena."

(pause)

Hypnotherapist: "Can you help her enjoy the feeling of easy abundance for a moment? I'd like her to enjoy the feeling of full abundance for a moment - of plentifulness – of excess beyond your needs."

(pause)

Hypnotherapist: "I'd like her to experience excess coming easily to her, including in unexpected ways – to just feel that for a moment. What does that feel like for her?"

Higher Self: "That's an excellent visualization. She's never had that in this lifetime. She's never lived in that place. It's not been an easy abundance for her. She's managed to live in some nice homes through working very, very hard – the homes were often at risk."

(pause)

Higher Self: "We're moving her out of poverty consciousness now. We'd like her to keep doing that visualization a few times a week – to move the old energy out, and the new energy in."

(pause)

Higher Self: "We'd like her to feel the satisfaction, the joy, the elation – to have more than what you need. We will harmonize that with the new energy – it's happening NOW – everything she wishes for is here NOW."

Hypnotherapist: "That's fantastic. Anything else?"

←→

Higher Self: "Yes. You teach what you need to learn. She should update her financial abundance vision board quarterly and have fun doing it. The energy gets stale over a year's time."

Hypnotherapist: "How can she surpass her cash flow needs?"

Higher Self: "By acting on tangible, achievable ideas in a steady way. She can easily increase her monthly income a few thousand dollars to start."

(pause)

Higher Self: "It's a river to ocean flow – it's energetically happening now. She needs to understand that publishing the first couple books is quite important for her. We encourage her to keep her focus there and do so as quickly as she can."

Hypnotherapist: "How will that go for her?"

Higher Self: "It's not about the book income, per se. It's getting the energy to flow. It's the client sessions – it's the radio interviews – but it doesn't end there. The book sales will come in unexpected ways."

←→

Hypnotherapist: "That sounds great. Is Wendy giving more than she knows?"

Higher Self: "Yes, she is. This will be quite counter-intuitive for her. We want her to get off the cross – to let go of that crippling work ethic – that WASP work ethic she was raised with via both her parents and her grandparents that if you need more money – you work! If you need still more money – you work harder!"

(pause)

Higher Self: "She almost worked herself to death a couple

39

times. She didn't factor in she's doing big mission and service work for mankind. She didn't understand her own energy limits while in the current body."

←→

Hypnotherapist: "So improving her ability to receive is critical to her life purpose, is that what I'm hearing?"

Higher Self: "Bingo. She knows she's here to do philanthropy. She needs to graciously accept what to her may initially feel like money falling out of the sky. That then becomes a self-worth question. Do I deserve this?"

(pause)

Higher Self: "Perhaps it's a patron or sponsor to help her – an unexpected inheritance – a beneficial collaboration or partnership she didn't see coming – a marriage – a lottery ticket win. Something unexpected and quite beneficial to her cash flow and net worth because she does so much service work."

Hypnotherapist: "So she needs to go with the flow and to be able to graciously receive to fulfill her life purpose? And her purpose includes philanthropy?"

←→

Again there was the sense of a tipping point hanging in the balance – which way would the energy flow?

Chapter Three – Boundary Dispute

Higher Self: "Exactly. She needs to be able to graciously receive or she's not going to fulfill her purpose."

(pause)

Higher Self: "She continued studying with the Native American Shaman to become a spiritual teacher. He said she became known as 'Doctor No.'"

(pause)

Higher Self: "There was a lot of martyr and victim energy to transmute, particularly from her life as Magdalen. The attacks were intense. She began blocking any energy near her to survive."

(pause)

Higher Self: "But some of that energy was from God. He was trying to give her funds – this is so unusual. He intends it for her mission work – the philanthropy. She needs to be able to graciously accept not only funds that she will use for mankind and the animals, but beneficial introductions and networking of all types."

(pause)

← →

Higher Self: "She should visualize people coming up and giving her money toward her mission projects. She'll be an excellent financial steward for others."

(pause)

Higher Self: "She needs to enjoy that feeling so good – rather than setting off alarms. We want her to visualize people giving the funds and the help to her freely – no hooks, no agenda, no control attempts. Freely given."

(pause)

Higher Self: "We want her to vision this as a kind, pleasant

41

encounter. 'I'm sharing this with you because you mean something to me, and I believe in your work.' It's a thank you for her service to the planet."

(pause)

Higher Self: "She has full latitude to use it for herself personally or for her family if she's guided to, or to put it toward her big three philanthropy projects."

(pause)

Higher Self: "She needs to prepare to receive left and right from unexpected sources. She can meditate and visualize to seat that energy."

← →

Hypnotherapist: "Should she continue to facilitate some past-life regression sessions for people without charging them?"

Higher Self: "No. That will be a rare exception going forward. Gifting a past-life regression session is too big. They take as much as four to six hours of her time and the full preparation and recovery makes it longer."

(pause)

Higher Self: "She needs to learn to instead do a complimentary phone appointment for fifteen minutes. She can explore with people if they'd like to pay for a session with her. She can help get them on the right track if they're not ready. She's excellent at triage if they should be working with someone else instead."

← →

Hypnotherapist: "Thank you. Can you support the moving together with her next partner – her soul mate?"

Higher Self: "Yes. She needs to keep the faith – this is being managed at the highest levels. They have many divine matchmakers working on this – she needs to keep on practicing meeting."

Hypnotherapist: "Practicing meeting?"

Higher Self: "Yes. We sometimes guide her to go out and about. To go places alone that she either enjoys or needs to go anyway. For example, we have asked her to buy a movie ticket for a certain time and place. It's important that she not feel crushed if he's not there. It takes time for them both to practice this skill."

Hypnotherapist: "So they're going to meet organically somewhere out in public?"

← →

Higher Self: "Yes. She needs to learn to attract her partner without trying to control the process or the timeline. She can ask him during meditation for suggestions where he'll be? Their telepathy is a two-way street. They should practice it. She should not be chasing him, though, meaning trying to make it happen."

42

(pause)
Higher Self: "Women don't want to chase men. It's exhausting, and not a good energy. Let the men chase you. You choose the best one, like in nature."
(pause)
Higher Self: "That's hard for her as she hasn't seen it modeled. It doesn't fit how she grew up. Her mother is a chaser, so the daughter never saw her in the female place."
(pause)
Higher Self: "Her mother was a single mother from when she was in her twenties. She endured romantic heartbreak after heartbreak after heartbreak. Wendy is breaking that cycle. Her mother never did. It's one reason the mother clings too much at times."
Hypnotherapist: "So that's the love that didn't let her down – the daughter. Wendy."

←→

Higher Self: "Yes. Wendy is helping dissolve old family patterns. She has set up her own daughters for successful romances. 'That was then, this is now' is one of the most powerful statements a person can make.'
(pause)
Higher Self: "For example, apply that to the ear-ringing. She doesn't need to hear a World War II nuclear explosion. She doesn't need that reverberation in all its minute detail."
(pause)
Higher Self: "She recalls several of her World War II lifetimes in detail, including the one Joe DiMaggio spoke of earlier. She's healed those lifetimes. She gets it. She knows she's here to help bring Heaven to Earth, including the peace, love, and joy energies."

←→

Hypnotherapist: "So she has a different path than her mother when it comes to her romantic partner?"
Higher Self: "Yes. They're not the same person. She doesn't need her mother's imprint in this area. Her mother unconsciously chose difficult, heartbreaking relationships with men as a reflection of her own father wound. This is not the daughter's path – Wendy's path – healing it is!"
Hypnotherapist: "Concerning the partner that is now in Wendy's field – are there any blocks to resolve prior to their meeting?"

←→

Higher Self: "There are no blocks, *per se*. They both need to continue to progress separately. They're doing well now. This is the time to heal not useful tendencies. For example, Wendy can be an enabler and take on too much work in the relationship. She can do all the planning, which isn't good for either of them. She can call him out via telepathy, if

43

needed."

Hypnotherapist: "Can you give us an example of what that would look like?"

Higher Self: "She can ask him to do some date planning – to be fun and light about it. She can ask him to 'surprise me' – to put some effort into it – to be light and easy."

Hypnotherapist: "So she's doing it all?"

Higher Self: "She has in the past. This is the time to break that habit. He's extremely capable – she can have him heavy-lift – make him shine."

(pause)

Higher Self: "She doesn't know how to inspire a man."

Hypnotherapist: "What does that mean?"

Higher Self: "To do his best – to be the best man he can be, for her. To give her his best. It's an aspect of the Divine Feminine to inspire him to be the best man he can be."

Hypnotherapist: "Oh?"

← →

Higher Self: "Joe is asking if we can explain this together for clarity. This isn't meant to be sexist. Let me try to speak well from my heart – from my soul self, not just as Joe DiMaggio, born in 1914. It's her choice, of course."

(pause)

Joe/ Higher Self: "For example, she could choose to be a bit blonde – to give him a genuine smile and bat her eyelashes at him. Marilyn will show her how to do this as Wendy isn't a natural flirt. She could say honestly, 'I don't know how to do that or can't do that easily. Can you do that for me – for us? I'd so appreciate it.' "

(pause)

Joe/ Higher Self: "Make him her hero! This isn't about manipulation. Men crave approval and respect from the woman they love. Give him something to work with, is all I'm saying."

(pause)

← →

Higher Self: "Set it up in a genuine way so he can succeed and both partners will be happy. You need to show a man what you want and need. Don't expect him to be a mind-reader and be angry when he doesn't succeed."

(pause)

Higher Self: "Her former boyfriend asked her to be flirty with him as he enjoyed the repartee. Flirting can be light and flowy energy between partners. It helps keep things from getting stale. It's a way of saying 'I see you and I appreciate you – you're attractive to me.' "

(pause)

Higher Self: "She couldn't do it as she didn't understand the energy. She equated it with cheating, as he had a lot of cheater energy, but that wasn't his intent."

Hypnotherapist: "Thank you. This is making more sense to me now."

←→

Higher Self: "Good. She's spent fifty-five years trying to do everything, for everyone. Working to serve her family and many friends. To parent her parents, at the soul level. To help her dead brother energetically – her children – her former husband. The soul mate who woke her up. Her clients. She's taken on a lot."

Hypnotherapist: "Speaking of her daughters – her former husband – the ex- boyfriend she had so many lives with – her mother – her children. Let's have them all sit in a circle, please."

(pause)

Hypnotherapist: "Wendy, I'd like you to stand up with love and appreciation for all they've meant to you. I'd like you to describe to them that it's time to cut the cords on anything holding you back from walking into a healthy, happy relationship and romance at this point. Do you feel you're prepared to do that?"

Wendy: "Yes, I can do that. I love and appreciate all of you. It's time to focus on your own lives – go do what you need to do. It's time to give me the space and privacy that I deserve to have a wonderful romance now. This doesn't take away from my caring for you, but it's my time now."

(pause)

Higher Self: (*more strongly*) "There are multiple blocks. You are not able to block this from me any longer – I won't tolerate it."

←→

Hypnotherapist: "What was their reaction? Let's go person by person. What do you observe?"

Higher Self: "Wendy's eldest daughter is quite supportive of her mother. There is no issue there. Her former husband is chagrined – he didn't know he was energetically blocking her. He said he won't do that any longer." (*Midnight, Wendy's cat meowed angrily a few times to help move the blocking energy.*)

Hypnotherapist: "What's happening now?"

Higher Self: "He's withdrawing and will not be an issue. My sense is he will deal with his own issues better now – heal his own wounding."

Hypnotherapist: "Great!"

←→

Higher Self: "Her younger daughter is progressing by leaps and bounds. She's away at college, even though it's local. It's a confidence-builder for her that she chose the right major and that she can afford college with her scholarship and help from family."

(pause)
Higher Self: "She's managing her energy from being tripled in a small dorm room. That is extremely intense for her. So many people in that large dormitory building. Also living in Seattle. She's never lived in the city before."

(pause)
Higher Self: "She said, 'Mom, go do your thing.' This is big progress as she was energetically blocking Wendy from a romance when she still lived at home."

←→

Hypnotherapist: "So she's adjusting well to college?"
Higher Self: "Overall, yes. She's busy. She's happy. You won't really see the change until it's Christmas and she comes home and goes back to school again. She needs to get through the firsts – her first semester grades and everything else."

(pause)
Higher Self: "The young woman's health is stabilized from the extreme difficulties last year. She almost went Home to the Light. The poor quality of the college food is a major bump in the road. She's being quite careful. There are so many foods she can't eat due to food sensitivities and intolerances."

Hypnotherapist: "So in general she's made a good adjustment? This is a happy time for her?
Higher Self: "Yes, it can be."

←→

Hypnotherapist: "What about Wendy's former boyfriend? She knows he's been blocking her. She's worked hard to complete their lessons and cut the cords."
Higher Self: "Her former lover is finally letting go. This is crucial as she was afraid writing the book about his session would call him back. It did the opposite. It closed out their old entanglements."
Hypnotherapist: "She mentioned she's been worried – should she send him a copy or not?"
Higher Self: "Yes, she should. It will provide additional closure."
Hypnotherapist: "Is he on Facebook?"
Higher Self: "Yes. We asked her to gently block him there. No emotion other than gratitude and peaceful closure. We asked her to block him on email and in her phone, and she did so immediately. Just part peacefully. She gave him warning and allowed for closure."

←→

Hypnotherapist: "What does the Higher Self advise whether she should forward a copy of her book to him?"
Higher Self: "She should, but in a specific conscious manner. We'd like her to put a copy of the book on her altar

46

and to give thanks for their relationship. To see it as closed out peacefully. She can give her thanks for their relationship and express her gratitude it's a wrap."

(pause)

Higher Self: "This is unusual we coach someone to do this. She is to close out their relationship for all space and time. She doesn't need to see him on the Earth plane again. Only at Home, if she chooses."

Hypnotherapist: "So their relationships is truly complete?"

Higher Self: "Yes. This is rare as they were primary soul mates coming into this life. But their relationship has run its course. She's to close it out. She doesn't need the heartbreak he engenders. She's outgrown him."

Hypnotherapist: "It's good to know when done is done."

Higher Self: "Exactly. It's like the Kenny Rogers song, *'The Gambler* - know when to walk away.' She can now gently neutralize and dissolve the last of their energy together."

Hypnotherapist: "Excellent. What is her mother's reaction?"

←→

Higher Self: "This is the most difficult piece to manage. She's finally truly clear with her former boyfriend, her ex-husband, and her daughter - it's just her mother. She should dialog with the mother's Higher Self now."

Hypnotherapist: "Excellent."

Higher Self *(on Wendy's behalf)*: "Mom, I love you. I appreciate everything you've done for me. I'm requesting pristine boundaries with you. You need to allow me the time, space, and privacy to have my new relationship. I will be holding you accountable."

(long pause – no reply from the mother's Higher Self)

Higher Self: "If that doesn't occur the way I need, we will need to negotiate new house rules. I'll need to lock the fire door pass-through connecting our homes. I prefer not to do that. You've done well with the recent changes including my youngest moving out for college – you went through that empty-nest adjustment at some level like I did."

(long pause – still no answer from the mother's Higher Self)

Higher Self: "This allows us to see each other every few days, to do a couple things together a week because you're no longer expecting me to be your one and only friend and companion. That was too heavy a burden for me to carry. I'm not willing to play that role – I'm here to live my life, not yours."

←→

Hypnotherapist: "Would it be helpful to encourage her to join a group? To take up a new hobby? To volunteer?"

Higher Self: *(ruefully)* "I wish! She won't do it. Wendy has made suggestions in that area until she's blue in the face."

Hypnotherapist: "Okay, so Wendy needs to let that go

and just hold her boundaries as to what she needs – is that what I'm hearing?"

Higher Self: "Yes. Her mother is stubborn as a mule – she resists and fights back great suggestions. She joined a gym after years of refusing to do so, but it's closing. That's likely to be a problem."

(pause)

Higher Self: "The mother keeps trying to make it Wendy's problem to find a new gym for her. Wendy needs to keep returning that task. Her mother needs to find her own new gym, which also brings her much-needed socialization – or not. This is not that difficult. The mother is creating drama."

←→

Hypnotherapist: "We want to dissolve the existing blocks – the resistance from the mother, the former boy-friend, and any other resistance."

Higher Self: "Yes. We've told her she needs to play this new relationship differently. When she starts dating her new partner, she cannot bring him to her house in the beginning. Wendy needs to more be out and about with him and over time, to go to his home. We've told her she needs to hear a sincere 'I love you' from him before she brings him to her home. Her mother will not be able to create a block at that point. It will be a *fait accompli*."

(pause)

Higher Self: "Wendy needs to honor herself in this area as it's her deepest desire. She needs to be strategic and not waffle on this issue. She should not fool herself, 'Oh, it will be fine,' and bring him to her home prematurely. Bad move!"

Hypnotherapist: "Thank you so much. Having addressed them in the circle, do you feel stronger now?"

←→

Higher Self: "This was a wonderful idea for her – she never thought to approach it this way. She has talked with each of them separately Higher Self to Higher Self during meditation. It was a lot of work. There was a lot of blocking energy as there were four of them. This was powerful work in circle today."

Hypnotherapist: "She can do this again at any time in the future in her own meditations as needed to keep up her boundaries."

Higher Self: "Exactly. She's had wishy-washy boundaries."

Hypnotherapist: "Well, she hasn't had any time to herself before, so this is a bit new to her?"

Higher Self: "That's correct. As strange at that sounds, it's exactly right. She's now living alone for the first time at the age of fifty-five. She now can practice strong pristine boundaries particularly with these four individuals."

(pause)

Hypnotherapist: "She's an adult. She owns her own home. She has the right to privacy."

←→

Higher Self: "Yes, that's what 's been challenging for her – her boundaries were too soft and ill-defined. She'd get angry when people crossed them. People would then be surprised by her strong push-back. She needs stronger boundaries which allow for more spaciousness and graciousness in her life."

(pause)

Higher Self: "Her boundaries were too narrow. They were too close to her so when they were crossed, she'd push back hard. The solution is better boundaries with more spaciousness for her."

Hypnotherapist: "So she'd go from appearing mushy to a firm boundary and people were confused, thinking she'd changed the rules with no notice?"

Higher Self: "Exactly. She has new boundaries now, and everyone is aware. And she should give reminders from time to time as needed so it doesn't get to a blow-up."

Hypnotherapist: "How might that look for her?"

←→

Hypnotherapist: "Can she tell her mother, 'Mom, I love you, but when I lock my fire door it means you're not to pop over unexpectedly. I'm fifty-five years old and deserve my privacy.' "

Higher Self: "She's told her that quite clearly. Multiple times. It hasn't gone well. She's going to have to continue to do that. It was no one's business when she and her boyfriend chose to become an intimate couple, yet her mother and her daughter were popping in at awkward times."

Hypnotherapist: "How did Wendy feel about that?"

Higher Self: "It was problematic. It made it not her own home. She had no privacy that she could count on. She couldn't relax into a relationship she had worked hard to attract and was committed to."

(pause)

Higher Self: "It didn't work well for her boyfriend, either. It made him on edge and brought up a lot of his old issues from not feeling accepted by family members in previous relationships."

Hypnotherapist: "So that clearly hasn't worked for Wendy?"

←→

Joe began answering the questions again.

Joe: "You're correct. It's the only downside to their amazing duplex. Overall, it has worked out brilliantly for all concerned. This is the one area that really allows Wendy to practice having pristine boundaries. It's the one dynamic her mother will need to adjust to."

(pause)

Joe: "Over time, Wendy's mother will enjoy having a man around the house again as she is appreciative of the tiniest little acts of service. It's her primary love language – something being done for her. She pushes for it hard."

(pause)

Joe: "If Wendy's new partner is the least bit handy or simply good-natured about helping her mother carry this or reach that, he will be greatly appreciated. She's going to need more of that help as the years go on."

Hypnotherapist: "So there's light at the end of the tunnel for them both – both Wendy and her mother?"

Joe: "Absolutely. Elizabeth – her mother – just came back to the table and said, 'What's in it for me?' "

(Sound of Wendy and her friend laughing)

←→

Joe: *(dryly)* "Let's start with a truly happy, fulfilled daughter. Elizabeth just said, 'Oh, I didn't think of that.'"

Joe: "I'm replying to her, "Maybe this guy's handy or can cook dinner or help you from time to time.' She's saying again, 'I hadn't thought of that.' "

Hypnotherapist: "What's Wendy's new guy going to think of this arrangement with her mother living next door?"

Joe: "It's going to be okay. It won't be overdone or overwhelming for him. She won't ask him will you spread four hundred pounds of bark chips around my entire yard – she can hire for that. It's the little one-off, more time-sensitive stuff."

(pause)

Joe: "Elizabeth has a housecleaning service, a yard service, a handyman and plumber as needed. She has someone to go up and clean off the roof and gutters and to put down moss preventer. She's good at finding and managing those services to keep her home and property in great shape."

←→

Hypnotherapist: "That's wonderful. Alright, let's shift gears to false holograms. We'd like to ask the Higher Self what exactly is a false hologram? This is from Wendy's list of questions for today."

(Joe stepped back as the Higher Self was being requested)

Higher Self: "Picture energy going along in a nice clean energy stream. Things are going along as they were planned. There's a nice calm, high vibration flow but suddenly there's a major interruption – say a jarring, unplanned death – a war, a major explosion."

(pause)

Higher Self: "I'm using big examples for illustrative purposes. There's a tremendous interruption. That can cause the timeline and the energy stream to fracture in an uncontrolled, unexpected way that can lead to a false hologram."

Hypnotherapist: "Yes? Please tell us more."

←→

Higher Self: "A false hologram is like a House of Mirrors, for example. Are you familiar with those fun house mirrors where the refraction is purposefully off to make everything look distorted – quite weird? The reflections aren't a true representation of reality?"

Hypnotherapist: "Yes, I am. So, what's the impact?"

Higher Self: "The issue with false holograms is the energy can't get back to the Light. Picture trying to find your way out using those fun house mirrors. The energy is too twisted and bent and misdirected to return to the Light."

Hypnotherapist: "Was there a false hologram interfering with the three or four meetups Wendy and her partner attempted? She's been hearing the term 'false hologram' during meditation and wasn't sure how and if it pertained to her."

←→

Higher Self: "No, it was more a matter of timing. Wendy tends to be too much of a driver. She tries to control the energy when she should instead relax into it and continue to raise her vibration to obtain better outcomes."

Hypnotherapist: "Yes?"

Higher Self: "She's been waiting for her partner for a long time. She divorced in early 2005. That's a long time to wait to meet her Divine Right partner."

Hypnotherapist: "Yes. More than ten years."

←→

Higher Self: "There was a lot of galactic oversight and interest in their first attempted meeting this past July. They're Twin-Rays – cosmic Twin-Flames."

(pause)

Higher Self: "They were so close to meeting! They both knew where they were supposed to be that night. Both went to the Don Henley concert partly to meet one another, but it was too soon."

Hypnotherapist: "Oh? Did more energy need to build?"

Higher Self: "There was plenty of energy between them. But there were too many eyes on them. It wasn't advisable, so we backed it down and there was no meet."

(pause)

Higher Self: "We told her to stand down and she was disappointed but did so immediately. She pulled in her energy."

Hypnotherapist: "Oh? What happened exactly? Is this okay to talk about."

←→

Higher Self: "Thank you for your sensitivity. Wendy saw the galactic guard disguised as Security. She made him. He was on her far left just behind a fence in the tree line. He gave himself away when he took his sunglasses off. She caught him scanning the crowd too rapidly."
(pause)
Higher Self: "No human could move their eyes that rapidly and take in so much information that fast. He saw her really see him. He put his glasses back on to shield his eyes, as did she. He knew she knew he was there in a benevolent role, helping to hold the space for she and her new partner to meet outdoors under the Full Moon at the Henley concert."

Hypnotherapist: "But they didn't meet?"
Higher Self: "No, they did not. There are many at the highest level helping them connect in person."
(pause)
Higher Self: "There are a few who don't want them to meet due to the amount of Light they'll provide mankind as a Twin-Ray couple. Those few won't prevail."

Hypnotherapist: "So that failed meet wasn't the reflection of a false hologram?"
Higher Self: "No – it has nothing to do with it. She was just hearing the term to learn what it was for the future as it may be helpful for a client or another scenario."

←→

Hypnotherapist: "Okay. What's next for them to meet – is it appropriate for us to learn more?"
(Joe stepped back in to speak in place of the Higher Self)
Joe: "We backed it down to simpler organic meetings. She understands to not be disappointed if she doesn't encounter him at any given location – she knows there's to be a series of potential meetings."

Hypnotherapist: "Can you tell me how she will feel when she does meet him?"
Joe: "Fulfilled. There will be an instant connection. It will finally be easy! So joyful. She can finally relax. Romance has never been easy for her."

Hypnotherapist: "Oh! That's marvelous to hear. Why has it been so difficult?"

←→

Joe: "She was programmed to fail romantically with men. Mind-control. She was loaded up with negative programming and implants that repelled most men. Typically, all were repelled but the most self-confident men or the ones who had a strong soul contract with her. This was despite her good looks, integrity, intelligence, and sense of humor and fun."

(pause)

Joe: "This is her first opportunity to meet someone new without that programming aboard since the Shaman removed that old junk."

Hypnotherapist: "So she'll recognize him?"

Joe: "They both will recognize one another at some level. That doesn't mean they won't ever have to learn and correct along the way. We've all chosen a human experience, after all – but it will be fine. It will be easy! It will be happy and fulfilling."

←→

Hypnotherapist: "That's wonderful! Does she hear him correctly as to his name, where he lives and his occupation? How is their telepathy with one another?"

Joe: "What she's hearing is correct. There's been some learning curve to it. What you said to her earlier is correct. Sometimes our Guides are just playing with us to go here or to go there at a certain time. It's good practice, and we learn. Just being relaxed and releasing the outcome is best."

Hypnotherapist: "So regarding their telepathy and speaking to one another, if she's worrying is it true, should she not put any credence into what she's hearing? Should she just let it go and return to it another time?"

Joe: "Yes."

←→

Hypnotherapist: "Will she be open to others who might be a superb match but don't bear that name?

Joe: "Absolutely! She's finally embracing life is full of wonderful surprises. No problem."

Hypnotherapist: "So she's open."

Joe: "She's completely open. She's happy – she's open. She wrote down for fun what she heard as his demo-graphics. She would be happy to laugh uproariously to be so wrong, yet to have it be so right. She doesn't have a 'need to be right.' "

Hypnotherapist: "That's great – so she's open."

←→

Joe: "Yes. She taped a small journal box with what she heard from her Guides about him to the back of her vision board. If it's inaccurate, she'll be the first person to laugh at herself and not be bothered. She knows to have fun with it – to keep it light and easy. Her ego is well-balanced at this juncture."

Hypnotherapist: "Is he a Leo? I feel Leo energy here."

Joe: "Yes, he's a Leo. He was born right at the tail end – he's the last day of Leo."

Hypnotherapist: "So he's a weak Leo?"

Joe: "He won't be what she fears when she thinks of the classic Leo – what both of you fear – bossy men."

(pause)

Joe: "Bossy men aren't attractive to strong women like the two of you. It's a non-starter for her to be with a domineering man. It's not instructive. She's outgrown that energy."

Hypnotherapist: "But his ascendant could be more important – the ascendant is what we show to the world."

Joe: "You're right."

Hypnotherapist: "He seems like a Leo when I tune into his energy – he's gregarious like a Leo. Hopefully, that will be a positive quality."

Joe: "Yes – he won't be unbearably selfish. She's already done her time with that incredibly selfish boyfriend. I'm not talking about occasional moments of needing to be a little selfish to re-center oneself. She has them, too. We all do when human. I'm talking about that being the predominant trait."

Hypnotherapist: "So no history repeating itself?"

←→

Joe: "No, history won't repeat as she got the lessons. It won't be like the former boyfriend – the former primary soul mate she concluded her work with."

(pause)

Joe: "We asked her to have her former lover's astrology done in combination with hers, with his permission. What it showed them was he has a profound number of planets in the first house – the House of Self. That helped them both understand it wasn't her fault, or his, that their romance needed to end. They both wanted it to succeed with every ounce of their being-ness. Both tried so hard – they gave it all they had."

Hypnotherapist: "So there was no way it could work for them this lifetime, given their astrology?"

←→

Joe: "Exactly. He needed to maximize his 'self' lessons this lifetime. That's why he chose that date, time and place of birth that gave him so many planets in the House of Self. It makes him remarkably selfish, despite the many attractive qualities that drew her to him initially."

(pause)

Joe: "He also has a fatal flaw she can't work with. He's not interested in monogamy or a committed relationship. He was born on March 15th which is the 'Day of the Great Betrayer' in numerology – the Ides of March."

Hypnotherapist: "Okay, so it's best she moved on. We'd like to inquire about Twin-Rays. What are Twin-Rays that you mentioned earlier?"

←→

Joe: "Her spiritual teacher Roberta – the one that she calls Birdie - gave her the correct definition. A Twin-Ray is a specific type of soul mate. It's most analogous to a Twin-Flame, but it's the galactic – the other planetary – Twin."
Hypnotherapist: "Oh? Can you tell us more."
Joe: "Certainly. Let me back up. We all have many types of soul mates. Many are not romantic – they are simply people we travel with many times – our best friends, perhaps a child, a favorite teacher. Your worst enemy. They're soul group members we incarnate with numerous times.
Hypnotherapist: "What purpose do they serve?"

←→

Joe: "Soul mates are primarily for lessons. There's the companionship and support function, too, but they're mainly for lessons. There are also romantic soul mates who we contract with for 'a reason, season or a lifetime.'"
(pause)
Joe: "Many people – women especially – my sincere apologies for stereotyping – can become upset if the romance doesn't last a lifetime. But when the teaching is done, it's best to part. The contract is complete. Take the time you need to digest and recover, and then move onto a new adventure and experience. This is how you learn and grow as a soul."
Hypnotherapist: "Thank you. Anything else?"

←→

Joe: "Yes. It would be best for people to stop beating themselves or others up for the quote – 'failed' relationship. It didn't fail. It simply ran its course. The lessons are complete. Be gracious and move on. Part peacefully."
(pause)
Joe: "I'd like to congratulate Wendy's former primary soul mate as he helped her understand this concept, along with many others. It gave her the opportunity to heal."

←→

Hypnotherapist: "Where do life partners fit into the equation? Are they different than soul mates?"
Joe: "There's nothing wrong with a well-matched life partner. It may not be as profound a connection, but it doesn't carry the soul mate charge."
(pause)
Joe: "A few soul mates are incredibly happy as they've mastered or are mastering their lessons well. From my vantage point, these couples are rare. Look at me and Marilyn – love did not conquer all."

←→

Hypnotherapist: "Are there other types of romantic

partners?"

Joe: "Yes, there are Twin-Flames."

Hypnotherapist: "Thank you. What's a Twin-Flame?"

Joe: "It's a specific type of soul mate. We have only one Twin-Flame as it's the other half of our soul from our Earth lives."

(pause)

Joe: "It's a soul that agreed to be split in two to go off and have different experiences before reuniting. Not everyone has one. It's a free will choice made to progress at the soul level."

←→

Hypnotherapist: "So Wendy has a Twin-Flame?"

Joe: "Yes. Wendy is a Twin-Flame with the man in her office building that she worked to reunite with for three or four years. She did the right thing to move on. He needs to heal on his own at this point – or not. He's too wounded for her."

Hypnotherapist: "So he needs to heal more?"

Joe: "Yes. Her Guides asked her to move on because he's no longer a suitable partner for her. We're proud of her – she worked to connect with him daily for over three years – she helped heal him for that long. That took immense patience and trust on her part to do."

Hypnotherapist: "It was hopefully a good lesson, also?"

Joe: "In what way?"

Hypnotherapist: "She spent three years of her life trying to make that work, but now she's asking for a suitable partner to present in the physical."

Joe: *(sharply)* "She's already been praying for that for years. Her request was spot-on and practical. We thought her Twin-Flame could heal and they could reunite in the physical to light up the world."

(pause)

Joe: "He wasn't capable of it."

←→

Hypnotherapist: "So it's time."

Joe: "Yes. That's what was so difficult for her. That relationship would progress – then it would stall. It would progress as he tried to heal, then stall again as his progress wasn't sustainable."

(pause)

Joe: "She was getting mixed messages from the healers and psychics around her who first could and then couldn't see him. He kept fading in and out. He couldn't hold his energy signature. Therefore, they didn't meet."

Hypnotherapist: "That does sound frustrating."

Joe: "Yes. That's what was so hard on her. She kept asking us, 'Why is this so hard? This is supposed to be easy as a new

56

experience for me. I've done hard multiple times. I'm ready for a new romance that's easy. You know – like hitting the big red 'easy button' that office supply store used to sell?' "
(laughing)

←→

Hypnotherapist: "So this is meant to have an easy flow to it?"

Joe: "Yes, we're looking for easy for her now. She deserves it – she's earned it – she's ready."

Hypnotherapist: "Yes. She said she felt like she was trying to boil the ocean trying to heal him, to move forward with their reunion."

Joe: "Yes."

Hypnotherapist: "So it was good for her in many ways, but now it's time to shift into the physical plane."

Joe: "She always wanted physical. She's been specific with her request and timeframe as to present day, but not overly specific. We just haven't been able to make it happen yet."

←→

Hypnotherapist: "So let's change that. May I ask is the new partner healthy? Is he ready to commit to a relationship with her?"

Joe: "Yes to both."

Hypnotherapist: "Wonderful. So, he's healthy and is ready for a nice relationship with her?"

Joe: "He's healthy, he's successful, he's ready for a committed relationship with her over time."

Hypnotherapist: "So that fits with her desire, too – that's a good match?"

←→

Joe: "Yes, it is. He's more newly divorced than her, but it's been about two years. There's been enough time. He already had his messy, drama-filled relationship that many people engage in after a long-term marriage or relationship ends."

Hypnotherapist: "So he's already done that?"

Joe: "Yes. He did that right away – crossed off the list."

Hypnotherapist: "So that's completely closed out? He's healed and free and ready to commit?"

Joe: "Yes. He had the rebound affair. He's ready for something much deeper and a better fit."

←→

Hypnotherapist: "So where does this Twin-Ray energy fit in, if at all?"

Joe: "The reason it's important for this couple is they hold the energy for that template pattern. They're not the only ones, but they're important to help other Twin-Rays successfully meet and be happy together. It's important not only on the planet, but for the Cosmos."

Hypnotherapist: "Is Wendy destined to meet her Twin-Ray?"

Joe: "Yes, that's who her new partner is. He's her Twin-Ray. That's part of what has taken her aback to switch her energy focus to someone new."

←→

Joe: "Her Twin-Flame that was too wounded was Yeshua ben Joseph when she was Magdalen. To have to let that go, and to wrap her head around a Twin-Ray has been an issue for her ego."

Hypnotherapist: "How so?"

Joe: "Because her ego is a little small for some of the energy work that we ask her to do. Her ego is well-balanced in most ways. But we need her to find a cause and to stand up for it. To use her power to help others."

(pause)

Joe: "She needs to move toward her North Node in Leo and to allow herself to radiate passion, enthusiasm, and leadership. She needs to help excite and entertain others, so they get on their spiritual path and do their life purpose work in an enjoyable way."

(pause)

Joe: "We don't want her to repeat her South Node and to let the group or family come before her, or to be excessively generous and give too much of herself away. The boundary issues we discussed – It's right there in her astrology."

(pause)

Joe: "It's been a big deal for her to have recognized she was to reunite with a Twin-Flame – who used to be Jesus, no less? And then to be asked to match with a Twin-Ray right when she was sighing with relief asking for a superb life partner instead of a soul mate, let alone a Twin..."

Hypnotherapist: *(interrupting)* "That sounds like a reasonable request."

Joe: "Yes. So, to instead be told we'd now like you to match with your Twin-Ray to help the Cosmos, her initial response was, 'Oh shit!' "

(Both women laughed heartily)

←→

Hypnotherapist: "So maybe that's why you're playing big league now, Joe, as a type of Guide for Wendy. Can you help show her how to succeed well in the big leagues?"

Joe: *(enthusiastically)* "I sure can! That's a great analogy."

Hypnotherapist: "Can you tell us more what a Twin-Ray is?"

Joe: "Sure. A Twin-Ray is the other half of your soul like a Twin-Flame. But a Twin-Flame correlates to your Earth lives and a Twin-Ray to the galactic lifetimes – lives lived on other planets."

(pause)

Joe: "A Twin-Ray relates to the Cosmos – the bigger picture – the Twin-Flame is like half-way to the Twin-Ray. The Twin-Flame is a subset of the Twin-Ray because it's only your Earth lives. Some souls choose to experience incarnating on other planets, to be other life forms, and in other dimensions."

←→

Hypnotherapist: "But the Twin-Ray can be met on Earth in the physical, right?"

Joe: "Absolutely!"

Hypnotherapist: "So it's a cosmic relationship."

Joe: "Yes. You can term it intergalactic or cosmic. It's multi-dimensional, too. Examples include the fairy kingdom and the dragon realm."

Hypnotherapist: "Wow. This does get deep. And it can be happy and healthy here on Earth for her now – for Wendy now – and for her new guy now?"

Joe: "Yes, absolutely. She knew she was to open the portal so more Twin-Flames could reunite. The purpose was to increase the light on the planet. She opened the Twin reunion portal successfully first from Mt. Shasta, California with Birdie holding space for her, and then from another private location on her own when we asked her to."

←→

Hypnotherapist: "Was there a particular driver why she was to get involved with the Twin-Ray energy?"

Joe: "Shrewd question. Yes. She has a friend who was told she was to meet her Twin-Ray. That friend expressed to Wendy she's received zero help. She asked Wendy, 'When you do your work for the Twin-Flame portal, would you be willing to do it for the Twin-Ray portal, too?'"

(pause)

Joe: "Wendy told her yes after checking with her Guides, not knowing that it would become important for her personally. A year later she learned that work was to benefit her directly."

(pause)

Joe: "If we'd asked her to work with the Twin-Ray portal earlier, she would have freaked and said the Twin-Flame energy is intense enough for me and turned us down. She grew into the assignment. It was easier for her to say yes to help a friend who truly needed the assist."

Hypnotherapist: "Great. Anything else on this topic to help broaden our understanding?"

←→

Joe: "Let's make this simple. A Twin-Flame is a unique

59

soul mate. It's a lot of labeling – it's just a numbers game. You have lots of soul mates that you work with again and again. A subset of them are romantic soul mates. And then you have your primary soul mate – who may or may not be your Twin-Flame. They are rare to meet on Earth. The Twin-Flame is a much smaller subset of the types of soul mates. There's only one, and not everyone has one. And there's the galactic Twin-Ray – there's also only one, if you ever have one. It's a choice."

←→

Hypnotherapist: "Thank you – that's a good summary. I'm going to continue now with the questions Wendy wrote before we began today for her Higher Self and Guides to answer. Does Wendy understand her connections to a member of the Eagles band?"

Joe: "Yes, she has that all straight. She's incarnated with the soul now known as Don Henley multiple times. The most recent time was in the 1800s when she was one of the Louisa May Alcotts. There have been many Louisas, as timelines repeat. Henley was Ralph Waldo Emerson."

(pause)

Joe: "Another member of the Eagles was Henry David Thoreau. They were Transcendentalists together in Concord, Massachusetts."

(pause)

Joe: "Why do you think Henley saved Walden Pond from development? He's spent years fundraising to save it in perpetuity."

(pause)

Joe: "He'd spent decades there in a previous lifetime and Walden Pond holds a special place in his heart. I doubt he's consciously aware of it."

(pause)

Joe: "Her memories from that timeline began to flow back in when she read 'On Walden Pond' in college. She didn't fully understand them until recently."

(pause)

←→

Joe: "We'd like to encourage her to visit Concord again on her own when she can. She can enjoy and celebrate that life quietly. Her father now was her father then. He introduced her to the Eagles music when she was only about ten or eleven years old when they first began playing in the early 1970s."

(pause)

Joe: "She later recognized two of the band members from the earlier life with her father when he was Amos Bronson Alcott, the educational reformer."

(pause)

Joe: "She should think about why her former husband lived in Concord in the present lifetime and loves the Eagles, too. It's deeper than them being a popular group who've enjoyed a lot of success."

Hypnotherapist: "Thank you. Can you share more?'

←→

Joe: "I'll simply say the writer becomes the songwriter – it's not such a stretch Henley perfected the energy this lifetime. And he had the same best friend in the 1800s in Thoreau and as an Eagles bandmate."

(pause)

Joe: "It's been hard for Henley being such a public figure, though he chose it. The amount of fame has dismayed him many times – more accurately, people's reactions to it."

(pause)

Joe: "He'd just like people to act normally when they do recognize him or approach him for an autograph or to thank him for his music. Just be understated and be real. Better yet, let his family eat their dinner out in peace. That would be the best gift to him."

(pause)

Joe: "I can relate from my lifetime. Let's let it be. She's got it all straight."

Hypnotherapist: "I understand. We'll let it be."

←→

We'd suddenly arrived at the million-dollar question...

Chapter Four – What's a Parallel Life?

Hypnotherapist: "Did she experience a lifetime as an athlete?"

Joe: "Yes. We went straight to my lifetime – her lifetime as me, as Joe DiMaggio. This was key for her to find because she had not realized the implications on her current life. This provides the opportunity to now heal much more easily."

(pause)

Joe: "She also hadn't realized the block she had to attracting a new life partner because of the heartbreak her soul – our soul – was still feeling from having lost Marilyn."

←→

Hypnotherapist: "Are you saying she had an actual lifetime as Joe DiMaggio? It's not imprinting from the collective, or someone else from that life who knew him well? Didn't he have a lot of brothers and teammates, for example."

Joe: "Yes, I certainly did. Her soul – our soul – lived an actual full past life for eighty plus years as me, as Joe DiMaggio. More accurately, she lived a parallel/ past life as Joltin Joe DiMaggio – the Yankee Clipper."

←→

Hypnotherapist: "What's that been like for her to try to accept?"

Joe: "She didn't want to believe it. She's been blocking it for a year or more as it made her uncomfortable. She didn't want to accept the possibility of another famous past life."

(pause)

Joe: "She's well-aware of the public scrutiny that will likely come. We've told her she needs to stand tall and share her own truth and let go of the outcome. That takes courage to do in these sorts of cases."

(pause)

Joe: "We – meaning her Guides – remind her often she needs to let go of 'what will other people think' to fulfill her life purpose. We had her former boyfriend coach her on that several times. He had some fame of his own to manage. He was a Kodak All-American quarterback drafted to the NFL. That's a big achievement as was becoming a sportscaster on television."

(pause)

Joe: "He shared his father's wisdom with her. His father told him, 'Never believe the press written about you. It's not about you. It's more a reflection of the writer's or the publisher's agenda.'"

(pause)

Joe: "Her boyfriend was able to help her with these areas – to prepare her for her future. Now she needs to step to the plate! Pun intended."

(sound of laughter)

←→

Hypnotherapist: "And what about you both being alive at the same time? Tell me how that would be possible."

Joe: "Great – I wanted to cover that next. She was perturbed at first because there's an almost forty-year overlap between when she was born and when I died in 1999. We can refer to her life as me as a past life, but it's more accurately a past-parallel life."

(pause)

Joe: "I was born as Joe in 1914 and Wendy was born in 1961, but we're the same soul."

Hypnotherapist: "I see. So how and why might a soul choose a parallel life? You're saying Wendy and Joe are the same soul and lived a parallel life incarnated into two different bodies at the same time?"

←→

Joe: "Yes. I'm going to step aside for the Higher Self to explain this better. I'll sit in the dugout and listen."

(pause)

Higher Self: "Wendy and Joe DiMaggio lived parallel lives. They're the same soul. The soul chose two incarnations at the same time. Souls have plenty of energy to incarnate into parallel lives once they learn how to be efficient with their energy."

(pause)

Higher Self: "Some Higher Self soul energy always remains Home with the Light. You can choose to live parallel lives to experience more, to learn more, to transmute or clean up more karma faster, and to assist mankind."

(pause)
Higher Self: "A parallel life can be quite mission-driven. There are many reasons for an experienced soul to choose this strategy. The planning is done carefully at Home first with one's Guides and typically with key people you'll interact with during the lifetime."

← →

Hypnotherapist: "Thank you. Can you clear up why this was so confusing for Wendy to figure out who she was in that lifetime? Wouldn't it have been easier to be some bit player in that timeline as Joe was so well-known?"
Higher Self: "Easier, yes. Instructive – no. This is a highly experienced soul who is pushing for and capable of complex experiences and learning, and to share them with others. She's able to express herself eloquently as an expressive soul type."
(pause)
Higher Self: "That's why she 'volunteered' to be here at this time. She was drafted by Yeshua to help others with their spiritual awakenings, and to help land peace on Earth."
Hypnotherapist: "So was she clear she might have been Joe for a long time – even from childhood?"
Higher Self: "Yes, she has memories from childhood. But at one point she felt she might have been Joe's wife. She thought that she might have been Marilyn as she kept getting visions of Marilyn and seeing her with Joe."
Hypnotherapist: "So what was really going on?"

← →

Higher Self: "The visions were from Joe's vantage point – his point-of-view. Joe's wife – his second wife – was a Mary Magdalen. Marilyn had a past life as a Mary Magdalen. There's a clue right there in the initials."
(pause)
Higher Self: "Don't forget Norma Jeane chose her stage name. She reinvented herself. She evolved into that more glamorous name."
(pause)
Higher Self: "Marilyn had the same initials in both lifetimes as Marilyn Monroe and as Mary Magdalen. Wendy now has those initials on her palms – two clear letter "M's," which isn't all that common. Not everyone has that palmistry."
Hypnotherapist: "Can you verify who you're referring to as Joe's wife?"

← →

Higher Self: "I'm referring to Marilyn Monroe. Let me explain. The energy was so similar between Mary Magdalen and Joe's second wife Marilyn for a reason. Marilyn has a past life as a Magdalen, and Wendy has also served as Mary

Magdalen."

(pause)

Higher Self: "Wendy was confused for several months as to her identity in that timeline, which was as Joe DiMaggio. That's why she kept seeing Marilyn – she was seeing her from Joe's eyes from their shared lifetime."

(pause)

Higher Self: "Once she was willing to explore the possibility of who she'd been in that timeline, the memories flooded in and made more sense. She'd had some of these memories as Joe since she was a child."

←→

Hypnotherapist: "So why would Wendy see them both?"

Higher Self: "Joe and Marilyn are just extremely close. They kept coming to Wendy together for her to accept this life."

(pause)

Higher Self: "She would see Marilyn, but she would feel and hear Joe. Typically, she feels him first come in through her left thigh."

←→

Hypnotherapist: "Is it possible it's an imprint, where there's a picking up of energy from another?"

Higher Self: "That's an excellent question. It's always possible, but it's not what's occurring in this case. There's too much emotion for it to be an imprint. There are too many memories – there's an incredible backlog of specific memories. Many of them are mundane things that you won't read about but that were emotionally important to Joe – to this soul."

(pause)

Higher Self: "Also she's healing amazingly well both physically and emotionally from learning about the life as Joe DiMaggio. That doesn't tend to happen at this depth with a mere imprint or with a fantasy."

(pause)

←→

Higher Self: "We are not interested in trying to prove the point. It's not possible from a materialist perspective. We don't find the materialist viewpoint useful. It's too limited."

(pause)

Higher Self: "We only wish for her to be well. To be happy and healthy and well. That is the purpose of today's session. To let go of other people's opinions."

Hypnotherapist: "I understand. But this can be made clear for her. I'd like to speak with the Higher Self now."

Higher Self: *(nodding)* "You already are. Joe's still sitting in the dugout listening to us converse."

Hypnotherapist: "Does Wendy now understand why this was confusing?"

Higher Self: "Yes, she understands now based on our conversation today. She can answer any future questions via meditation, auto-writing and via conversation with her Higher Self and Guides. Her clairaudience is highly accurate and will continue to develop."

←→

Hypnotherapist: "Is hypnotherapy still useful for her?"

Higher Self: "Absolutely. It's an incredibly efficient way for her to get a lot of information in a few hours. Just put aside a single day and get a tremendous download like this – thank you for helping her! Her muscle-testing is equally accurate."

Hypnotherapist: "That's great to know."

Higher Self: "Unless she's feeling monkey-mind or fear or anxiety, in that case what she's hearing won't be accurate. She knows to then stop, take a time out and re-center herself."

Hypnotherapist: "Good – so she knows what to do."

Higher Self: "Yes. She knows she's on the right path in so many ways as her life keeps improving."

Hypnotherapist: "Great – so she's on track."

Higher Self: "Yes. Things keep getting easier – going better."

Hypnotherapist: "So she has more confidence."

Higher Self: "Yes. She's more healed – she's more together – there have been many useful soul retrievals."

←→

Hypnotherapist: "That's wonderful. She had a question does she need healing around fame and fortune? Now I see why she wrote that question."

Higher Self: "Yes. That was crucial for her. We've been resolving it today."

Hypnotherapist: "Why was this presenting at this time?"

Higher Self: "To prepare her for the future. We showed her the contrast in how fame was handled by Joe versus by Marilyn."

(pause)

Higher Self: "Both knew to be kind and appreciative to their public. But Joe was able to keep his center and not be owned by his fans, despite his fame."

(pause)

Higher Self: "Marilyn became owned by the machine that made her. There's a sharp contrast between the two. Marilyn got chewed up and spit out by Hollywood, while Joe was able to keep his center. That's why he banned them from her funeral."

(pause)

66

Higher Self: "He had such strong roots from his good family life – his parents, his siblings, his genuine friends. He never forgot who he was as Joe – as a simple man."
(pause)
Higher Self: "Marilyn didn't have any of that. She got put through the wringer. Joe had his roots to pull strength from and to provide a healthy perspective. She didn't have a foundation to draw from."
(pause)
Higher Self: "I don't recall who said Marilyn needed a savior, not another husband. They were right. She overcame so much in a difficult life. She should be proud of her accomplishments."

←→

Hypnotherapist: "So Wendy is to learn from the contrast – the difference between how the two were able to handle their fame and fortune? Is this resolved for her now?"
Higher Self: "Yes. This is now comfortable for her. This is a tremendous healing around fame and fortune so she will be able to fulfill her life purpose to help others."
(pause)
Higher Self: "Let's use a baseball analogy. She's been given every resource to know when to choke up on the bat to increase her bat speed. She won't choke when she steps to the plate. She knows how to breathe and to ground herself."
(pause)
Higher Self: "She also knows when it's time to step to the plate, or to be on deck or elsewhere on the field, or to be in the dugout or at home relaxing, watching the game."
Hypnotherapist: "Good – so she's following her guidance where to be when, and what her role is to be."
Higher Self: "Exactly. What else does she need help with?"

←→

Hypnotherapist: "Does the Camelot life need more clearing?"
Higher Self: "Perfect – we want to do that right now. Wendy has done a lot of work with her memories from that lifetime. Her memories are detailed and accurate, but we want to take it to the next level."
Hypnotherapist: "Why is this presenting now?"
Higher Self: "The reason we had her write that question is she's had three or four people show up recently with a lot of rancor toward her. It seemed to come out of left field."
(pause)
Higher Self: "She'd only just met the person, but she surmised correctly there was past life energy to release

67

from when she was Guinevere as she would hear, 'Past life – Camelot.' "

Hypnotherapist: "What's the best way to address this rancor?"

Higher Self: "We'd like to use your technique to bring everyone to the Round Table. We invite forward anyone who has any issues with Queen Guinevere of Camelot in Britain to come forward now."

(pause)

Higher Self: "The parameters are this must be peaceful. It's to be resolved now or you are to hold your peace. You don't need to hold back or lay in wait for her to try to take her down. That is not productive and will no longer be permitted."

Hypnotherapist: "Has that happened before?"

←→

Higher Self: "Yes. This happened with her most recent radio show where she was asked to be a guest. The host didn't do any of the preparation or promotion he was hired to do. He became too angry to function once he tuned into her energy."

(pause)

Higher Self: "He didn't show up for their production planning meeting. He didn't provide a word of explanation before or after the missed meeting. He didn't read her book to prepare for the interview or promote the event."

(pause)

Higher Self: "He suddenly left town to take a class, not really knowing why, making himself unavailable to host his own radio program. He did this mainly to avoid direct contact with her, but without understanding their past life energy at Camelot."

(pause)

Higher Self: "Fortunately his co-host was a lovely fit for Wendy. She read the book in record speed and hosted a good interview once Wendy reached out to her."

←→

Hypnotherapist: "Thank you for that example of how past life energy can show up where we're unconscious of it. I would like to request that those who have issues with Guinevere that they're willing to peacefully settle now step forward."

Higher Self: "There's a lot of movement."

Hypnotherapist: "Tell me who shows up."

Higher Self: "It's more and more knights, including the Higher Self of the radio host I mentioned. It's all men at this point."

(pause)

Higher Self: "She's resolved the low vibration energy

with the women. There was a lot of unpleasantness with many women – a lot of jealousy. Guinevere was a beautiful, unusually powerful young queen. She had many supporters, but also many detractors – enemies, even."

←→

Hypnotherapist: "So who's coming to the table?"
Higher Self: "There are several knights presenting – they're expressing what she did that made them so angry."
Hypnotherapist: "Why are they angry?"
Higher Self: "They felt she betrayed Arthur – their friend, their leader, their beloved King."
(pause)
Higher Self: "They then internalized it. It's the male fear of being betrayed sexually – of being cuckolded. It's the fear of a woman lying with someone other than her husband or partner. It's compounded by a huge resentment that she sat at the Round Table with them as not only their queen, but as their equal at a time when women were not equal to men. There's lots of anger bubbling up here."
Hypnotherapist: "Tell me more about that."

←→

Higher Self: "The Round Table was a wedding gift from Guinevere's father King Leodegrance to his daughter and new son-in-law. It symbolized what Camelot stood for. Guinevere brought it with her as part of her dowry when she traveled to Arthur's court for their marriage."
(pause)
Higher Self: "Every man has an equal seat at a round table. There is no head or foot of the table with its implied power."
Hypnotherapist: "You said every man has an equal seat – are we to take that literally? What about a woman in that time – a queen?"
Higher Self: "Guinevere was the only woman who ever sat at the Round Table. She was highly intelligent and intellectually and emotionally strong. She was trained by her father as a military strategist and was more educated regarding geography and history than many of the knights."
(pause)

←→

Higher Self: "Traditionally only the noble-born had a formal education in what we now consider the Dark Ages. Guinevere sat at the table in Arthur's place during his many absences."
(pause)
Higher Self: "It's important to understand this wasn't for an occasional meeting. It was for up to a year at a time when Arthur was on the front line of a war campaign or on a diplomatic mission which took him away from home and

his young wife."

(pause)

Higher Self: "She wasn't at the table as a figurehead or simply to listen or sit in. Guinevere was most often running the meetings with her closest advisors backing her, which not many people know."

Hypnotherapist: "So how can we resolve this?"

←→

Higher Self: "Now that I've provided the insights as to how this originated – now we can heal it. Let me ask them a question. 'What do you gentlemen need to make this right? I see more and more of you coming in – how can we make this right? What do you need from Guinevere?' "

(long pause)

Hypnotherapist: "What are they saying?"

Higher Self: "They're saying 'We want you to apologize!' Let me clarify. What would you like Guinevere to apologize for?"

(pause)

Higher Self: "We want you to apologize for betraying Arthur by cuckolding him – we need nothing else but that."

←→

Hypnotherapist: "What does this betrayal really boil down to?"

Higher Self: "They want Guinevere to apologize for having an affair with Lancelot in Arthur's absence. Lancelot was Arthur's best friend, so it was an especially hurtful betrayal."

(pause)

Higher Self: "It became public the King was cuckolded and that was the final blow to end Camelot."

Hypnotherapist: "Would Guinevere like to speak?"

(Wendy began speaking as Guinevere)

Guinevere: "Yes, I would. I truly apologize for having betrayed my husband, and my court as well as my marriage vows. We had no children – I was lonely – I was weak."

(pause)

Guinevere: "I should have kept to my marriage vows despite my husband's continual decision to be gone from home for up to a year at a time. He did that so many times! He could have made a different decision."

(pause)

Guinevere: "Arthur wouldn't agree to my repeated requests to be at home and to be in the marriage with me. That doesn't excuse what I did."

(pause)

Guinevere: "It's why we had to meet again in a future life to work it out. Wendy's boyfriend that woke her up was Arthur long ago."

(pause)

Guinevere: *(humbly)* "I sincerely apologize to all of you for having let you down and betrayed you as well as Camelot. You needed more from me as your Queen, as your leader, as your friend. Will you accept my most sincere apologies?"

←→

Hypnotherapist: "What are they doing now?"
(long pause)
Guinevere: *(beaming)* "The men said they accept my apology! They are bowing to me now, and quietly backing away from the table and out of the room. A weight is coming off my shoulders."
Hypnotherapist: "Wonderful. Is there anything you'd like to say in return?"
Guinevere: "I'm truly grateful for your forgiveness – I so appreciate your divine grace for my terrible mistake."
Hypnotherapist: "That's wonderful – let's fully express your gratitude. What else is now clear to you from this episode?"
Guinevere: "That was not a comfortable feeling they would keep showing up and would try to sabotage me as Wendy. Thank you for helping me ask for forgiveness in this powerful way."
Hypnotherapist: "Does this feel settled and resolved on all levels – all accounts?"

←→

Guinevere: "Yes. This was all that we – that all the parties involved - needed. Thank you. Wendy knew something was wrong."
(pause)
Guinevere: "Her boyfriend in this life that used to be Arthur kept talking in current time about how hard it was to trust a woman to not cuckold him. Cuckold is an old-fashioned term that few men use today. Wendy knew there was old energy to release."
Hypnotherapist: "And that's resolved with the present-day Arthur?"
Guinevere: "Yes – completely resolved. They both worked hard in present day to forgive one another and to forgive themselves. It's done. That had to be done to be able to part peacefully."
Hypnotherapist: 'Wonderful. May I speak with the Higher Self now for the next question?'
Higher Self: "Yes, you may."

←→

Hypnotherapist: "Wendy would like to know what's her best role with the deceased soldiers she sees clairvoyantly from what looks like World War II. Should she continue to help walk them Home? She believes she's to help the soldiers from World War II but it's an immensely huge project with millions of people still stuck on the Earth plane."

(pause)

Hypnotherapist: "She feels many of the soldiers went Home, but it's not just the soldiers – it's the victims of a World War – the impact on the animals and the Earth herself, too. She wants to serve, but she's concerned with the scope and the best approach."

Higher Self: "We're looking for the most efficient way to resolve this. We're not going to outline it now – it's too soon. She knows she'll work on this with her teacher Birdie at the right time in the right way, with clear signals from both their Guides what and how to do it."

Hypnotherapist: "Okay. May we know more, if appropriate?"

← →

Higher Self: "They will host it as a public event when the time is right. They have the famous name on the other side helping with this immense project. The spirit of Marilyn Monroe will help them."

(pause)

Higher Self: "The three public conference call events that Wendy, Birdie and the Shaman have organized to clear and bless the White House has had a large and positive energetic impact. The White House is a symbol of the U.S. government. They became aware it was filled with ghosts and other low vibration energy, so they worked to clear it just as the Presidential election cycle was reaching its completion."

Hypnotherapist: "Yes?"

Higher Self: "They'll model from the White House clearing work. We need to scope the World War II clearing quite carefully. It will be a public event spearheaded by Birdie with Wendy."

(pause)

Higher Self: "We need to manage it carefully as there will be some public outcry – why not Vietnam, why not Korea? They need to know how and when to scope things the way they do, which Birdie is a master at."

(pause)

Higher Self: "This is not to be outlined today. Today is simply a confirm they are meant to do this sacred work together."

Hypnotherapist: "So when it's time she'll know what to do?"

← →

Higher Self: "Yes. They're not to try to do this during Birdie's own past life regression she's planning with Wendy – it will sweep her away as it's so vast. They can plan it then

72

but are not to do it then."

Hypnotherapist: "Because it's too large?"

Higher Self: "Exactly. In a past-life regression with a different client Wendy and the client helped almost four thousand people Home. They were waiting for everyone to be ready to go Home as a group after a great flood."

(pause)

Higher Self: "This caused a huge depletion of their chi – their personal life force energy. It was a grave depletion of their energy. She won't make that mistake again. She was a new therapist then."

Hypnotherapist: "So she and her teacher are not to do this work on their own?"

Higher Self: "Certainly not. And it's more complex than calling in the Divine – they'll know what to do at the right time."

← →

Hypnotherapist: "So when she does these huge projects, she's to do them with her Guides and with others as a team?"

Higher Self: "Yes, that's correct."

Hypnotherapist: "It appears to me she needs more rest."

Higher Self: "Yes, that's a valid reminder. We've put in checks and balances as she's been experiencing 'scope creep' in the size and number of projects she's taking on to serve mankind."

(pause)

Higher Self: "She was taking on too many large projects as she slept at night and burning up too much of her human energy."

Hypnotherapist: "Does this happen often for her? How about for other people? What would you advise?"

← →

Higher Self: "Anyone who wakes up feeling more exhausted than when they went to bed at night would be wise to work with their Guides to stay home at night in their body and to heal it instead."

(pause)

Higher Self: "Ask to go to a Healing Temple and to stay there for the night. That is the purpose of sleep – to be fully restorative – to heal the human body. Today will help her fully recognize and change that. Thank you for helping her."

Hypnotherapist: "It takes a lot of energy for the work she's doing for mankind. She'd like to reclaim some of her energy and rest well."

Higher Self: "Yes, we agree. Consider it done."

Hypnotherapist: "Good. Let's switch to the next topic."

← →

73

Hypnotherapist: "How accurate is Wendy's written channeling?"

Higher Self: "Highly accurate. They key is meditating first – asking the critical questions that she does, without doubting the information that comes through. She's right where she needs to be, thinking with discernment, but trusting. It's perfect."

Hypnotherapist: "So she's doing great with the written channeling – she's right where she should be?"

Higher Self: "Correct."

←→

Hypnotherapist: "She wants to know when she should begin the verbal channeling?"

Higher Self: "That's an amusing question as she's already doing it. She just doesn't fully realize it. She channels what she says on the radio, usually – she invites in Mary Magdalen."

(pause)

Hypnotherapist: "It's that simple for her to accurately channel?"

Higher Self: "Yes. She doesn't fully realize how well and how naturally she channels as she's seen other channels – other different types of channels with different processes."

(pause)

Higher Self: "She's used to seeing this awkward, painful full body channeling that many have experienced. The person's eyes are closed, they're jerking all over the place – that's not how she channels."

(pause)

Higher Self: "Her channeling is subtle, it's easy, but no less beautiful and accurate. She's done this in many lifetimes. She has soul contracts in place to do so again now."

←→

Hypnotherapist: "Does she know when she's channeling?"

Higher Self: "She'll fully understand it after today. She suspected she was channeling because she didn't recall much of what she said during the radio program."

(pause)

Higher Self: "She began as a conscious channel after years of work to balance her ego. She has the capability to be a full-body channel and can do so eyes open, which is a bit unusual."

Hypnotherapist: "Oh? Please tell us more."

Higher Self: "If she hears the different voice and energy when she listens to the program recording and can't remember what she said on the radio interview, she knows she was full-body channeling."

(pause)

Higher Self: "She's been getting nervous waiting to hear

74

her interviews. We want her to calm down and trust nothing will be said that she would be uncomfortable with. This is a beautiful progression."

(pause)
Higher Self: "We won't share anything she isn't ready to share. We want to reassure her she does a wonderful job on-air. She's a voice healer and belongs on-air."

←→

Hypnotherapist: "Wendy has experienced some attacks in a spiritual group she's a member of. Is she learning what's needed?"

Higher Self: "She's handling it very well. She knew typically the best response is no response unless it's truly defamation of character."

(pause)
Higher Self: "She was guided and measured in her neutral, yet powerful response. She knew not to respond the same day. She knew to be her highest vibration when she responded – if you are truly guided to respond at all. It's stooping to a lower level and a losing game for you in most cases."

(pause)
Higher Self: "She'll have to do a lot more 'no comment' in the future as she becomes well-known. Her boyfriend understood this well from his career as a successful athlete. He was right to tell her 'Don't read your publicity. Be careful if you chose to read your book reviews. Do not respond to them. Play your own long game – this is how you will achieve excellence.' "

Hypnotherapist: "That sounds like great advice!"

←→

Higher Self: "Yes. Don't get addicted to seeking approval from others. That's a losing game. That is how you squander your soul, piece by piece. It can be a surprisingly short, slippery slope."

(pause)
Higher Self: "It's part of what happened with Marilyn as well as with many other celebrities."

(pause)
Higher Self: "She knows she has a life lesson to 'let go of what other people think' and to be true to herself. She should simply be thoughtful and take a pause. Ask herself truthfully am I meant to read my reviews – am I meant to do so now – am I my Higher Self?"

Hypnotherapist: "That's great advice."

←→

Hypnotherapist: "Did she successfully astral travel to the Mary Magdalen sacred tour site that her friend was on?"

Higher Self: "We'd like to ask Joe to come forward again.

He can best answer the remainder of today's questions."

Hypnotherapist: "Very good. Welcome, Joe. Are you here as a Guide?"

Joe: 'Yes, I am. She successfully traveled to the tour site in France. Her friend asked Wendy her impressions and she sent them via private messenger. She should let go of her friend may or may not respond. She's quite busy on her trip and doesn't always have good connectivity."

(pause)

Joe: "We want to confirm the astral travel was an effective technique. Wendy checked with her Higher Self and Guides first, and it was done for a divine purpose."

Hypnotherapist: "So this helped her regardless of whether her friend responds?"

←→

Joe: "Yes. It helped her bring in her writer blueprint – her ability to write the book again in the future that Magdalen wrote before. Magdalen's Book of Love. Wendy is to write her own book again."

(pause)

Joe: "We want her to understand something important. She is not to be concerned with what the historical documents or public records state. A portion of people in Southern France – including a large percentage of Catholics – believe Mary Magdalen was repentant."

(pause)

Joe: "Many believe she was a penitent whore. This is what they were taught by their man-made religion. That religion was created in large part to crush the Divine Feminine. Notice I said man-made – the holy women were pushed out after Jesus' death, including his wife and mother."

Hypnotherapist: "So what's Wendy's highest truth?"

←→

Joe: "That's the perfect question! Wendy doesn't have those memories or beliefs because it's not what she experienced or chose in that lifetime. I want to encourage you – to inspire you – don't bow down or feel badly when your memories don't match the – quote – 'history.' "

(pause)

Joe: "After this session, she's going to want to read about me. To look up Joe DiMaggio. She's never read about or researched me. She's going to want to judge herself for what she 'got right' and didn't get right from the historical records."

(pause)

Joe: "We'd like to ask you what can be more 'right' than your own memory and experiences? Much of the public record may be unclear. It's always a reflection of that writer, patron, or publisher at that point in time."

(pause)

Joe: "Isn't it better to honor yourself – to trust yourself? Keep digging to learn your truth. There are many timelines. Memory is not a perfect mechanism. It serves us to the best of its ability."

(pause)

Joe: "We may be tapping into parallel lives is another issue – a different experience would have evolved if she followed one of those splits."

←→

Hypnotherapist: "Is your point that she shouldn't feel badly when people ask her, 'Why don't you talk about or remember those years in the cave when you were Mary Magdalen?"

Joe: "Exactly. She needs to speak her own truth. She can state, 'I remember going to the caves from time to time, but I certainly didn't spend most of my thirty plus years in France there."

(pause)

Joe: "Speak your truth with conviction and without apology. Own your power. Live your life! That was her boyfriend's message to her many times. That was their contract, for him to inspire her to step fully into her power, without abusing it."

Hypnotherapist: "It sounds like their relationship was multi-layered and important for her – for them both."

Joe: "It was. Back to our discussion of the caves. She can state, 'I recall meditating in the caves. I recall being in solitude there. I remember doing some writing there. I didn't live there for thirty years."

Hypnotherapist: "Thank you for that clarity."

←→

Hypnotherapist: "Should she walk the labyrinth at St. John's in Kirkland?"

Joe: "Yes. It's why we drew it to her attention. We had her drive home a different route when there was an accident on the highway. She got stuck in traffic next to the labyrinth so that she would notice it."

(pause)

Joe: "That was not a coincidence. There are no coincidences – only synchronicities as we work to get your attention."

(pause)

Joe: "Walking that labyrinth will help her easily connect with the Chartres Cathedral labyrinth in France. It doesn't matter if she connects with her friend via private message during her Magdalen trip to France – their energy will connect."

(pause)

Joe: "Many labyrinths including St. John's are designed

based on the Chartres Cathedral in France. Wendy was quite excited to learn that fact. These are the types of synchronicities that mean you're on the right track – pursue them!"

(pause)

Joe: "It's important for her to walk the St. John's labyrinth on the same day her friend's group tours Chartres Cathedral. If it's rainy in Seattle – so what, take an umbrella. She won't melt and it will keep any crowds down."

(pause)

Joe: "She's meant to go next Thursday – that's the day the tour group is going to Chartres Cathedral in Chartres, France an hour or so outside of Paris."

←→

Hypnotherapist: "Thank you. Those were all the questions Wendy wrote for today. Has the Quantum Healing Hypnotherapy session concluded for the moment?"

Joe: "It has."

Hypnotherapist: "May we request the healing continue..."

Joe: *(interrupting)* "Wendy can continue to connect with her Higher Self and Guides and with me, with Joe. We're becoming more one with her to help her."

←→

Hypnotherapist: "That's wonderful – thank you, Joe. Is there anything Wendy can do to support today's healing?"

Joe: "The simplest thing she can do to heal and keep her energy up is to get enough sleep. She needs seven to eight hours a night minimum, as do almost all souls when in a human body."

(pause)

Joe: "It's time for her to trust her intuition – to act decisively on it. The time for questioning is no longer needed. Her discernment is now highly honed. She can move forward smoothly without the indecision and attacks she's endured."

(pause)

Joe: "We encourage her to give over anything troubling her to the Universe. She can now do what she is supposed to do. She can now fully relax into her life purpose. We also encourage her to 'be' versus always 'doing' – this is problematic for so many. She can now be at peace – she can be peace."

←→

Hypnotherapist: "Thank you. How does Wendy best receive her guidance?"

Joe: "She's in constant communication with her Guides. She hears at the deepest levels. She no longer needs to meditate to hear us, which is a bit unusual."

(pause)

Joe: "Meditation and muscle-testing as well as hypno-therapy is still excellent for her more complex questions and to help level up to the next stage."

(pause)

Joe: "Each course she takes – each technique she re-learns – helps her hear and understand more from the Divine. This is a wonderful place to be. She's earned it through many lives."

← →

Hypnotherapist: "Thank you – that's amazing! Is there any closing message for me?"

Joe: "It's the same message for you. Trust your intuition and act on it decisively. You're both truly blessed. You have both surpassed expectations as to what was planned for this lifetime."

Hypnotherapist: "Thank you. It's been a pleasure, Joe."

← →

Our session was concluded and closed out. I felt so grateful for it. Such a wealth of information had come through for me!

Unfortunately, over time my ego started to niggle at me, "What if you're making this all up? Who are you to think you were Joe DiMaggio, one of the greatest ball players of all time?"

I asked my Guides to enlighten me. Had I really lived a life as Joe DiMaggio? Was he truly now one of my Guides? I did my best to surrender any remaining doubts to the Divine. I was grateful it didn't take long for definitive proof to arrive on my doorstep...

Chapter Five – Forgiveness

A remarkable potential client was referred to me a few short weeks after the session in which I first explored my life as Joe DiMaggio.

Maria (name changed for confidentiality) described having memories from Marilyn Monroe's viewpoint since she was a child. She wondered if these recollections might relate to or be the cause of her nightmares, anxiety, and intermittent depression, as well as certain phobias.

We spoke via phone to discuss the challenges Maria was facing. We assessed if we communicated well enough to have a productive session as English was not Maria's first language.

I needed to assess if Maria had realistic expectations for a past-life regression. She understood that a past-life regression is not a psychic reading, and that her Higher Self and Guides would architect what she would experience.

It was important we both release any expectations, particularly as I recalled being Joe DiMaggio. I would not mention Joe, Marilyn, or any information from that timeline during Maria's session. I'd follow my client's lead.

We synched our calendars for a four-hour session in November of 2016. It was a plus that Maria knew how to meditate and had a lot of specific dream recall.

The following are excerpts from Maria's transcript. I normally purposefully ask only open-ended questions. Maria requested I provide her with examples to choose from if she needed help describing in English what she was seeing and experiencing.

I posed my questions as carefully as I could. It's crucial to not 'lead the witness' during a hypnotherapy session to not influence the client's memory recall. I asked Archangel Gabriel to help with our communication.

←→

(session in progress)
Wendy: "What's the first thing you see as you come off the boat and find yourself at a very important time and place?"
(long pause)
Wendy: "Are you coming off the boat? What's the first thing you see or experience?
Maria: "People."
Wendy: "Good, you see people. Look down at your feet first for me, please, and then we'll look at the people."
Maria: "Okay."
Wendy: "Are you wearing anything on your feet?"
Maria: "Shoes."
Wendy: "You're doing great. What type of shoes are you wearing?"
Maria: "High heels."
Wendy: "Okay, you're wearing high heels. What color are they?"
Maria: "They look like they're black."
Wendy: "You're doing great. You see black high heels – as you look up a bit at your legs and body – what are you wearing on the rest of your body?"

←→

Maria: "I'm wearing a dress."
Wendy: "Ok, wonderful. What color is your dress. What does it look like, specifically?"
Maria: "It's black with black or white or something..."
Wendy: "Very good. How long is it – to the knees or longer? Can you tell what length it is? It's fine if you don't know."
Maria: "It's to my knees."
Wendy: "Can you get a feel for the fabric? Can you reach down and touch it with your fingers? It's fine if you don't get an impression."
Maria: "Umm – it's kind of – I don't know – I think it's some kind of slippery material?"
Wendy: "You're doing very well. Are you wearing long sleeves, or sleeveless or do you sleeves go part way down your arms?"
Maria: "It's sleeveless."
Wendy: "Very good. How would you describe your neckline?"
Maria: "It's like – it goes down from the shoulders – the chest is kind of – I don't know how to say it in English right now."

81

←→

Wendy: "It's okay – you're doing great! Does your body feel female?"

Maria: "Yes."

Wendy: "Does your body feel healthy?"

Maria: "Yes. I'm healthy."

Wendy: "Wonderful. Do you feel young, or old or middle-aged?"

Maria: "I'm in my thirties."

Wendy: "Wonderful. Look down at yourself again – are you wearing anything on your fingers or around your wrists?"

Maria: "I'm wearing globes."

Wendy: *(confused)* "You're wearing globes?"

Maria: "No, I'm wearing GLOBES – you know, on my hands?"

Wendy: *(laughing)* "Oh, excuse me, you're wearing gloves. Are they short or longer in length?"

Maria: "They're short."

Wendy: "Wonderful – you're seeing very clearly now. Is there anything you can see or feel around your neck?"

Maria: "No – I don't think so."

Wendy: "How about on your head?"

Maria: "No."

Wendy: "Are you carrying anything with you?"

Maria: "My handbag."

Wendy: "Oh, you have a handbag. What does it look like?"

Maria: "It's little – it's black – maybe leather? It has some gold hardware."

Wendy: "Excellent. What a great description. Now that we've thoroughly explored what you look like and are wearing, let's check out your surroundings."

←→

Wendy: "Where are you standing? Are you outside, or inside – how would you describe where you're standing?"

Maria: "I'm standing outside a door."

Wendy: "Okay, you're standing outside a door. What else can you see around you?"

Maria: "I see the Hollywood sign. It's not too close, but I see it – I recognize it."

Wendy: "When you say you see the Hollywood sign, is Hollywood written on a street sign? Or is it the big white letters spelling Hollywood out on the hillside? Or are you seeing it somewhere else?"

Maria: "I'm seeing the last one you said – the big one on the hillside."

←→

Wendy: "Wonderful. You're seeing so clearly now. Carry

on your natural course. Do you want to go inside that door?"

Maria: "The house – I want to see inside the house."

Wendy: "That's a great choice to explore. You can just open the door and go on in. What do you see inside or experience as you first enter the house?"

Maria: "Ummm – it's white – it doesn't feel like my house quite yet."

Wendy: "That's fine. Do you know who's house it is or if you've been here before?"

Maria: "I don't know whose house this is."

(pause)

←→

Wendy: "That's fine. We can explore inside, and it may become clear to you, if it's important to know. You mentioned seeing or sensing white. Do you see lots of white inside the house or the exterior, or both?"

Maria: "It was the outside that was white – but it has a dark brown door."

Wendy: "That's great. You're seeing very clearly now. Is there anything on the door – maybe a hanging decoration, or a sign or house number or something else? How about on the doorframe?"

Maria: "No, it's just plain."

Wendy: "Okay, so you're seeing a white house with a dark brown door. Do you enter on your own with a key, or is the door already open? Do you ring a bell or knock? How do you enter the white house with the dark brown door?"

Maria: "It's open. It was left unlocked for me, I think."

←→

Wendy: "Great. Let's go on in. What do you see as you enter – do you enter straight into a room or maybe into an entryway or foyer?"

Maria: "It's a room. I'm in a room."

Wendy: "What do you see around you in that room?"

Maria: "I see two chairs."

Wendy: "What do the two chairs look like?"

Maria: "They're brown – they're not straight chairs – more like sofa chairs."

Wendy: "Are they like upholstered living room chairs?"

Maria: "Yes, exactly."

Wendy: "What else do you see? Did you enter the living room, or maybe you're seeing a different type of room?"

Maria: "Living room sounds right."

Wendy: "You're doing great. Is there anything else that catches your eye or looks interesting that you'd like to examine more closely?"

←→

Maria: "There's a fireplace made from bricks but built in the wall."

Wendy: "Very good. What kind of shape is it as you observe that fireplace built into the wall?"

Maria: 'It's a square kind of shape, this fireplace."

Wendy: "Very good. Does it have a mantel or shelf above it, or do you just see the brick?"

Maria: "Just the brick – there's no mantel – it's set into a white wall."

Wendy: "Do you see anything else that captures your attention?

Maria: "No."

Wendy: "Okay. Is there any carpeting–"

Maria: *(interrupting excitedly – sense of her clarity increasing)* "Oh, I see a window!"

Wendy: "Excellent! Does it have any curtains or blinds?"

Maria: "It has large white curtains."

Wendy: "Very good. Look down at the floor – is there any carpeting or rug you can see or is it some sort of hard-surface floor?"

Maria: "There's no carpet here or elsewhere I can see. They're hard-surface floors."

Wendy: "That's great. Can you see what type of hard floors are in this house?"

Maria: "They're brown wood. Light brown wood. I don't know what it's called."

←→

Wendy: "That's okay. You're doing great. Have you been here before, do you think?"

Maria: "I believe I have some connection to this house."

Wendy: "Okay, that makes sense as to why you'd want to revisit it. Plus, the front door was perhaps left unlocked for you?"

Maria: "Yes."

Wendy: "Would you like to explore another room in the house?"

Maria: "Yes, I do want to."

Wendy: "Great, where would you like to go? Do you have a favorite spot in this house?"

←→

Maria: "I want to go to the bedroom."

Wendy: "Okay, let's go to the bedroom. Is the house one-story or do you need to go up or down some stairs to get to the bedroom?"

Maria: "I need to go up – to go up some stairs. I need to ascend."

Wendy: "Great. Be there now!"

Maria: "I'm up. I'm there in the bedroom."

Wendy: "Great – good job. Is this the only bedroom upstairs or are there others?"

Maria: "There are more rooms – but this is the only

bedroom upstairs or in this area."

Wendy: "Very good. Describe what you see or experience in the bedroom, please – your first impressions?"

←→

Maria: "There's a huge white bed. There's no pillows or anything. It's so huge! There's nothing on it – there's normally something on it. I'm not sure why nothing is on it right now?"

Wendy: "You can see quite clearly now. Why is the bed looking so white? Is there a comforter or bedspread on it, or are you looking at just a bare mattress or box spring or something else? What are you seeing right now?"

Maria: "It looks like it was just placed there. The room is not yet finished. There are no pictures, no tables – oh, wait, there's just one bedside table."

Wendy: "You're doing great. Where is the bedside table positioned as you enter the room in comparison to the bed?"

Maria: "The bedside table is to the right as you face the bed. You know, from the foot of the bed?"

Wendy: "I understand. Is there anything on the night table?"

Maria: "Yes, I see something on the night table."

Wendy: "What do you see on the night table?"

←→

Maria: "I see some letters. I don't think they're finished. There's something else there, too."

Wendy: "Why don't you pick up the letters? Are these letters you're writing, or do you see someone else's writing on the letter?"

Maria: "It's my writing. I see my handwriting."

Wendy: "Very good – are these letters you've started writing?"

Maria: "Yes."

Wendy: "Excellent. Let's look at these more closely. Who are you writing to? Did you write a salutation at the top?"

Maria: "It looks like I wrote 'Bobby.'"

Wendy: "Very good. Please help me understand – are all the letters written to this Bobby, or to different people? It's okay if you don't know."

Maria: "They're to different people."

Wendy: "Who are the other names written there, or can you simply sense who you are writing to?"

←→

Maria: "They're to my lovers. The other letter is to Joe, but it doesn't say more."

Wendy: "So does it look like it's just a start – the two letters are unfinished?"

Maria: "Yes, they're unfinished – that's right."

Wendy: "Thank you for clarifying. Is there anything else

85

on that bedside table?"

Maria: "Yes."

Wendy: "What else do you see there?"

←→

Maria: "I see empty bottles."

Wendy: "Okay, you see empty bottles. Can you tell what they contained?"

Maria: "I'm not sure what they contain – I'm going to pick one up to look at it better."

Wendy: "That's a great idea. What does it look like? How would you describe the color or size of the bottle? Can you tell what it's made from – perhaps glass or plastic or something else? Is there a label you can read."

Maria: "It's an orange bottle – I'm trying to read it now." *(pause)*

Maria: "It's sleeping medication. It's orange in color. It's not very big, this bottle."

Wendy: "You're doing great. Is there anything else on your bedside table?"

←→

Maria: "It's white."

Wendy: "What's white – is this another bottle you're seeing? Is there anything in it?"

Maria: "Yes, a white bottle."

Wendy: "What's inside it?"

Maria: "Just pills. There are pills in the bottle."

Wendy: "Very good. Can you read any label or product information?"

Maria: "Yes."

Wendy: "What does it say?"

Maria: "The label says the side effects. There could be negative stomach impact or effect on the body when you take the pills. It says how many pills to take."

Wendy: "Do you mean the recommended dosage? How many pills to take and how often and with or without food, that kind of thing?"

Maria: *(nodding)* "Yes!"

Wendy: "What's the best dosage for you to take from this bottle you're now examining?

Maria: "It says two."

Wendy: "Two pills once a day, or as needed, or a certain number of hours apart? What is the recommended dosage for you for this medication?"

Maria: "Two per night."

Wendy: "Is this a sleeping aid, did you say earlier?"

Maria: "Yes, I believe that's what this medicine is."

←→

Wendy: "Super. You're seeing extremely clearly now. Do you see any other information about the sleeping pills?

Maybe the medicine's name or the doctor's name? Or perhaps your name, address, or phone number?"

(pause)

Wendy: "What can you read on that label? You can put on your glasses if you need reading glasses or turn on the light to better examine that pharmacy label."

Maria: *(slowly)* "Something – something – B – A – something - something – it's hard to read this tiny label. That's the type of sleeping medicine I'm taking."

Wendy: *(repeating what her Guide whispered, which was unusual because it's important not to lead the client experience. She did so because her Guide asked her repeatedly to ask the question.)* "Barbital, perhaps - barbiturates?"

Maria: "Yes, that's one of them. One of the prescription medications - I think I know this name you just said."

Wendy: "Anything else you need to know will fill in later. Is there anything else on that bedside table?"

←→

Maria: "I see a picture."

Wendy: "Why don't you pick it up and describe it? Is the picture loose or framed?"

Maria: "Framed. It's a child and a mother."

(pause)

Maria: "It's me with my mother.

Wendy: "Oh, it's you with your mother. How old do you look in the photo?"

Maria: "I'm a little girl of two or three years old."

Wendy: "Where are you, do you think?"

Maria: "We're on the beach."

Wendy: "Oh, that sounds nice. What are you doing on the beach in the photograph?"

Maria: "We're standing in the sand looking right into the camera – we're playing in the sand."

Wendy: "That sounds fun. Is there anything else on that bedside table?"

Maria: "No – there's just a little lamp. There's nothing more."

Wendy: "Okay. What does the bedside table itself look like? Can you tell me what it might be made from?"

Maria: "The bedside table is brown wood."

←→

Wendy: "Okay. Now that we've been here for a while, do you get more of a sense of who's house this is?"

Maria: "Yes, I do."

Wendy: "Who's house is this?"

Maria: "This is now my house! I just bought it recently."

Wendy: "Oh, it's your house – how wonderful! Do you get a sense of where your home is located geographically?"

Maria: "It's somewhere nice and warm – I see my flowers."

Wendy: "What types of flowers do you see around your

home? Do you see flowers inside or outside your home, or both?"

Maria: "I see roses – mostly roses. Some new plants are going in – someone has been working in the garden."

Wendy: "That sounds beautiful. What else can you see?"

Maria: "To my left, I see a glimpse of a big swimming pool – I see the blue sky up above."

Wendy: "What else do you see or hear or notice outside your home?"

Maria: "It's very quiet here. Peaceful."

Wendy: "Sunshine and quiet – that sounds wonderful. Is there anything else you can see out your bedroom window?"

Maria: "No, the bushes are too high, I can't see more than what I described."

←→

(This was interesting since Maria felt she had gone upstairs to get to her bedroom. I tried to understand more how bushes could be obstructing her view.)

Wendy: "Where are the bushes located?"

Maria: "There's a high hedge between me and the street but I can see out my door around my own property."

Wendy: "Do you now get a sense where you are geographically?"

Maria: "Yes, I'm in California. I'm in the United States."

Wendy: "Great job pinpointing that. What's your neighborhood like if you're on the other side of the high hedge?"

Maria: "There are not many people who live here. Not many people are here as they want privacy. They choose this neighborhood for its privacy factor."

←→

Wendy: "Do you know who any of your neighbors are even if you haven't yet met them personally?"

Maria: "Yes, I do know who lives near me, but I don't know them personally yet. I'm just in the process of moving in."

Wendy: "Can you say who else lives in the neighborhood?"

Maria: "Do you mean their names?"

Wendy: "Yes."

Maria: "There's a guy named Paul or Frank or something like that – hmmm – I don't really know. This house has so much protection and privacy that I barely know who's in my neighborhood."

Wendy: "It sounds quite idyllic in many ways – is it?"

Maria: *(smiling)* "Yes, it is."

←→

Wendy: "Is there anything else you'd like to explore?"

Maria: "I'm not sure."

Wendy: "Okay. Let's learn more about the letters you're writing – the ones on your nightstand. Do you know the last name of the Bobby you were writing to?"

Maria: "Yes – it's a nickname that I call him Bobby."

Wendy: "Do you know Bobby's last name?"

Maria: "Kennedy. I think it's Kennedy."

Wendy: "Are you referring to Bobby Kennedy – Robert Kennedy, President John F. Kennedy's brother?"

Maria: "Yes."

← →

Wendy: "Okay, very good. You're seeing everything quite clearly. You mentioned you had started a letter to another lover. Do you know who else you were writing to?"

Maria: "Yes, it's to Joe."

Wendy: "Does it say anything more?"

Maria: "It just says Joe, nothing else."

Wendy: "So if this is an informal letter you wouldn't write the person's full name at the top of the page. But do you know it? What would you write on an envelope if you were to mail this letter rather than giving it to him in-person."

Maria: "It's to you – it's to Joe DiMaggio."

← →

Wendy: *(feeling suddenly emotional)* "Oh my goodness, that's truly special. You're writing a letter to me – to me when I was Joe?"

Maria: "Yes."

Wendy: "Okay."

(I was struggling not to burst into tears. I did my best to put my emotions aside to keep my focus on what Maria needed.)

← →

Wendy: "Did you say there were three letters?"

Maria: "No, there are just two letters. The one to Bobby and the one to you. I see a manuscript on the bed – it's not actually a letter."

Wendy: "Is the manuscript for a book or play or something else?"

Maria: "The manuscript is for a movie."

Wendy: "Can you read the name of the movie on the cover of the manuscript?"

← →

Maria: "Let me look. The manuscript reads, *Something's Got to Give!* That's the film name."

Wendy: "Great job – you're seeing and sensing so clearly now. Is your name on the manuscript? Or did you sign it at the bottom of the unfinished letters by chance?"

Maria: "No, nothing has my name on the manuscript. There's just the names of the other actors and actresses. If you turn the page, you can see my lines."

Wendy: "Are your lines highlighted for you already, or

89

do you mark them yourself?"

Maria: "I'm marking up my lines myself now while we talk."

Wendy: "What's your character's name in the movie?"

←→

Maria: "I don't see it. It just says my full name instead."

Wendy: "How is your name written in the manuscript? Can you read it to me, please."

Maria: "It says *MM*. Then when I turn the page, it says *Marilyn Monroe.*"

Wendy: "That's quite clear, Marilyn, excellent job. How are your name and initials written – by hand or some other way?"

(I now began addressing Maria as Marilyn)

Marilyn: "It's written almost like from a computer nowadays, but it's very distinct and clear. Maybe a typewriter?"

Wendy: "So you can read your name clearly on the white paper. Is the paper white? What does your manuscript look like physically?"

Marilyn: "It's not white, the paper, it's cream-colored."

←→

Wendy: "Very descriptive – you're seeing so clearly. So, it's a clean manuscript with very clear body writing..."

Marilyn: "That's right."

Wendy: "Is there anyone else in the house with you? Are there any people or pets or is it just you, Marilyn?"

Marilyn: "It's just me – it's very quiet."

Wendy: "Wonderful."

Marilyn: "I don't hear any street noises – it's very quiet."

Wendy: "What's your favorite place in the house to sit or relax or simply be."

Marilyn: "I love sitting in the garden, and also in the living room. I love to sit in one of those good chairs that were placed there - those comfortable brown chairs I told you about?"

Wendy: "Yes, the chairs you saw when we first entered the house?"

Marilyn: "No, wait – there's a weird wood chair in the other living room. There are two sections to the room – I don't know why it's set up like this."

Wendy: "Do you mean the room is split on the two sides of the front door?"

Marilyn: *(nodding)* "Yes, sort of."

←→

Wendy: "Okay. Would you like to have a meal in your home?"

(no answer)

Wendy: "Do you want to go to the kitchen for a meal?"

Marilyn; "No, I don't eat much."

Wendy: "That's fine. Marilyn, do you get a sense of the year?"

Marilyn: "Yes, I do. It's the late 1950s – no, it's later."

Wendy: "Was there a date on the manuscript? Or on either of the letters you're writing. Can you find a date? You can see this very clearly now."

(long pause)

←→

Marilyn: "I found it! The manuscript says June 13, 1962."

Wendy: "Okay, you're doing marvelously. Is there anything more to learn from that time and place?"

(no reply)

Wendy: "Is there anything more to explore?"

Marilyn: "No, not in this house. Everything looks undone. It's not yet set up. It's a Mexican style kitchen."

(pause)

Marilyn: "I think I ordered things but they're not here yet. That's why the living room and bedroom still look so empty. My things haven't come yet."

←→

Wendy: "That makes sense. Now that we understand what you were shown, let's move forward to the next important day for healing and understanding. What's the first thing that you see?"

Marilyn: "I see the sky – it's a beautiful afternoon."

Wendy: "Great – are you inside or outside?"

Marilyn: "I'm outside."

Wendy: "So you're outside. What time of day is it? What are you doing?"

Marilyn: "It's turning to early evening. I'm leaning on the balcony. I'm drinking something."

Wendy: "What happens next as you look out and lean on the balcony and have your drink?"

Marilyn: "I'm waiting for someone to come. I'm waiting."

Wendy: "You're waiting for a visitor? Are you home or somewhere else?"

Marilyn: "I'm somewhere else. There's no balcony at my house."

Wendy: "So you're somewhere other than your home. What happens next?"

←→

Marilyn: "There's this guy – this man – he just appeared."

Wendy: "What does he look like? Is he walking toward the house, and you see him from the balcony?"

Marilyn: *(smiling)* "No, he's walking toward me with his camera."

Wendy: "What does he look like? What's he wearing?"

Marilyn: "He's wearing beige. It's a T-shirt. He's wearing pants or shorts with it. I'm not sure how long his pants are."

Wendy: "Very good. What does his face look like?"

Marilyn: "He has dark brown eyes."

Wendy: "What's his name. Does he introduce himself to you? Or do you already know him?"

Marilyn: *(no hesitation)* "It's George."

(pause)

Marilyn: "Can I ask him if his name is George? I want to make sure."

Wendy: "Of course. What's the photographer's name?"

Marilyn: "Well, another guy was supposed to come. Oh, God - I really want to get this right!"

Wendy: "It's okay. Just breathe. You're doing fantastic. We can figure this out. Picture him introducing himself, even if he doesn't do so today. What does he say his name is?"

Marilyn: "He just says George."

Wendy: "Okay, he just says his first name – that's fine. Where do you take the photos?"

← →

Marilyn: "On the balcony."

Wendy: "So you're up on the balcony together taking pictures. What are you wearing?"

Marilyn: "I'm wearing an orange sweater with pants. They're white – they're just above the ankle."

Wendy: "How about on your feet?"

Marilyn: "I'm barefoot."

Wendy: "Very good. Do you like having your photo taken? Is this something you're comfortable with or even enjoy? Or is it a duty from the studio or someone else assigning it to you?"

Marilyn: *(smiling)* "I'm just having a good time. These pictures are not going to be published – it's just for fun!"

Wendy: "That's wonderful. How long do you take the photos for, do you know? It's okay if you don't know."

Marilyn: "For a few hours."

Wendy: "What do you do when you're done? Does he just leave right after your photos?"

Marilyn: "Yes. He had to go home to his wife. Plus, we don't live here, so we couldn't have a drink or a bite to eat. He needs to travel home."

← →

Wendy: "I understand. Did you get a sense of where the building was with the balcony? Did you choose the location or did George?"

Marilyn: "We agreed to the location because it was such a nice place. It was good for photos in natural light and shaded this time of day."

Wendy: "Are you in the L.A. area, or did you travel

further to meet George?"

Marilyn: "We're somewhere in L.A.."

Wendy: "Great. Is there anything else to learn from that time and place when you're wearing your orange sweater and having George take your photos for fun?"

←→

Marilyn: *(quietly)* "I remember being very depressed."

Wendy: *(gently)* "Ahh – do you know why you're depressed?"

Marilyn: "I was very depressed because there'd been another divorce. I had a lot of things to clean up.

(long pause)

Marilyn: "Some people wanted me dead."

(I drew in a deep breath - it was important to not over-react)

Wendy: "You said you recently divorced?"

Marilyn: "Yes, but that's mostly okay now. We've made our peace. The more immediate issue is my difficult love situation with another man."

←→

Wendy: "What's your difficult love situation?"

Marilyn: *(sighing)* "We tried being married before. It didn't work out, though we'd been great friends and went slow. We got divorced a long time ago. That was a different divorce than the first one I mentioned. He wanted to try again to make it work for us both. He wanted us to reconcile."

Wendy: "But what do you want, Marilyn? We're here for you today."

Marilyn: "It was difficult to forgive him."

Wendy: "Who was it difficult to forgive?"

Marilyn: "Joe. You – Joe DiMaggio."

Wendy: *(sucking in another deep breath)* "What was difficult to forgive Joe for?"

Marilyn: "Joe's anger took over his actions. He became very angry with me and then he hit me. I had bruises on my shoulder and on my back."

Wendy: "I'm truly sorry, Marilyn. What happened next?"

Marilyn: "I had to be in the movie the next week. The makeup team had to cover up the bruises with makeup. I felt hurt and embarrassed. It wasn't only the physical pain – it triggered a deep emotional pain."

←→

Wendy: *(crying silently)* "I'm so sorry that happened to you, Marilyn. Is there a way you could possibly forgive him now so that you are no longer carrying that pain in your body? It would be so good for you. It doesn't condone his actions – you can forgive him without that."

Marilyn: "I'm trying to forgive him, but he wanted me to be a housewife. I couldn't do that. I had my job. I tried to respect my husband's feelings, but I needed to be working to be truly me. We tried and tried to make our marriage

93

work, but we had to separate and then divorce."

Wendy: "That sounds so difficult. What happened next?"

←→

Marilyn: "Joe kept saying he loved me. He was so sorry, and it wouldn't ever happen again."

(pause)

Marilyn: "But I didn't know how to forgive him. I went through things that hurt me physically and emotionally when I was younger. It was hard to feel love and acceptance from him once he'd crossed the line because it triggered when I was younger."

Wendy: "I'm sure he'd love to ask your forgiveness right now, Marilyn. We can't sweep what Joe did under the rug. You have every right to your feelings – I can see why'd you be upset at every level."

(pause)

Wendy: "Forgiveness is a challenging life lesson. When we forgive, we free ourselves and the other person. We set ourselves free."

(no reply)

Wendy: "Let's ask your Guides if it's best to help you forgive him – Joe – me – now? What's best for you, Marilyn?"

(no reply)

←→

Wendy: "Are you hearing your Guides to consider forgiving Joe? Or is that not your path at this moment?"

Marilyn: *(slowly)* "I do forgive him. I don't hate him – I don't hate anyone."

Wendy: *(quietly)* "That's a big gift to him – and an even bigger gift to yourself. You're a kind and generous person to forgive him."

(pause)

Wendy: "Is there anything further to learn from that time and place? Or are we ready to move forward?"

Marilyn: "That's all that's needed for that piece. I had to become a good role model for myself."

Wendy: "In what way?"

Marilyn: "Daniel is helping explain this to me. Daniel is my Guide. Because no one showed me how to have self-confidence. I had to develop it myself. I had to continually change – to invent and then re-invent myself."

Wendy: "It feels like you did an amazing job with that in your lifetime."

Marilyn: "Thank you."

←→

Wendy: "Did you complete your main mission that lifetime?"

Marilyn: "No, I died way too young. It's time for me to cross over to the Light. Daniel my Guide is going to meet

94

me there."

Wendy: "Wonderful. Let's do that now."

(Wendy helped Marilyn cross over to the White Light of Home.)

←→

Wendy: *(gently)* "Let's look back on your life from this higher plane, where everything can be made clear to you. I'm asking your Higher Self – your eternal soul – and your Guides to speak through you. Is there anything that could have been done better? Or differently?"

Higher Self: "There's nothing I could have changed, given the circumstances."

Wendy: "Okay – you did the best you could. You over-came a lot."

Higher Self: "Yes."

Wendy: "What else do you see around you as you have this lovely reunion with your Guide Daniel and with the White Light?"

(Marilyn begins speaking in place of the Higher Self)

Marilyn: "Not much else. It's so lovely, it's warm – it's the White Light! It's nothing negative. It's all peace and unconditional love..."

Wendy: "Can you take a moment and really absorb that through your whole body – your whole entire being, through all space and time – to always be with you?"

(pause)

Wendy: "I'll be quiet and hold sacred space for you, and you can tell me when you're ready to move on."

(long pause)

←→

Marilyn: *(sounding stronger – cheerful)* "Ok, I'm ready!"

Wendy: "Okay, wonderful – how does the Light make you feel?"

Marilyn: "Umm – warm..."

Wendy: "Wonderful – very good. You can feel that blissful feeling at any time. You can choose to merge with the Light more – to feel it purifying your energy – reenergizing you – rejuvenating you – making perfect every cell of your body. It will uplift your spirit, your emotions, your mind..."

Marilyn: "Okay."

Wendy: "What do you see around you now?"

Marilyn: "Trees."

Wendy: "Wonderful. What do they look like?"

Marilyn: "They're huge."

Wendy: "What else do you notice?"

Marilyn: "It's a nice summer day."

Wendy: "Where are you in comparison to the huge trees on this nice summer day?"

Marilyn: "I'm sitting in the grass in my heels – I see the flowers."

(pause)

←→

Wendy: "That sounds wonderful – what types of flowers do you see?"

Marilyn: "They're small."

Wendy: "Do you know what type of flowers they are?"

Marilyn: "I don't know what kind they are."

Wendy: "That's okay. What colors do you see?"

Marilyn: "I see yellow."

Wendy: "That sounds beautiful. Do you notice anything else?"

Marilyn: "Not really."

Wendy: "Do you feel loved and supported in this place?"

Marilyn: "I feel that, yes."

Wendy: "That's wonderful."

(pause)

Wendy: "Do you feel a connection to this place?"

Marilyn: "Yes, I do."

Wendy: "You'll remember this when we're done. You can return here at any time. Would you like to remain a bit longer to feel bliss? To recharge your soul?"

Marilyn: "No, I'm ready to move on."

←→

Healing Temple

Wendy: "We can go straight to a Temple of Healing – a place of healing. Would you like to go there?"

Marilyn: "Yes."

Wendy: "What do you see around you in that place of healing?"

Marilyn: "Brick."

Wendy: "You see bricks?"

Marilyn: "Yes, an open tower of them."

Wendy: "You can feel Source is even stronger..."

Marilyn: *(interrupting)* "Oh, I feel wonderful here!"

Wendy: *(smiling)* "Now you will see a healing light. It will go to a specific place on your body to heal it through all space and time – through all dimensions – all life forms. Where does it go and what do you experience?"

Marilyn: "It's on my neck."

Wendy: "Wonderful. What color or colors do you notice? What do you experience with it."

Marilyn: "It's purple – it feels really good. I'm letting go of all that pressure from that life."

Wendy: "Wonderful! You can do that right now. Let go of all that pressure. Where do you notice any pressure?"

Marilyn: "My head – my brain – my thoughts."

Wendy: "Your thoughts – let's have those just gently flow away."

(pause)
Wendy: "That's very good. Is there a new healing light that would like to come to you now?"

←→

Marilyn: "There's the White Light again – I feel relief."
Wendy: "Why do you feel relief?"
Marilyn: "It gets my thoughts to calm down."
Wendy: "That's wonderful. Is there a new healing light presenting for you now?"
Marilyn: "Yes. It's going to my heart. It's a pink light. It's healing hurts I have been carrying as a soul for so long. I can release the soul level pain."
Wendy: "That's a powerful realization. Great job! Is there another healing light coming to you now?"

←→

Marilyn: "Yes, it's coming to my eyes."
Wendy: "What color is the healing light coming to your eyes?"
Marilyn: "It's blue."
Wendy: "What does it represent?"
Marilyn: "I can look differently at things in the future."
Wendy: "Is it like you can see through a new lens?"
Marilyn: "Yes, kind of."
Wendy: "Good. I'm inviting in a new healing light for you to powerfully yet gently heal your body, your mind and your soul through all space and time. Where does the new light go?"

←→

Marilyn: "To my feet."
Wendy: "What color is it?"
Marilyn: "It's green."
Wendy: "How does it make you feel?
Marilyn: "I feel relief. It will help me keep my feet on the ground, to be very grounded despite other people."
Wendy: "Wonderful. A new healing light can come to you now. What color is it and where does it go?"

←→

Marilyn: "The light is coming to my hands. It's a red color.
Wendy: "Great. What do you feel or experience with it?"
Marilyn: "It's helping make things less stressful. It's helping me do some de-stressing."
Wendy: "That's fantastic. Do you need more time to de-stress?"

←→

Marilyn: "No, the next healing light is coming. It's going to my ears – I see a dark brown color."
Wendy: "Do you know what that represents? It's okay if you don't."

Marilyn: "It's a reminder I don't need to maybe take in all the negative comments or believe them."

Wendy: "That sounds incredibly wise. Are you meant to be true to yourself – to let go of what other people think?"

Marilyn: "Yes. This provides me with a beautiful freedom."

Wendy: "This is fantastic work. Are there more healing lights for you?"

←→

Marilyn: "Yes, one is coming to my lips. It's a dark pink. It's to remind me to smile at stuff that I would normally be upset by."

Wendy: "Brilliant. Are there more lights?"

Marilyn: "There's a navy blue coming to support my entire back. It feels so good. It feels so warm, such relief, not so much pressure or responsibility on my back."

Wendy: "That sounds quite symbolic. Are there any more healing lights for you – perhaps one that will go all around you and fill your aura or energy field?"

Marilyn: "There are no more lights at this time."

←→

Wendy: *(smiling)* "You did fantastic! I'm asking your Higher Self and Guides to help you to continue to feel comfort and healing. To make perfect so many things you delineated so well. Are you ready to move on?"

Marilyn: "Yes."

←→

Temple of Knowledge

Wendy: "Excellent. Let's visit the Temple of All Knowledge to get the answers to your important questions you wrote for today. We'd like to understand why you chose your current life. I'd like you to imagine – to visualize – an amazing Temple of Knowledge just like you did your Healing Temple."

(pause)

Wendy: "I'm asking a Greeter or Guide to come forward to help you find the best information for your life today."

←→

Marilyn: "He's here – there's a Greeter here."

Wendy: "Wonderful. What does he look like? What name would he like us to use for him? What's your impression of him?"

Marilyn: "He has dark hair – he's a warm person. He's smiling at me."

Wendy: "Wonderful. Is he the same greeter as before? Was that an Angel we met?"

Marilyn: "No, he's a different one."

Wendy: "Okay. He has access to all knowledge – specifically to the knowledge that can best help you in your life now. The two of you are telepathically linked. I'll ask your questions and he will be able to answer through you. Do you understand?"

Marilyn: "Yes."

←→

Wendy: "Why was your mother born on the date of Marilyn Monroe's funeral? Does that have meaning?"

Marilyn: "She was born on that day to give birth to me as Maria to help me know who I am. It was to help me find my Marilyn Monroe past life to release all that energy."

Wendy: "Well, thank you to your mother for choosing that day to be born. We appreciate the synchronicity. It was a great clue you both noticed. Anything more on that point?"

←→

Marilyn: "The Guide is pointing out the intended meaning of that day was for a marriage. It was to be the day Marilyn and Joe remarried. Instead, it became a funeral day rather than a marriage – a wedding."

Wendy: *(soberly)* "Is it appropriate to heal that further for Marilyn, for Joe – for both of us? I feel a lot of energy there."

(long pause)

Wendy: "I feel healing coming through. I'm grateful you're doing this session today. It's unusual how strongly this session ties into my own heart. I appreciate your big heart for forgiving me in that lifetime."

Marilyn: *(slowly)* "I'm healing..."

Wendy: *(tearfully)* "That's excellent. I'm hearing we're both going to have happy lives, including positive relationships with men. Would your Guide like to confirm that for you?"

Marilyn: *(nodding)* "He says yes."

←→

Wendy: "Thank you. How can we best heal the loneliness and sadness you've experienced? Are we resolving them with today's session? How may I best be of service to you."

Marilyn: "Yes, this has helped me. It will continue to help me over time. I will heal more from today, but I will always feel a little sad. My soul won't one hundred percent heal, but this gets me on the best track."

Wendy: "Why is the soul not able to heal completely? Does more healing need to occur at Home after you drop your body this lifetime?"

Marilyn: "Because it will take more lifetimes."

Wendy: "I see. Can you expand on that?"

Marilyn: "There is so much debt and burden it's overwhelming."

Wendy: "Please tell me more. You're strong and brave and young – you're quite connected to God. We have incredible resources from the Divine and from the Light right now –

is this the best healing we can provide for you at this time?"
Marilyn: *(firmly)* "Yes."

←→

Wendy: "Thank you. Why does Maria have such 'intense and crazy dreams', in her words? Can you help her understand them better? Are they to help her understand her past life as Marilyn or more about her life purpose?"
Maria's Guides: "Her dreams have two main purposes."
Wendy: "What are the purposes?"
Maria: "I'll give you an example. The latest dream was in an office with a guy talking to me about my stage name. Aunt Grace was there with me. I had to change my name because I was 'discovered.' I was a little older than sixteen - somewhere around that age. It's like my age now, which is why the dream was presenting."
Wendy: "Thank you. What else do your dreams tell you?"

←→

Maria: "I have some dreams that are flashbacks to when I died. There's a dark tunnel – I know I'm dead."
(pause)
Maria: "There's also a modeling agency dream. This is another flashback because of things I'm doing in my life now. I'm releasing old energy through the dreams. It also helps you to see you have successfully done these things before."
Wendy: "Absolutely. This sounds like bringing forward past abilities to your life now. Would your Guide like us to know anything more about your dreams?"

←→

Maria: "Did I tell you about the first dream I had that made me think I might have a special connection with Marilyn or have even been her?"
Wendy: "Please ask your Guide if it's pertinent for our work today. I'm happy to listen."
Maria: "My Guide says to tell you the short version. I had this dream when I was young at a time when I was quite ill. I dreamed about a huge white bed – like today? There were two men in suits. One was Italian. One had glasses and was taller than the other. He barely had any hair."
(pause)
Maria: "I recognized them but didn't know their names. They started to introduce themselves and to tell me what they did for a living..."
Wendy: "Yes?"

←→

Maria: *(becoming increasingly upset)* "They handed me a mirror. I suddenly changed from a seven-year-old girl to a
100

woman with her hair all bleached out. She looked so tired."

(Marilyn begins speaking)

Marilyn: "The door to the bedroom opened. They just stared at me. More and more people came in and introduced themselves. Even my mother came. Each said who they had been in my life."

(pause)

Marilyn: "An Angel came and said gently, 'It's time to leave.' Nothing looked like modern day – meaning it was August 1962. I was dead."

(Maria resumes the narration)

Maria: "Then it happened today during my session!"

Wendy: "We are moving that experience out of your emotional field. You can have a much happier life this time around. You've done an excellent job really feeling these emotions, and now we can release them. Dreams help purge old experiences and emotions."

(pause)

Wendy: "Do you feel complete with that? Are you ready to move on to the next question or do your dreams require more healing?"

Maria: "We can move on."

←→

Wendy: "Excellent. When you reincarnate and chose your next life, do you physically look like you did in your previous life?"

Maria: "I'll ask my Guide."

(pause)

Maria: "He agrees with our earlier discussion we may or may not look alike. My looks this lifetime are to remind people of Marilyn Monroe. There are some differences. No one can be exactly the same."

←→

Wendy: "Thank you. May we have some insights into why Maria chose the current life?"

Maria: "I chose to have a loving mother because I didn't have one last time. My mother now is like I should have had when I was Marilyn, or like I would be as a mother. She's helping play a role for me as both."

Wendy: "Yes. You've described a challenging past life."

Maria: "The reason why my soul chose this life now is I get to relive a childhood I felt was missing last time. I never got one."

Wendy: "You chose your mother well. You've described a wonderfully positive parent and child relationship with lots of support for you."

←→

Maria: "Yes. But I have no idea why both my father and stepfather had to die. I have no idea why…"

101

Wendy: "Let's ask your Guide. Was there a soul contract to experience this loss? What was the teaching or purpose, if any?"

Maria: *(bluntly)* "My Guide says there was none. Both smoked – neither was aware of the consequences. They realized too late. There was no purpose to their early deaths. It was so unfair. They didn't know how to take care of the physical body for a lifetime."

Wendy: "I'm so sorry. Is there any further healing we can bring in for your heart right now? And what about your mother? Will she accept a healing at this time?"

← →

Maria: "I want her to find someone who loves her again like both my father and stepfather did – including as a best friend."

(pause)

Maria: "We are there for each other. We are supportive of one another. This is so important."

Wendy: "Yes, it is. Any other concerns in this area?"

Maria: "The thing is we forget them being here physically and we forget the emotional connection over time."

Wendy: *(gently)* "So time can heal it to a certain extent – the pain gets a little easier to bear? I'm not saying it's easy."

Maria: "Yes."

← →

Wendy: "Anything more about your current life purpose and mission?"

Maria: "No."

Wendy: "Okay. Why does Maria feel uncomfortable around children and about the thought of having children? What does your Guide say.?"

Maria: "I didn't get to be a mother when I was Marilyn. It was very upsetting. My body was afraid to have a child. I really wanted one."

(pause)

Maria: "I was in foster care with no father. I didn't know who my father was. He was one of three men – Edward – or a Mexican man – or a Norwegian guy?"

← →

Wendy: "I see. I have a gentle question for your Higher Self and Guides. This won't carry any emotional load. Are you meant to have children this lifetime? Can we heal this past life energy around being unhappy from not being able to have children?"

Maria: "I don't need children to have a happy life. If I'm meant to have them, I will. My soul wants to be young and carefree for as long as possible this lifetime."

Wendy: "I understand. I had my first child when I was

thirty-four. There's no rush."

Maria: "My mother was thirty-seven or thirty-eight."

Wendy: "Exactly. Anything more about children?"

Maria: "It's covered."

←→

Wendy: "Excellent. Why do you feel such a connection to Joe DiMaggio? Or has that been answered?"

Maria: "It's basically been answered. I feel a strong pull because we were the most emotionally connected of all the men I ever dated or married."

(pause)

Marilyn: "Joe understood me the most. He cared for me the most. We were maybe in the end soul mates just before I died. I would choose him for that role."

←→

Wendy: "Is it possible Marilyn and Joe were Twin-Flames?"

(pause)

Maria: "My Guide says yes – it's a possibility, but different, too. It's not useful to explore right now."

Wendy: "Okay, we'll move on. Is there anything else about the relationship with Joe to heal or to understand? We have this unique circumstance and opportunity with us here together – the former Joe and Marilyn."

Maria: "I miss him very much. He promised to always bring flowers to me every week after my death. He did so for twenty years. It was so important to me that he kept that promise. It showed he really cared."

Wendy: "Did you ask Joe to bring you flowers every week when you were Marilyn?"

Maria: "Yes, she – I – asked if I were to die first, would he put fresh flowers on my grave."

Wendy: "So it was a specific request?"

Maria: "Yes."

Wendy: "Thank you. That's such an amazing validation for me. I remember walking along the sidewalk as Joe, carrying flowers to take to Marilyn's grave. They were red roses a lot of the time."

(pause)

Wendy: "My spiritual teacher's husband used to work in downtown L.A. He would see me walking with the flowers when I was Joe. Over time florists delivered them as I didn't live in L.A., but I delivered some in-person, too."

(pause)

Wendy: "This makes me feel emotional. Thank you for clarifying this for me. I'm so glad we were introduced and can do this session."

Maria: "Same!"

←→

Wendy: "Let's return to your questions that you wrote

before we started today. Why have you not been able to avoid looking back at this past life? Is it a teaching tool for you?"

Maria: "Yes, and to allow me to release it. Now that I understand the lessons, I can release the energy I don't need."

Wendy: "You're exactly right – well done! Why have people told you that you look like Marilyn?"

Maria: "To help me to find and to understand the past life, and to release it. The recognition added to my dreams – it built more energy."

←→

Wendy: "How can we best heal your concern or fear men may use you. Is this a past life issue to release? How do we accomplish that or is it already done?"

Maria: *(sounding agitated)* "I don't know!"

Wendy: *(soothingly)* "Your Guide will know. How can Maria trust her instincts while still having an open heart? What's best for her?"

Maria: "My Guide said since I have already experienced men using people, I'm aware of the challenge. I know to be careful. I don't trust too many. I won't be naïve. I will be somewhere in the middle – I won't be fearful or closed-off either."

Wendy: "That sounds fantastic. You'll be wonderfully balanced. Am I hearing you'll be able to experience love in a healthy way?"

Maria: "Yes."

Wendy: "Excellent."

←→

Wendy: "How do we heal the fear of being alone? Was this triggered by past life energy from the Marilyn – the Norma Jean – lifetime?"

(Marilyn resumes speaking)

Marilyn: "When I wasn't married, I was alone. This included the last few months of my life. Arthur and I separated in 1961. I only had a couple of affairs after that – nothing real."

(pause)

Marilyn: "There was only me and Joe on and off. That was the only real thing."

Wendy: "How can we best address any fear of being alone now?"

(Maria steps to the forefront again)

Maria: "I have now learned to be alone and not alone. Being alone can be nice. You have some privacy. You have your freedom. You don't have to coordinate with someone else or ask anyone to do what you want to do."

(pause)

Maria: "It's also wonderful to do things together with

someone you care for. Can you see the beauty in each – the natural ebbs and flows?"

Wendy: "That's so well-put. I truly relate. I think you've just expressed being complete in oneself quite beautifully."

←→

Wendy: "You had a question why you love old Hollywood?

Maria: "It's another reminder of my past life as Marilyn. It was a timeless and classy period when women were women, and men were men. There were many remarkable things in the old Hollywood era. The beautiful styles – the ways women dressed up. It was more feminine."

Wendy: "I agree. I see Marilyn as such a glamorous depiction of the Divine Feminine. It's why she has such tremendous appeal. She's the most popular worldwide icon in existence, more loved now than when she was alive."

Maria: "I agree."

←→

Wendy: "Wonderful. Did we answer why you feel you should have been born back then?"

Maria: "Yes – answered."

Wendy: "Did we answer why you were missing Joe?"

Maria: "Yes. But there's more sad news about me missing people from that life. I have been researching people that might still be alive."

Wendy: "What did you discover?"

Maria: "I found Amy Green. She was Milton Green the photographer's wife."

(pause)

Maria: "George Barris died this year in 2016. That was truly sad for me. It hit me emotionally as we were good friends. He wasn't just my photographer."

Wendy: "I know you meditate well. Did you know you can ask to speak with his Higher Self and have a wonderful conversation?"

Maria: "I didn't think of that. That's good info. So, I could talk with my stepfather and father and my former photographers, too?"

Wendy: "Yes. You can ask to speak with their soul – they need to agree."

←→

Wendy: "Returning to your questions – we've certainly answered if you had an actual past life as Marilyn."

Maria: "Yes, I did."

Wendy: "May I ask gently how you died – how you passed on? There are conflicting reports in this area. We'd appreciate clarity if that is in your best interest to know. We only want to know what is best for you today."

Maria: "I died because of a sleeping pill overdose mixed up with other drugs – a drug interaction? But what happened after that – the dream I shared with you? I feel that was real. The men came, but I was dead. But I was there at the same time as I was dead? How can that be."

Wendy: "The soul can linger around the body until the funeral or much longer. Let's ask your Guide. Has every fragment of your soul from being Marilyn crossed over to the Light fully? Do we need to do a soul retrieval?"

(pause)

Maria: "My Marilyn energy crossed over."

Wendy: "Fantastic. Is that past life energy in the right time and place in your timeline – in your soul's entire timeline?

Maria: "My Guide says yes."

Wendy: "Wonderful – we're so grateful. Thank you for that. Is there anything else to understand about your death as Marilyn? We only want to know what's for your highest good."

←→

Maria: "Yes. So many claim to be Marilyn and also to be Natalie Wood. Why Marilyn? It hurts. I don't share my memories often and when I do so, I do so carefully as I've been attacked and betrayed."

Wendy: "Ask your Higher Self and Guides to teach you discernment, Maria. You can do this. Learn to read people's energy. Don't be fooled by their words or even their actions. Learn to read their soul energy. You're highly intuitive – you can do this!"

(pause)

Wendy: "My Guides say you will master this lifetime what you couldn't master as Marilyn. Sometimes people reappear in a Facebook group for example, using a new name or image. Notice their energy – learn to read energy. Pay attention to how it makes you feel."

(pause)

Wendy: "I've had to remove people like that in my role as group Administrator when my Guides show them to me. They've been removed from a group previously and then reapply using a new name and photo, but it's the same energy. Are you good with that?"

Maria: "Yes, I can do that."

Wendy: "You need to control your own narrative, Maria as I'm hearing you are likely to become well-known. Ask your Guides to help you. Marilyn can help you, too."

Maria: "Good."

←→

Wendy: "Excellent. Let's take a deep breath and re-center ourselves. You're with the Light. Your Guide is with us. We're in the Place of All Knowledge, as well as a place of healing. Did we do everything we need to do to resolve neck

106

pain and any other discomfort?"

Maria: "Yes! I'm very appreciative."

Wendy: "Wonderful. I'd like you to relax your body and mind – we're going to become pure consciousness only. Let's take a deep breath and then let it out very slowly. We'll repeat this three times."

(pause)

Wendy: "I want you to allow your body to complete its healing. We're now going to get a greater understanding as well as a permanent healing for the current body and emotions. Are there any questions we didn't ask that the Light – the Divine – would like to speak about?"

Maria: "No."

←→

Wendy: "You chose to bring forward a past life as Marilyn Monroe. Is there anything more to know about it?"

Maria: "It was chosen because it's the most powerful past life. It was also the biggest scandal."

Wendy: "Is our learning about it now complete? Is the healing complete?"

Maria: "Yes."

←→

Wendy: "Wonderful. Can your Guides answer the other important questions you have for today as we start to wrap up?"

Guide: "Yes."

Wendy: "Wonderful. Can a soul divide and go into more than one body at a time? Can we live a parallel or simultaneous life or lives?"

Guide: "Yes. There's plenty of energy to do so if that's the path chosen."

(Daniel began speaking as Maria's Guide)

←→

Wendy: "Was there anyone in Maria's past life as Marilyn that's in her life now?"

Daniel: "Yes. She knows who Arthur Miller – Marilyn's third husband Arthur – is now. She recognizes you as Joe DiMaggio in all those varying roles in her life."

(pause)

Daniel: "She already knows who the players are in her life now from the Marilyn life."

←→

Wendy: "Thank you. Can you provide Maria with messages and guidance during her dreams in a way that she can remember the information and interpret it accurately?"

Daniel: "Yes, we will. She's good with dream recall."

Wendy: "Absolutely. Can you help give her strength when needed?"

Daniel: "Certainly."

Wendy: "Fantastic. Will the Divine make its presence known when she meditates? Should she meditate any special way?"

Daniel: "Yes, it will. Meditating as she's falling asleep at night is a good time."

Wendy: "What else does she need for restful sleep? She is extremely busy with school and multiple lessons. She said she falls asleep easily but wake ups five times a night on average. That doesn't sound restful."

(pause)

Wendy: "She's experiencing a lot of nightmares. Is there a way to help ease that? Is there a better way to process that energy?"

Daniel: "The nightmares will be less based on today's healing work, but there will always be some."

←→

Wendy: "Are they serving her in some way?"

Daniel: "No, they don't serve her – they scare her."

Wendy: "Can we change that? How can we best help her?"

Daniel: "The nightmares are meant to change as they are negative. They are precognitive dreams. She's a High-Sensitive, like you."

(pause)

Daniel: "What we recommend for restful sleep is to clean out the negative thoughts, and then go to bed with a positive thought about her past life. This will help her re-program or re-frame as you say."

Wendy: "Wonderful. Will you help her with that change?"

(Sense of vibration rising and additional Light coming in)

The Light: "Yes, I *(the Light)* will help her do that."

Wendy: "Thank you. We're grateful. Would having any crystals or going to the Healing Temple like we did early in her session help her sleep better?"

The Light: "No. Just clear out the negative thoughts and reframe with a positive thought."

Wendy: "Thank you. Have we discussed all her questions fully?"

The Light: "Yes. You may ask a few more questions on her behalf, if you wish now that we finished her list."

←→

Wendy: "Thank you. Does Maria have a particular healing power or positive energy to share with others?"

The Light: "She brought her kindness, her caring for people."

Wendy: "Will that serve her well in a performing career if she continues down that road?"

The Light: "Yes. She needs to have the courage to let it

108

shine. She needs to be careful to ensure people don't manipulate or use her."

Wendy: "We discussed this before. Does she have good instincts – good discernment? Should she ask her Guides each time should I work with this person – should I accept this interview or role?"

The Light: "Yes, absolutely."

Wendy: "Will this help avoid the previous manipulations?"

The Light: "Yes, it will. And times have changed and continue to change..."

←→

Wendy: "Yes – so true. Is she helping others ascend – to raise their vibration or level of consciousness?"

The Light: "Yes."

Wendy: "What does it look and feel like for her to help others?"

The Light: "She already knows. She has a natural love and empathy for others. She wants to help them. She needs to watch she doesn't get enough time by herself due to helping others."

Wendy: "Can you protect her as a High-Sensitive to help her de-stress and to clear her energy? What does she most need?"

←→

The Light: "She's to continue her existing alone time. We'll tell her if she needs a day alone, in nature, by the water or the woods just as we tell you. You're also a High-Sensitive and need pristine boundaries."

Wendy: *(ruefully)* "Yes, thank you. I've been learning that the hard way, later in life."

←→

Wendy: "Can you bestow the true power of forgiveness on her?"

The Light: "She forgave Joe DiMaggio. That was our main purpose today."

Wendy: *(choking up)* "I'm so grateful."

The Light: "She understands."

Wendy: "Can she forgive herself when necessary?"

The Light: "Yes, absolutely."

Wendy: "Is there a best spiritual practice for her to raise her vibration?"

The Light: "Not at this time. She is to focus on school and her performing arts training."

Wendy: "Is she meant to move toward performing as her career?"

The Light: "Yes."

←→

Wendy: "I'd like to extend my immense gratitude for today's session. Do you the Light have any final message for the world?"

The Light: "Not currently. I'd like Maria to know I'll always be there for her. That bears repeating – I want her to know, 'I will always be there for you.'"

Wendy: "Thank you. Is there any final message for me today?"

The Light: "Thank you for talking to Maria and for being so positive. It really helped Maria. We met our goal for today."

Wendy: "I feel privileged to have done this session with her. Experiencing true forgiveness is a big deal and greatly appreciated."

The Light: "We are now complete."

←→

(Our four-hour session concluded with my counting Maria out and orienting her to the present day)

I was stunned and elated by this unique session. Who could better confirm the incredible truth that I had been Joe DiMaggio than my dear friend and former wife Marilyn Monroe?

I was thrilled to publish my first book, "Regression Healing I: The Huntsman, The Lord High Mayor and the World War II Soldier" in December of 2016. The theme once again was forgiveness. In the spring of 2017, I recorded and published the audiobook version.

Chapter Six – Prince & Yeshua Step In

On June 10, 2017. I had the good fortune to have a Life-Between-Lives session with a lovely new friend. Her hypno-therapy training included the (Michael) Newton Institute. She kindly came to my home so I wouldn't have to drive after my session.

The hypnotherapist led me through a long and relaxing induction. We revisited several happy scenes from my childhood. She asked me about my earliest childhood memory, and we then went back to my memories of being in the womb.

The following is the transcript of our session beginning at about the one-hour point.

Hypnotherapist: "Can you hear your mother's heartbeat?"

Wendy: "Yes."

Hypnotherapist: "Can you feel your mother's emotions?"

Wendy: "Yes, I can."

Hypnotherapist: "Are you able to influence your mother's emotions?"

Wendy: "Yes, I am. I ask her to rub her belly for a moment and that allows us to connect."

←→

Hypnotherapist: "When did your soul join the body in-utero?"

Wendy: "I came in early as a soul at three months gestation and stayed. This is unusual."

Hypnotherapist: "Why did you choose to come in early?"

Wendy: "Because a lot of adjustments were needed to the body I chose. Normally I arrive later and go in and out until birth, especially when the mother is sleeping."

Hypnotherapist: "What made this body challenging for you?"

Wendy: "It was hard to fit my soul essence into this small body. I have big, high energy and wisdom I'm meant to share. Yet I chose a body with severe scoliosis – curvature of the spine. I came in early to make the best possible fit for myself."

← →

Hypnotherapist: "How has that worked out over your lifetime?""

Wendy: "Western medicine did the best it could for me with a major back surgery when I was entering high school. But there's been daily pain since childhood. It's severe at times. There's a significant leg length difference which throws off the pelvis and hips and back, causing pain and mobility challenges."

Hypnotherapist: "How have you dealt with it?"

Wendy: "My first spiritual teacher was a tremendous help. I'll forever be grateful to her. She helped me repair my timeline and do some key soul retrievals. I received incredible healing, insights and clearings from her."

Hypnotherapist: "Is there anything else to understand in this area?"

← →

(My Higher Self began speaking – notice the third person references)

Higher Self: "Yes, her back being fused and having a fourteen-inch metal rod represents a lifetime with that same teacher two thousand years ago. The metal rod is the cross from the crucifixion."

(pause)

Higher Self: "She's healed that lifetime marvelously over the last few years. They both have. We don't need to focus on it now."

Hypnotherapist: "I'd like to look for a pleasant or uplifting past life."

Higher Self: "Yes, excellent suggestion. We have one final comment why she chose this body and life. It was to teach her to rise above challenges. She volunteered for something incredibly worthwhile to help mankind."

(pause)

Higher Self: "She has great empathy for others. It made her a more effective healer because she had that significant pain for almost fifty years and then healed it. That is incredible!"

(pause)

Higher Self: "She can teach others to do the same whether it's physical or emotional pain as they are closely linked. She has the first-hand experience versus teaching from an abstract place of theory."

Hypnotherapist: "Yes, I can see why that would be quite

valuable. I'd like you to prepare to move now to a significant scene in the most recent past life. We're now moving backwards in time. You have a protected shield of golden energy all around you – be there now!"

←→

(Wendy immediately begins sobbing)
Hypnotherapist *(gently)*: "What's happening?"
Joe *(DiMaggio)*: "I'm so sad she died when she wasn't grounded. She lost a part of herself. She didn't have enough support. There was too much drinking and drugs."
Hypnotherapist: "Who are you referring to?"
Joe: "I want to give her a dignified departure. I can't believe I'm burying her – burying Marilyn – on what was to be our wedding day."
(pause)
Joe: "We were remarrying."
(Continuing to cry harder)
Hypnotherapist: "Why the tears? What are you feeling now?"
Joe: "Marilyn chose the life. We all do, but I feel such anger and guilt. I wasn't a good husband for her the first time. Now I'm robbed of our second chance together. It was my chance to make things right, and now it's gone."
Hypnotherapist: "Are you feeling regret?"
Joe: *(sighing deeply)* "Yes – so much regret."

←→

Hypnotherapist: "Okay, let's work to reframe this and put it in perspective. I'd like you to go to the last day of this lifetime that we're exploring. Are you ready to do that?"
Joe: "Yes. I'm there now."
Hypnotherapist: "Excellent. What's happening? How old are you?"
Joe: "I'm in my mid-eighties. I'm ready for the end."
Hypnotherapist: "How do you pass on? This can be very gentle for you now as well as instructive."
Joe: "I die at home from lung cancer in that lifetime as Joe DiMaggio. I had a long hospitalization and then went home to die."
Hypnotherapist: "What do you think about your life as you review it in its entirety now?"
Joe: "It was a wonderful life! Amazing in many ways. I'm ready to go."
(pause)
Joe: "I'm fortunate to die at home with family and friends with me. There's a visiting nurse who comes in and helps me to stay as comfortable as possible. It's like having hospice care."
Hypnotherapist: "That sounds wonderful that you were ready to go and were surrounded by loved ones and feel

you had a wonderful life. What were some of the life lessons you learned?"

←→

Joe: "I learned two different outcomes for fame. There was a lot of contrast between my life and Marilyn's as famous individuals."

Hypnotherapist: "How so? Can you give me an example, please."

Joe: "I had an easy time handling my fame because I had good strong roots. I had a big, loving family with lots of siblings and two secure parents who helped keep me grounded."

(pause)

Joe: "They'd known me all my life, obviously. They didn't treat me any differently despite my having the good fortune to have success and become well-known from my years playing for the New York Yankees. I was still just 'Joe' to my family and oldest friends."

(pause)

Joe: "My teammates kept me grounded, as did the physicality of playing baseball and being outside so much."

←→

Hypnotherapist: "Yes, I can see why that would be an advantage. Was there anything else that helped you?"

Joe: "Yes. A professional athlete's career isn't long compared to most other careers. I was fortunate to be able to retire when it was no longer fun. My body was beginning to feel too much pain from playing. I knew when to retire and did so with gratitude and no regrets."

Note: Wendy's cat suddenly jumped on the couch where she was having her session. The TV came on unexpectedly as Midnight had leaped on the television remote on his way into her lap. Both women laughed as they realized the television was playing the "Joe TV" channel. What a fun synchronicity that they were indeed speaking with the spirit of Joe DiMaggio, who had died in 1999.

←→

Hypnotherapist: "What did you do after you retired? How old were you?"

Joe: "I was in my mid-thirties when I retired from the Yankees – maybe thirty-six or thirty-seven? I had the good fortune to become an early spokesman for some companies."

Hypnotherapist: "Do you recall which companies?"

Joe: "Yes, there was talk about my endorsing some golf products as I enjoyed golfing and played frequently. But that didn't come to fruition. I later became a spokesperson for Mr. Coffee and for a bank."

Hypnotherapist: "How did that come about?"

Joe: "The Mr. Coffee appliance changed the playing field

114

for how good consistent coffee could be made at home versus on the stove top or in the old percolators. It was a compact, easy-to-use machine."

(pause)

Joe: "The ad concept was that this new home machine was so simple to use that even a bachelor like me – I was twice divorced – could have his first cup of coffee in the morning at home. You didn't have to go to the coffee shop."

(pause)

Joe: "Wendy saw those ads on TV starting in the 1970s. They were on for many years. They stirred some memories for her, but she didn't know what to make of them. It seemed too outlandish at the time that she had been me, but she felt our energy connecting."

←→

Hypnotherapist: "Yes, I understand. And now we can integrate the energy. That sounds wonderful you became a spokesman. I'd like you to prepare to move away from the body. You've just died in that one lifetime and will not feel any pain or discomfort."

(pause)

Hypnotherapist: "Your mind is going to expand to the highest levels – your eternal soul is going to float out of your body when you were Joe. I'd like you to leave all pain and sadness behind. You can now return Home. This is a wonderful release – you can go straight Home where you will remember incredible details."

(pause)

Hypnotherapist: "You've now transitioned Home to your life as a soul. You can expand your awareness as you leave the Earth plane – releasing all negative physical issues. You'll be able to talk about all your lives with objectivity and full understanding."

(pause)

Hypnotherapist: "Let me know when you've crossed over, and who comes forward to greet you. I'm asking for a Guide or Greeter for you. Who comes forward?"

←→

Joe: "Oh, wow, do you see all the purple? There's so much purple!"

Hypnotherapist: "Who's coming forward to greet you?"

Joe: "He went by Prince. That was his stage name. Most people know him by Prince, rather than as Prince Rogers Nelson. He's high-fiving me and laughing. He's saying, 'Look who's Home – it's Mr. Coffee – my favorite cup of Joe!'"

Hypnotherapist: "What does he look like?"

Joe: "He's dressed up in the full Prince regalia. He looks handsome and beautiful both. He's quite androgynous. He looks wonderfully healthy. He looks like he did about ten years before his death."

Hypnotherapist: "Wait a minute – didn't Prince die years after you? I think he just died last year."

Joe: "Yes, but time is different on the other side. This is a great example of time being continuous. I'm meeting Prince's Higher Self in 1999 when I drop my body as Joe."

Hypnotherapist: "Got it. Thank you for clarifying that important point. Is Prince your Greeter or your Guide?"

← →

Joe: "He's my Master Teacher Guide. He's been a Guide to my soul for eons, both on-planet and off. Wendy only learned about him recently. It was a few months ago during her Certified Spiritual Teacher training. Prince came in then as her Master Teacher."

Hypnotherapist: "May we ask Prince directly how you did as Joe? What are his thoughts on how well you lived your life purpose as Joe DiMaggio?"

Joe: "Sure thing! He says my life was well-lived overall, but I need to release the emotions I'm still carrying at the soul level. They're showing up too big in Wendy's body."

(pause)

Joe: "No one could save her from her own choices. It was not in her power as a human to not make them. She needed to have the experiences she did to best progress at the soul level."

(pause)

Joe: "Some of those soul level choices are tough! Next time she'll be encouraged to step into her power earlier during the current lifetime – Wendy has been mastering that lesson."

Hypnotherapist: "What would that look like?"

Joe: "One easy way she can do that is to get the covers for her books earlier in the process. Don't wait until they're done. She can make a simple mock-up herself. It makes them more real in the physical world and easier to power through writing a book."

Hypnotherapist: "That sounds like an excellent idea – thank you."

← →

Hypnotherapist: "Does Joe need to go to a Place of Healing now that he's Home?"

Joe: "Absolutely! It's important not only for me but for Wendy as we're the same soul. She's carrying too many of my physical injuries. For example, her right foot bunion and dislocated toes were caused by my batting stance."

(pause)

Joe: "Grinding the top of my right foot and toes into the ground so hard so many times, hitting like that with all my might and then taking off at a run as fast as I could. I did that physically thousands of times for about thirty years. And cleats weren't great back when I played."

Hypnotherapist: "And that's affecting her right foot now?"

Joe: "Yes, she's had to have two painful surgeries on her right foot. She has right foot issues from other past lives, too. There's more past life bleed-through. But she can heal it with some work. She's made a lot of progress."

Hypnotherapist: "Is there anything else you need to heal that would help her?"

←→

Joe: "Yes – her hips and lower back. Sure, some of that pain is from the pelvis getting out of alignment from the scoliosis and leg length difference, but a lot of it is from all that power-hitting I did. She's feeling the impact of Joltin' Joe too much in her body – let's heal it!"

Hypnotherapist: "Perfect – we'd really appreciate that. Why is there such bleed-over between your two lives as Joe and as Wendy?"

Joe: "Because our lives weren't quite separate enough. I'm her most recent past life but it was a parallel-past life for almost forty years – we were both alive at the same time for almost forty years."

Hypnotherapist: "I see. Can Prince take you to the perfect Place of Healing now?"

←→

Joe: *(laughing)* "Yes, he's taking both me and Wendy on a two-for-one ticket as the same soul."

Hypnotherapist: "What does your place of healing look like? How would you describe it?

Joe: "It's a rose garden. This is my soul's favorite place to heal. There are so many colors of roses, and fountains and birds. Lots of beautiful trees, and Angels too."

Hypnotherapist: "That sounds beautiful. What else do you notice or experience there?"

Joe: "Yeshua and Magdalen are here with Mother Mary – Yeshua ben Joseph's mother, and her husband Father Joseph. Yeshua was later called Jesus."

(pause)

Joe: "Wendy was born at St. Joseph's Hospital. There have been many reminders for her to that lifetime with Yeshua."

(pause)

Joe: "We're in the Garden of Gethsemane. This is Wendy's favorite place of healing."

Hypnotherapist: "Is this the Garden of Gethsemane that was written about in the Bible? Isn't that where Jesus was taken from to be crucified?"

Joe: "Yes. It's a beautiful place of healing. He went there to pray for strength before being taken. He knew what was coming."

←→

Hypnotherapist: "Is there anything else your soul needs to heal?"

Joe: "Yes. My stomach needs healing. I had ulcers as Joe. Wendy has never drunk coffee in her life. I had enough of it as Joe, as Mr. Coffee."

(pause)

Joe: "I liked coffee but had to switch to mostly tea due to the ulcers. We should heal our shared pain here and any other pain she has – it's no longer useful."

(pause)

Joe: "She's learned the lessons from it and made the associations with many of her past lives. That part's done."

Hypnotherapist: "I couldn't agree more. What does Prince recommend for the best healing?"

Joe: "He's saying take the pain from your body. Take it out of your energy field – give it to us to heal. Give it up to the Light or ground it – give it to Mother Earth to transmute."

(pause)

Joe: "She should stop trying to heal it herself. She's maxed what she can heal. She's worked hard and learned a lot. It's time for her to push the pain and physical challenges away from her body – to move them out of her field. The Angels will take them from her."

Hypnotherapist: "That's amazing! Is there anything else she should do?"

←→

Joe: "Yes. She should ask to go to a Healing Temple every night while she sleeps. She's not getting enough sleep. She's also not in her body enough, due partly to the pain. That leads to all kinds of issues. She should let her Guides choose which Healing Temple to take her to. Trust them."

Hypnotherapist: "Thank you. Any more specifics around that?"

Joe: "Yes. She does well with planned timeframes as her life is so highly scheduled with working full-time outside the home. Mondays through Fridays she should ask to go to the Temple for healing. Saturday and Sunday nights, she can astral-travel to help others."

Hypnotherapist: "Great – that's quite specific. Anything else to help her heal?"

←→

Joe: "Yes. She should be in nature more. It can be as simple as sitting on her front porch swing. She should stop by the lake on her way home more often – even ten minutes would help. She should walk around her yard daily – it's grounding for her as well as healing."

Hypnotherapist: "Any particular schedule?"

Joe: "No, but please listen when she feels the urge to go. It's important. Being by the water and trees is beneficial to her as well as to most people. Being out in the rain is okay – she won't melt. She can change her clothes if she needs to when she gets home."

Hypnotherapist: "Thank you. What else?"

←→

(There was a sense of the vibration rising as the Higher Self came in)

Higher Self: "Joe is receiving absolution for his marriage with Marilyn now that she has forgiven him. He is releasing his guilt about how he treated her during their marriage, and for her death."

(pause)

Higher Self: "He now knows she wasn't meant to be the little Italian wife. He didn't have another model to look to. He was born in 1914 and they married in 1954. He didn't understand she needed to be a star and to make movies the best way she knew how."

Hypnotherapist: "Let's ask Marilyn Monroe to come in. What would she like Joe to know?"

Higher Self: "He's asking her to forgive him. He's bowing down before her. She's telling him there's nothing to forgive. Marilyn is happy and grateful they are reunited on the other side. She has no regrets and no longer blames him. She appreciates he was so faithful after her death. He brought her fresh flowers to her burial site in the mausoleum for many years."

Hypnotherapist: "That's wonderful. Is there anything else?"

Higher Self: "No, that's complete."

←→

Hypnotherapist: "Thank you. Wendy had a question whether she should fictionalize this book or blind her identity. She feels uncomfortable talking about the possibility of having been you, having been Joe DiMaggio."

Higher Self: "I know. But it's part of her life lesson to 'let go of what other people think.' Let it go! She needs to step to the plate, and this is a great opportunity to do so. She needs to speak her own truth and let the chips fall where they may."

Hypnotherapist: "Thank you – that's helpful to know."

←→

Hypnotherapist: "May I ask a few more unrelated questions?"

Higher Self: "Yes, you may. I've got all day!"

(Higher Self laughs)

Hypnotherapist: "May I ask her soul's name? Is she allowed to share it?"

119

Higher Self: "Her soul name is Gwendolyn. Her mother chose her name well, as Wendy is a derivative, as is Gwen. This symbolizes her life is to be lived as a soul who is fully awakened – enlightened, even – not that she doesn't have her moments of human emotions and frailty and make mistakes and suffer for them."

← →

Hypnotherapist: "Thank you. Has she more often chosen female or male lives, or have they been somewhat balanced?"

Higher Self: "She's chosen more female lives. We've been helping her find and recall more male lives to help her balance up the energy. Everyone has both male and female energy each lifetime. But she's both needed to more recall the male perspective from being a male and to be able to more embrace her female energy now."

(pause)

Higher Self: "It's why she immediately went to a male life during her first Life-Between-Lives. It's why she reunited with a male Guide then and now – to balance the energy."

← →

Hypnotherapist: "That's wonderful. Is she ready to meet with her Council of Elders now?"

Higher Self: "Yes."

(long silence)

Hypnotherapist: "What is she experiencing?"

Higher Self: "The room is exceptionally beautiful with a high-domed ceiling. The table is in the shape of the letter V for Victory with seven elders seated to assist her. She's standing in front of them – her Guide Prince is to her left and a little behind her."

Hypnotherapist: "What would the Elders like her to know?"

Higher Self: "They are greeting her warmly, welcoming her Home. Several are smiling gently as they find it amusing that she has so many questions. She wrote so many questions for today."

(pause)

Higher Self: "They want her to know she is doing exceptionally well with her continual contact with her Guides. She hears and heeds them exceedingly well."

← →

Hypnotherapist: "She'd like to know why she still has so much left ear-ringing?"

Council Spokesman: "The ear-ringing is because there are so many galactic beings who wish to speak with her. Her ability to hear the galactic languages well is not yet resolved, hence the ear-ringing."

Hypnotherapist: "What do you suggest?"

Council Spokesman: "We suggest she use Prince as

triage. He can help her hear one at a time. She should be selective and focus on the highest Beings of Light from three specific planets. Prince will assist."

←→

Hypnotherapist: "May we know what the three planets are?"

Council Spokesman: "Yes. The first is the Purple Planet. It is her planet of origin with Prince. They both incarnated there for their first incarnations. That makes it their planet of origin."

Hypnotherapist: "Thank you, I was just going to ask you that. Can you tell us more about the Purple Planet? Is that a symbolic name?"

Council Spokesman: "It is a new planet in the sense it has not yet been discovered by astronomers. You may consider it an etheric or an energetic planet."

(pause)

Council Spokesman: "Its energy is much like the Violet Flame. It is extremely high vibration. It first showed up when Prince dropped his body and went Home."

Hypnotherapist: "Does it have a specific purpose?"

Council Spokesman: "The purpose is to help heal mankind and Earth. The simplest explanation I can give you is that the Purple Planet helps beam the Violet Flame energy of transmutation to Earth and her inhabitants. This is the reason Wendy works so well with the Violet Flame and why it's her primary flame this lifetime. Reading 'The Seven Sacred Flames' by Aurelia Louise Jones will provide more information on this topic."

←→

Hypnotherapist: "Thank you. And the second planet she's meant to connect with through her Guide Prince?"

Higher Self: "The Pleiades – the Seven Sisters – the cluster in the night sky most visible to the naked eye."

Hypnotherapist: "Anything more to know about the Seven Sisters?"

Council Spokesman: "No. I'd like to leave it at that for today. The third planet is Venus – the planet of love. She thought Venus was her home planet as she's spent so much time there. But the Purple Planet is her true planet of origin."

(pause)

Council Spokesman: "What do you think inspired Prince's biggest hit 'Purple Rain'? He had some memories of the Purple Planet at a subconscious level. It provided creative impulse. It's why Prince so often wore purple and chose it in his decor. Wendy does, too."

←→

Hypnotherapist: "Thank you. What else should she know

121

on this topic?"

Council Spokesman: "She should just relax and breathe as she uses Prince as her gatekeeper. Ask him to bring in one message at a time from one of those three locations."
(pause)

Council Spokesman: "Prince will be her Spirit Bouncer. This way she won't waste time with any message or information that is anything other than the highest vibration of love. She will hear it directly in fluid English."
(pause)

Council Spokesman: "She won't have to translate and try and interpret symbols and signs clairvoyantly like a lot of psychic mediums do – this channeling will be very smooth. English to English."
(pause)

Council Spokesman: "She's going to be an excellent communicator – a superb channel for us. There are no stops and starts and she doesn't have to repeat the message like some channels do, creating a distracting echo of sorts."
(pause)

Council Spokesman: "The two spiritual teachers she trained with to become a Certified Spiritual Teacher are both highly capable channels. But they have been translating galactic languages since they were children. Neither knows how to teach this skill."

Hypnotherapist: "And she's having a different experience?"

Council Spokesman: "Yes. She's starting in her mid-fifties, so we've worked with her to have the messages already be translated. It will already be in English, triaged through Prince."

Hypnotherapist: Thank you. That's so helpful. What else would you like her to know? We so appreciate your high-level insights."

←→

Council Spokesman: "Her next trip to Mount Shasta, California is important. She is to reunite with her wand. She is to make a connection that is only for her. She is to use her wand only for herself, not for the people she serves or for family members. Just for herself."
(pause)

Council Spokesman: "Her crystal wand will help her with her health, her work, and her ear-ringing. She is to meditate while holding it and to call in Prince. As she practices speaking what she hears aloud, she will hear better. She can then speak more, and then hear better once again. Do you understand?"

Hypnotherapist: "Yes. This sounds like a great protocol. Is there anything else you recommend?"

←→

Council Spokesman: "Her throat was blocked. No further work is needed on the throat today. She dug out the obstructions – the implants – meant to silence her. That will no longer be an issue."

Prince: *(interjecting a comment)* "Over time she'll be able to ask me to turn on the 'mixer faucet.' Messages from all three planets will merge beautifully into one cohesive message. But we'll start one at a time to not overload her. It takes a special kind of high energy to accurately channel galactic messages in this manner."

Hypnotherapist: "Thank you. Anything else on this topic or may I ask her next question?"

← →

Council Spokesman: *(smiling)* "Ask away. It's why we've gathered here together for her today."

Hypnotherapist: "She'd like to have an update on meeting her new life partner."

Council Spokesman: "There will be a lot of serendipity around their meeting they will both recognize. It will catch their attention to be ready to meet organically – to bump into one another unexpectedly, perhaps literally. But it's not truly unexpected. Their souls have been planning the meeting."

Hypnotherapist: "Is it appropriate to know more, or do we leave it as a fun surprise?"

← →

Council Spokesman: "She's done her work with both her Twin-Flame and her Twin-Ray. That has ended. That energy is complete before meeting in the physical. Her Twin-Ray is helping her new partner come in. He stepped aside as he was no longer a match as he changed his mind about wanting a committed relationship."

Hypnotherapist: "What type of relationship does he want now?"

Council Spokesman: "He now wants light and casual. Multiple romances at the same time. He would have been another heartbreaker for her like her former primary soul mate, so we moved him to a helper role – an introducer."

(pause)
Council Spokesman: "She doesn't need a soul mate. There were plenty of difficult lessons with the former husband. There were then tremendous lessons with her former primary soul mate we had intended to be a wonderful mate for her, but their relationship had become too karmic. They were teaching soul mates for one another. It was extremely hard on her."

Hypnotherapist: "So what's next? My goodness, it sounds like she needs a vacation partner!"

Council Spokesman: *(laughing heartily)* "Touché!"

Hypnotherapist: "She mentioned she's interested in attracting a romantic partner with high integrity and some common interests. Is there any action for her to take to meet him – like going to Meetups or joining Match or some other on-line dating?"

Council Spokesman: "No. She's already done all that and more. Her last step was to learn to happily vacation alone. She'll have mastered that with the trip to Mount Shasta."

(pause)

Council Spokesman: "What she needs to do now is to listen to her divine guidance. She works it too hard, and then we can't help. She needs to release it to us. She needs to ask for our help more often."

(pause)

Council Spokesman: "She needs to spiritually surrender. To be willing to say, 'Please help me with this certain task or situation – please make it better.' And she then needs to trust, and to leave it alone."

(pause)

Council Spokesman: "Yeshua would like to address her directly now. He's here on her Council."

Hypnotherapist: "Wonderful!"

←→

Yeshua ben Joseph (Jesus): "Self-forgiveness was Joe DiMaggio's life-lesson. She needs to get comfortable having a light touch and her natural sense of humor writing about him. His story is her story. Own it."

(pause)

Yeshua: "I'm here to help her release her fears around being criticized regarding that past life, the past life with me, and with the other – quote – 'historic, Biblical and famous past lives.' "

(pause)

Yeshua: "We encourage her to master her life-lesson of self-acceptance and to share her memories and experiences without needing others to believe them or to accept them. She needs to own them to set herself free."

Hypnotherapist: "Thank you. That's very powerful. Is there anything else for her to understand?"

←→

Yeshua: "Yes, we want to help heal her energetic – and sometimes physical – flinch regarding 'what will other people think.' She is overly vigilant – overly prepared for attack. She therefore experiences more attacks than is instructive or necessary. Over-vigilance is a sign of PTSD. It's exhausting."

(pause)

Yeshua: "She needs to truly understand the Law of

Attraction. You attract based on your own thoughts and energy. It's important to find a way to balance your emotions and to be love and peace and joy as often as you can. Vibrate with joy at least once a day."

(pause)

Yeshua: "It's important to find a way to forgive easily and to be in a place of gratitude for what you have, and you will attract more of it. If you expect negativity based on past experiences – and she's had a lot of challenging experiences – you create more of them. It loops and loops again. It can become an insanity loop."

←→

Hypnotherapist: "So what can she do to resolve this?"

Yeshua: "I'm inviting her back with me to the Garden of Gethsemane. It's a profound place of healing. It's her favorite place to heal. She comes here often. She remembers when we were here together over two thousand years ago."

(pause)

Yeshua: "We can spend time in the garden to heal the hyper-vigilance and being overly concerned what others will think."

(pause)

Yeshua: "We prepared well with her to be able to shine some light on the truth around famous lives. This is an area that's not well- understood. We will be with her every step of the way."

Hypnotherapist: "Thank you. Does she need to just spend time in the garden to heal? Can you let me know when that's done?"

(pause)

Yeshua: "I am taking her through the life cycle of a rose – just a moment more..."

(pause)

Yeshua: "The healing is now done!"

←→

Hypnotherapist: "That's wonderful. Thank you. Is there a lesson about simply being willing to be honest and to speak publicly about her lives?"

Yeshua: "Her role is to help people remember how magnificent their souls are – their own souls, as well as others. Do not confuse the soul with a single human incarnation. We need to let go of the judgments including of ourselves, and to continue to find ways to be kind and loving."

(pause)

Yeshua: "Her ego is quite well-balanced almost all the time. We've worked with her on this extensively. It's a little too shrinking at times which is why she hasn't wanted to share of historic, famous and Biblical past lives she's had."

(pause)

Yeshua: "I haven't counted them recently, but even if there's a dozen that's a small percent of the thousands of lives she's lived both on and off-planet. She has more of them than the norm as it correlates to her life purpose work to help others with this subset of past lives. Does that make sense?"

← →

Hypnotherapist: "It certainly does to me. It's the bigger picture that's important – the soul journey."

Yeshua: "Exactly! It's why we ask her to spend significant time helping in Facebook's largest reincarnation group. She can help with the famous lives as those often need the most support. She also understands multidimensionality and intergalactic lives on Earth and other planets."

Hypnotherapist: "That's fantastic. That's a fuller picture than most have been able to understand, yet it only scratches the surface."

Yeshua: "That's a profound remark. Thank you for helping her so much today. We know you went to a lot of time and effort."

Hypnotherapist: "It's my pleasure and fascinating for me! Is there more for her to know on the topic of the famous lives – for example, why do so many people recall being one famous person? What are some of the possible reasons for that?"

← →

Yeshua: "Let's use the example of Marie Antoinette, reigning queen of France at the time of the French Revolution. Marie had a large destiny, so she was what we call a shared soul. Multiple souls were serving as Marie at the same time. This can happen with a President or a Pope, too. It can be for just the time they are in office, or it can be for a lifetime."

(pause)

Yeshua: "There are also different timelines. Various people are correct in recalling being Marilyn Monroe, but it was at different times. They had some unique experiences and therefore memories."

(pause)

Yeshua: "Time is better described as a loop than a line of past-present – future. That's a human construct for simplicity. It's more continuous than that – it's more quantum with everything happening in the now."

(pause)

Yeshua: "Different souls can choose to be Marilyn in my example and have different experiences, leading to some confusion in the historical records. It's all rather complex, isn't it?"

Hypnotherapist: "Yes, it is."

Yeshua: "There can also be imprinting on a soul from the Collective Consciousness. The soul downloads the information without having technically lived that life. It's rather like a computer chip or program that allows the person to have some knowledge to make better decisions in their subsequent lives."

Hypnotherapist: "That is complex!"

←→

Yeshua: "Yes. I could go on with more examples, but that's enough for now. My best advice is don't judge anyone exploring a past or parallel life, no matter how far-fetched it may sound to you. It's not your role to judge, unless someone is specifically asking you for validation or input to help them put their own puzzle pieces together."

(pause)
Yeshua: "We more often see this unfortunate 'keyboard warring' and arguing on social media. It is lowering your vibration at precisely the time we need to be raising our vibration and frequency to match Gaia's – Mother Earth's. She needs to raise her vibration to survive, as does mankind."

←→

Hypnotherapist: "That's marvelous. Anything else?"
Yeshua: "Yes – I encourage you both to be colorful! You're to help lead the way. You're over fifty now – just be yourselves with a big smile on your face as you speak your truth and let the chips fall where they may. It's not your issue."

(pause)
Yeshua: "Wendy's daughters are old enough now she can really begin publishing what we ask her to. Her parents will be okay with it though they don't currently understand what she's called to do."

(pause)
Yeshua: "They are now elderly. When it's their time to go Home, they will then both help her with her writing from the other side. They have shared lives together which may come into play in future books."

←→

Hypnotherapist: "Thank you. Wendy posed an interesting question have she and I shared any past lives together? We hit it off so well from our very first conversation which can be a hallmark of that."

Yeshua: *(smiling)* "Yes, you do. The most notable was a lifetime when you were seers together in the fourth century. It was in Spain – the Iberian Peninsula. One of you was blind from birth and the other was purposefully blinded due to a primitive belief you needed to be blind to hear Spirit well."

(pause)
Yeshua: "In general, you were treated well. You both meditated and channeled for most of your time. You weren't allowed to marry or to have a romance or children, but you chose the life."

(pause)
Yeshua: "I see you both wearing warm, beautiful flowy white robes in that lifetime. You were both well-respected and well-liked in your small group of five or six seers. You have met again this lifetime so you can be supportive to one another in your energy work."

Hypnotherapist: "Thank you. That's lovely. I appreciate all the detail. What else would be helpful for Wendy to know at this time?"

←→

Yeshua *(bluntly)*: "She blocks easy abundance. There are unconscious beliefs she's not aware of. So many Light-workers think they need to be poor to do their holy work. It's an old habit that no longer serves them in a capitalistic society."

(pause)
Yeshua: "They are remembering lives with vows of poverty, but it's not serving them to do their current life's purpose work. She can manifest, but it's painful. There's too much bootstrapping - struggling to get by month-to-month as a single mother, paycheck to paycheck."

Hypnotherapist: "What should she do instead?"
Yeshua: "It's time to change this in a big way! We'd like her to surrender her abundance – not only her wealth, but her health and her relationships – to us in a big way."

(pause)
Yeshua: "She now trusts the Divine again which has taken her years of hard work after what she endured at my crucifixion. She was at my feet helping me go Home in the best possible way as was my mother. My wife and my mother were at my feet, assisting me. That was not an easy life."

(pause)
Yeshua: "But she is now overly independent from Spirit when I look at how she's lived her life so far."

Hypnotherapist: "What would benefit her more?"

←→

Yeshua: "The MAP *(Medical Assistance Plan)* meditation technique works fabulously well for her. The reason is it includes surrender to the Divine. She is to call in Spirit – to ask for our help – to give the challenge over to us, to give it fully over."

(pause)
Yeshua: "It is a sign of strength to know your worth and

128

to turn things over to the Divine, not of weakness. We are helping her build her receptors to receive so that she may live her life purpose to help others in a meaningful way. She will put the funds to great, thoughtful use per the Divine."
(pause)
Yeshua: "She is to take care of herself first, in delightful ways and then her children, without spoiling them – with our divine guidance. Next, she is to help the animals in a meaningful way. She is to assist Earth and mankind via clean, affordable water projects as 'Water is Life.' She is to help end human slavery and trafficking."
(pause)
Yeshua: "She will be receiving divine and human assistance to set up foundations and charities to do what I have outlined. This won't feel like work to her, it will feel like play! It's her life purpose. She will need to keep her vibration high to accomplish this but is more than capable."

←→

Hypnotherapist *(shrewdly)*: "Are there any blocks to this? She's going all the way from blocking easy abundance to what sounds like philanthropy?"
Yeshua: "There are no blocks. We have worked with her on this extensively. Six months ago, there were still blocks – now there are none. The wheels are all in motion."
Hypnotherapist: "Thank you, that sounds amazing."

←→

Hypnotherapist: "She doesn't understand why she had so much trouble getting her website built. She got it started, but it wouldn't function correctly and she couldn't find anyone to help her complete it?"
Yeshua *(calmly)*: "That's because we shut it down."
Hypnotherapist *(sounding surprised)*: "You shut it down? Was she not correct she was asked to build a website? That's a big piece of how business is done nowadays. We talked about moving from vows of poverty to a capitalistic society. She's not a monk or a nun anymore."
Yeshua: "We shut it down as the wrong people would have come, wasting her time and theirs and causing frustration. She needs to learn when she tries and tries to do a task that we've asked her to do and it has no flow, she's to pull back her energy. She's meant to ask if the Divine Right Timing is now? It was not. The time was not ripe."
(pause)
Yeshua: "She needs to break her old habit of having been socialized to try again and again to the point of exhaustion and even insanity. She's meant to find flow – Divine Flow. She can now return to her same website build and it will flow easily as there are people at the same vibrational level who will find it. They will find her and be a good match as

clients or colleagues – perhaps even a few friends."

←→

Hypnotherapist: "Thank you – now that makes sense! She'd like to know if she has a soul contract to work with the dog rescue where she's volunteering? She feels quite called to volunteer."

Yeshua: "Yes, she has soul contracts with both the husband and the wife. She has contracts with the woman who started the rescue and with the rescue founder's husband. Wendy has known them both in previous lives. They agreed before incarnating she would help with the rescue."

Hypnotherapist: "May we know more what that's to look like?"

Yeshua: "Over time she is likely to make a large donation to this specific dog rescue. It's important her donation be tied to a specific business plan. She may be involved with helping expand the network of foster families who are the backbone of the organization as there is no physical shelter. Quality fosters are the lifeblood of the organization."

←→

Hypnotherapist: "She's feeling some angst she had a casual discussion with the owner of the previous rescue she volunteered with that perhaps she was meant to write a book for that organization? That is extremely time-consuming."

Yeshua: "No, she is not meant to do that. That volunteering is complete. It was a segue to get her to the new rescue which hadn't yet begun."

(pause)

Yeshua: "The lesson is she doesn't release well – picture a dog that will not release a bone. She's overly responsible at times which can make her feel exhausted and/ or ener-getically scattered."

(pause)

Yeshua: "It can make her energy unnecessarily heavy and weighed down. The over-responsibility comes from being the oldest child of an alcoholic, as well as from some of her past lives. She can ask to release this tendency. It does not serve her."

Hypnotherapist: "What would help resolve this?"

←→

Yeshua: "I'm inviting her to step through a beautiful waterfall. She can let any ties with the former rescue go. She keeps stepping back into old residue she's outgrown."

(pause)

Yeshua: "This is important. I want her to be clear it harms her body. She needs to change this habit. She needs to learn to close things out graciously and to move on. Let the energy go – let it flow!"

Hypnotherapist: "That's an important skill for anyone."

Yeshua: "Yes, it is. Returning to the topic of both health and wealth, I'd like to pull the thread a bit more cohesively. We'd like her to vibrate with joy daily to receive her abundance package. She knows how to do this and can teach others."

(pause)

Yeshua: "It only takes seventeen seconds a day. It needs to be done consistently, meaning daily. The practice won't work if you do it just once, or here and there and then forget about it."

(pause)

Yeshua: "Really feel the joy of being in a human body and being on the Earth to the best of your ability! It's a privilege and a gift. It's part of raising your vibration."

(pause)

Yeshua: "People who aren't able to do that are going to opt out and head Home – to drop their bodies – as Earth continues to raise her vibration."

←→

Hypnotherapist: "That's powerful advice. What else would you like her to know?"

Yeshua: "She needs to get enough sleep to allow her body to not only truly rest, but to heal. We'd like her to find a way to consistently sleep at least seven to eight hours a night. Her girls are old enough now she can do this again. It's part of loving yourself first."

(pause)

Yeshua: "We'd like her to keep up her excellent meditation practice. She meditates for five minutes a day and then auto-writes a message from her Guides for five more minutes. She's an accomplished enough meditator at this point to be able to get right to it in ten minutes a day."

(pause)

Yeshua: "Doing a thirty to sixty-minute meditation at least once a week would round out what she needs at this time. Be prepared it will change again in the future."

Hypnotherapist: "Thank you. Anything else?"

←→

Yeshua: "Yes. She needs to be out in nature more. Even a five to fifteen-minute walk or being by the water or trees would help her clear her energy. We invite her to turn over to God her life partner match and requests for financial abundance needed to fulfill her life purpose."

(pause)

Yeshua: "I repeat my earlier points she works it too hard. Please surrender it. She can use the affirmation, 'I am fully aligned with my infinite wealth and abundance' as that will include her health and harmonious relationships."

(pause)

Yeshua: "She should write this out by hand and put it on her bathroom mirror, her computer monitor and on her auto-writing notebook so she'll see it until she believes it!"

(sound of laughter)

← →

Hypnotherapist: "Thank you for those specifics. Why is she experiencing a left knee buckle? She feels it's energetic."

Yeshua: "It is. We remind her to breathe first before taking a step. The left knee buckle is an energetic flinch. She subconsciously expects a smack or an attack when she tries to receive."

(pause)

Yeshua: "The left side – the female side – is about graciously receiving. This is the Divine Feminine energy. We all have both Divine Masculine and Divine Feminine energy in every lifetime."

(pause)

Yeshua: "She will heal her left foot and leg when she visits Glastonbury. It's why we've been asking her to go to England. When she opens herself to it and stops telling us how far it is and how expensive it is to travel from Seattle to England, it will be easy."

(pause)

Yeshua: "It's called getting out of your own way! She knows how to do this. She did it with getting her training to become a hypnotherapist specializing in past-life regression."

Hypnotherapist: "Thank you. I'm hearing open to the miracles of life – let go of trying to control them?"

Yeshua: "Yes! Well-said."

← →

Hypnotherapist: "She's had some pelvic floor issues and was told surgery was perhaps indicated?"

Yeshua: "We feel she can heal it by strengthening her own sacral and root chakras to support the pelvic floor. We don't want her to give up. This function should be able to be restored without surgery. We invite her to call on Dr. Lorphan to do psychic surgery instead."

Hypnotherapist: "Does she know how to do that?"

Yeshua: "Absolutely. We'll explain in detail another time for those who aren't familiar."

← →

Hypnotherapist: "Okay. She's experiencing a lot of skin tags as well as dry skin that can become uncomfortable. Any recommendations there?"

Yeshua: "Yes – release the old energy! Remember my comment that's not her forte? She can step through the waterfall again to release the many lives when she was burned as a witch. The skin tags and dry skin are from being

132

burned."

(pause)

Yeshua: "We've all been burned as witches as well as having thrown the match or the torch. Let it go! This doesn't need to present. Visualize her skin being in perfect balance and healthy."

← →

Hypnotherapist: "Thank you. She's noticing her sternum moving and cracking a bit. She said she feels like she's getting energetically larger, but there's no weight gain?"

Yeshua: "She's exactly right. This is a keen observation. This is part of the heart opening as she continues to raise her vibration to 5D and higher."

(pause)

Yeshua: "We grow energetically larger as Beings of Light. The physical body needs to adjust. She is growing her light well – returning to her light body while still in a human body."

(pause)

Yeshua: "She is de-aging, also known as youthing. She doesn't need a medical doctor. I will gently adjust her bones in that area for her right now so this can be more comfortable."

(pause)

Yeshua: "She's also more fully activating her thymus gland which will help her bring in additional light. She will continue to heal and to de-age. Everyone is capable of this. She's welcome to share this knowledge with anyone interested."

← →

Hypnotherapist: "We appreciate your perspective, Yeshua – the entire Council's perspective. She has concerns about how and when she's to transition to full-time spiritual employment – meaning to quit her day job? She has a family to think about in addition to herself."

Yeshua: "We'd like her to give this over to her Guides instead of worrying about it and trying to plan what she can't plan."

(pause)

Yeshua: "We like it when she jokes and asks us for help by saying, 'Please help me with this challenge – this is above my pay grade!' and then laughs. Laughing helps her reach her highest vibration so we can work together in the best possible way."

(pause)

Yeshua; "Spiritual surrender is a critical skill, as is trusting the Divine. We will help her serve as she should be serving, which will be working with Spirit full-time. We want her to know all outcomes are good in this area and to just breathe."

Hypnotherapist: "Thank you. I want to ask this delicately. If we're not meant to known more, that's fine. She has some challenges at work with non-human 'Watchers.' She feels one may cause her to lose her job. She feels they are aliens experiencing their first lives on Earth and does not enjoy having to work with them. What is the lesson? Her request is to close this out for the highest good of all involved."

Yeshua: "She's exactly right she recognized two non-human 'Watchers.' Their roles were to be low-key and to report back to their superiors on their home planet. They were meant to watch and to learn how humans live their lives. They were not meant to interfere with people's life paths and to wield their power so heavily. That was unfortunate."

(pause)

Yeshua: "Most people who've had contact with these beings didn't recognize fully what was going on. They simply knew these were not trustworthy individuals. They over-played their hands again and again."

Hypnotherapist: "Has she been able to learn from these experiences?"

← →

Yeshua: "The upside was they helped Wendy move fully into her sovereignty. They can no longer track her or bother her, but she can't see them either. Nor should she try to. It's time to move on. Lesson complete. Don't look back or re-engage."

Hypnotherapist: "Thank you. Anything else about that topic?"

Yeshua: "Yes. She learned she remembers her white witchcraft quite well. She realized she had dropped her hairbrush at work one day once she was already home after work. She did not want those Watchers to access it. She simply rendered it invisible until she could find it and secure it the next day. It was that simple, and that profound. A wonderful lesson for her, and quite empowering."

← →

Hypnotherapist: "Thank you. Should she build her website herself or via the media company she'll be working with to host her new radio program?"

Yeshua: "She should do it herself. The media company is going to be a short relationship, but quite beneficial. They will part peacefully, which is a beautiful practice."

(pause)

Yeshua: "She'll need to learn how to create a YouTube channel as well as to do Facebook Live. People will come forward over time to help her with these technical skills that she doesn't yet have."

(pause)

Yeshua: "Her friend Karen can help her get started with keywords. Key words are important for her website to come up in searches germane to her service offerings – the past life regression healing sessions and the channeling, for example."

(pause)

Yeshua: "We want her to be confident she will know who to work with. She needs to remember to ask for help and to be in joy to receive, including via her daily meditations. Remember to be in gratitude and to 'ask – receive – thank' as a cycle, and to vibrate with joy."

←→

Yeshua: "This may surprise people that we keep up with changes in technology, read current books, watch YouTube and even Netflix. It's part of how we can advise those we guide. It's important we stay relatable and relevant in our roles as Guides and Ascended Masters."

(pause)

Yeshua: "This is especially important for me as a World Teacher – I'm not stuck in a time warp from two thousand years ago!"

(Sound of Yeshua's delighted laughter)

Hypnotherapist: *(smiling)* "That's fabulous. Thank you for explaining that to us so well."

←→

Yeshua: "My pleasure. We would like her to move forward with the Dr. Brian Weiss full-week training at the Omega Center in New York next summer. She can easily combine that with her annual trip to visit her father. We don't recommend she train with either of the other big two hypnotherapy schools directly but rather work with their founders who are on the other side. We know you both sensed them here as we began today's session."

(pause)

Yeshua: "Both Dr. Michael Newton and Dolores Cannon's Higher Selves are here with us today. You are both welcome to work with them in Spirit. You're ready – congratulations!"

Hypnotherapist: "Oh my goodness – thank you! That's a privilege to know. She'd like to know how she can write faster so she can help more people by having more books available?"

←→

Yeshua: "She can meditate for fifteen minutes before writing and then call in Archangel Gabriel and Serapis Bey. Light a candle and have a favorite crystal nearby. They will help her write high-quality materials as quickly as possible all day long!"

(pause)

Yeshua: "She could complete three to four books a year in this manner. Her ego is now well-balanced ninety-nine percent of the time, which is a major accomplishment."

(pause)

Yeshua: "She no longer allows her ego to torture her. She comforts it, confronts it, or makes fun of it as is appropriate. She's accepted the ego is a part of her, as is the shadow self and the wounded child to use all your current healing buzz words."

(pause)

Yeshua: "Getting comfortable with famous and Biblical past lives was the last major piece. She is to be a leader in this area, as we discussed. We recommend she write more books in the 'Regression Healing' series as it is quicker and easier for her to write non-fiction than fiction; it requires less editing; and more directly correlates with her healing services for clients."

(pause)

Yeshua: "She needed to write *The Flow I: Plimoth Plantation* as there was such a tremendous energy bolus there to release. It was quite the energetic hairball is my best description!"

(Yeshua's rich laughter rang out again)

Yeshua: "It took a huge weight off her to publish that story after five years of work. She is to return to *The Flow* fiction series later. It will most likely best be published after her parents pass on."

←→

Hypnotherapist: "Is Wendy to write a book to help the rescue dogs?"

Yeshua: "Just let it be. If the perfect easy opportunity comes up in that area, we'll help her jump on it. She'll have a lot of fun with it."

Hypnotherapist: "What about Magdalen's Book of Love?"

Yeshua: "We will speak privately with her about that book. She is hearing us correctly to not research before she writes so that the information is as pure as it can be from her Guides – from Spirit. It's why we don't have her read about that timeline – my time on Earth."

←→

Hypnotherapist: "I understand. Is she to write a universal healing book that updates Reiki?"

Yeshua: "Yes, but not until her former spiritual teacher that she did the work with drops her body. The teacher will enjoy writing it with her from the other side."

(pause)

Yeshua: "She will also get assistance with some of the technology and perhaps business and legal aspects of publishing, speaking and client work from her new partner over time. This will be a welcome relief for her, and interesting and instructive for him. It's a wonderful partnership on all levels."

←→

Hypnotherapist: "That sounds fantastic. Is she correct two of her books may be made into films? She keeps being shown this in meditation."

Yeshua: "Yes, we'd like to accomplish this together, so we send her the vision. But Hollywood needs to grow up first. It needs to raise its vibration from the metaphysical and energetic being scary and unnatural and that a ghost can hurt you."

(deep sigh)

Yeshua: "As mankind's vibration rises, Hollywood will grow up, too. Then the pieces will come together exactly as they're meant to because she's open to it."

←→

Hypnotherapist: "Thank you. Another delicate question. This is a family where the mother and daughters have experienced more than their share of psychic attacks and implants that did not serve them. Has that been resolved? Wendy's daughters are now college-age."

Yeshua: "Yes, it has been resolved. She was right to stop protecting them and clearing their spaces once they moved out. They are capable young women and continue to bump up their own protection. She is simply to send them love, which she does daily."

Hypnotherapist: "Thank you. We're so grateful for this information. Is there anything else to discuss on her behalf?"

Yeshua: "Simply know you are both completely loved and on track with your destiny. This session is complete."

Hypnotherapist: "Thank you from the bottom of my heart. Namaste."

←→

I was stunned and grateful for the information that came through during this remarkable session. I didn't have any sense of how serendipitous the timing was.

A few weeks later I was laid off from a fantastic job I really enjoyed. I had been with my employer for almost ten years and had planned to retire from that healthcare system.

I was a fifty-five-year-old single mother with no income and two daughters in college. I was assisting both with tuition and living expenses. I had never received child support or alimony. Their father and I had cost-shared our daughters expenses until they graduated from high school.

This was going to be a true test of my faith. I sequestered

myself for several days to cry and release the emotions to the best of my ability, and then updated my family. I told my daughters that we would figure it out. They needed to stay in college and to trust all would go well.

I filed for unemployment insurance, gratefully accepted my severance package, and began looking for traditional employment. I also began building my own business as a solopreneur. I knew I was being given the opportunity to resolve my financial abundance fears. It was time to step to the plate in a higher-stakes game.

My Guides encouraged me to attend some inexpensive group past-life regression sessions during this time of rapid change. I asked them to bring the best ones to my attention. They did so within a few short days!

Chapter Seven – Three Group Past-Life Regressions

On June 24th, 2017, I attended my first group past-life regression via Meetup. I made sure my energy was well-grounded and clear and that I had no expectations as to what I'd experience.

I trusted my Higher Self and Guides would "take me to the time and place with the most healing and information for my life today." This is the prompt I use with most of my own clients.

I immediately returned to the past life as Joe DiMaggio. My Guides showed me I had done the work to forgive myself for Marilyn's death as well as the other parties involved. I was shown I would be able to handle the amount of fame necessary to fulfill my life purpose. I'd already done extremely well as Joe and now had more experiences under my belt.

My Guides commented I had the opportunity to be a better mother in my current life than Joe had to be a father. Progress had been made in that area. I was shown it was more important that Joe be Marilyn's friend than her husband or lover, and that he had excelled in that area including after her early death. I heard the comment again that "Marilyn needed a savior, not another husband."

I was told I had learned well not to be prejudiced from painful experiences in that lifetime as Joe, including being derisively called a "dago" by my own teammates back in the 1930s. I silently shed some tears during the group regression as I healed those emotions that Joe had never fully released.

My Guides confirmed that my present daughter had been my son Joe. They also commented how truly fortunate

I was to have had the Marilyn client not only be referred to me but that she forgave me for my regrettable actions during our short marriage.

They confirmed my former boyfriend had been the brash and beloved Babe Ruth who had played for the Yankees for many years and retired shortly before I was called up to the big league as Joe.

I was so pleased with how much information came to me during a simple, affordable group regression that I began offering them myself shortly thereafter.

←→

I attended another group regression with the same hypnotherapist on July 6th, 2017. My Guides said there was only one thing I needed to hear that day. They told me, "DiMaggio's life lesson is applicable to your life now – wear your power and popularity lightly." I nodded my earnest agreement and never forgot the advice.

←→

On October 28th, 2017, I attended one more group past-life regression workshop with a different hypnotherapist. I again made certain to ground and clear my energy and to release my expectations as to which past life I might explore.

My Guides provided a tremendous heart healing from the lifetime as Joe DiMaggio. They healed my lover's heart as Joe had been without a romantic partner for almost forty years after Marilyn's death.

My Guides told me they were breaking the cycle of my not having a romantic partner. I needed to surrender by visualizing physically jumping off a cliff.

I was to practice physically falling backwards to both sides – to the right and to the left – to know I would always be caught as I was fully supported by the Divine. I would be lifted to a higher level – a higher vibration and frequency, or level of consciousness, each time I practiced this falling – this surrendering.

My Guides said it was time to practice not making any requests, goals or plans as they were clear what I needed. That I was to simply practice the surrender exercise to turn my life over to them and to surrender so they could lift me up.

They added that our shadow can present as shame if we don't accept this part of ourselves. I had done well to not have addictions. It would help me to bring in Light to transmute the shadow self. It was best for me to forgive myself to accept and light up the shadow. Accepting and loving the inevitable duality would be the healthiest thing possible for me.

A few weeks after my June 2017 layoff, the perfect client

contacted me for another session at the exact right moment. I do so love Divine Right Timing!

Chapter Eight – "Happy Birthday, Mr. President!"

In August of 2017 I facilitated a second past-life regression healing session for Maria. Her session lasted three hours. I didn't assume additional memories as Marilyn Monroe would present. We had already done a four-hour session that focused on the Marilyn lifetime.

The energy that most needs to be healed and released is what presents during a past-life regression. The suggestion I give to my clients, with their permission, is to "go to the time and place with the most healing and information for your life now."

My Skype recorder would not record our call, which was unusual. We both could feel so much energy crackling about! Normally I simply share the session audio file with the client for them to receive additional healing and insights.

Maria and I discussed rescheduling. But since it had taken time and effort to synch our calendars and she was so primed for her session, we agreed to move forward that day. I would take more detailed notes than usual to share with her.

Maria had emailed her questions ahead for her Higher Self and Guides. Her Guides started the session with answers to her questions. They are the architect of the experience, along with the Higher Self.

I asked the following questions on Maria's behalf. Her Higher Self and Guides replied through her.

← →

(session in progress)
Wendy: "Am I on my life path?"
Maria: "Yes."

Wendy: "What is my life purpose, path or mission?
Maria: "You are not to know at this time."
Wendy: "Thank you, I understand. We appreciate you only sharing what's best for Maria to know at this time."

(Note: This is not unusual with younger clients who have not yet had their first Saturn return at the ages of twenty-eight to thirty. Dr. Michael Newton did not work with clients under the age of thirty when he was in active practice, but times have changed.

I occasionally work with clients who are in their late teens or college- aged if their intent and expectations align well with the type of healing I can help facilitate for them.

I love the check and balance that our loving, wise, supportive Guides only share with us what is in our best interest to know at that time.)

←→

Wendy: "What career(s) are best suited for my life path?"
Maria: "Acting – you should act in both films and plays."
Wendy: "Thank you. Anything further on that topic?"
Maria: "Not at this time."

←→

Wendy: "Are Maria's lessons this lifetime related to her past life experiences?"
Maria: "Yes."
Wendy: "Which ones are related? How is Maria doing with any continuing lessons?"
Maria: "She had a tough childhood, but different than the previous challenging childhood. She continues to learn how to release sadness."
Wendy: "What is the best way for her to release sadness?"
Maria: "Her Guides recommend she continue to do formal healing work like today's session."
Wendy: "Thank you for being here for her today. Any suggestions for what types of additional healing she should consider?"
Maria: "She'll know."
Wendy: "Meaning it will come across her path naturally and she'll be drawn to it?"
Maria: "Exactly."

←→

Wendy: "What can I do to contact my Higher Self more easily?"
Maria: "Meditate. Breathe. Recharge."
Wendy: "Thank you. This is so helpful as she is already a great meditator. Any additional advice on breathing or recharging?"
Maria: "Just look for opportunities to build this more

143

into daily life."

Wendy: "Thank you."

←→

That concluded our discussion of the questions Maria submitted before her session. Maria was able to journey easily, like she had done during her first session. She answered questions quickly and fluently and didn't need a lot of prompting.

I helped her "land" in the first scene and ground her energy. We oriented her to her own body from the feet on up. I then encouraged her to look around her and share her first impressions.

←→

Wendy: "You're doing really well! What do you see around you?"

Maria: "I see a building."

Wendy: "Wonderful. So, you see a building – what does it look like – what's your impression of it?"

Maria: "It's quite big. It's very old."

Wendy: "Very good. What else do you notice around you?"

Maria: "I see people now. They're dressed in old-fashioned clothes."

Wendy: "They're dressed in old-fashioned clothes. What do they look like? Do you get a sense of the time period? It's okay if you don't – you're seeing quite clearly now."

Maria: "They look like normal people."

Wendy: "What do their clothes look like?"

Maria: "They're regular clothes, not uniforms."

Wendy: "Okay, they're wearing regular street clothes. What happens next?"

←→

Maria: "A woman is walking beside me."

Wendy: "Yes? What does the woman look like?"

Maria: "She's not especially tall. She's wearing a dress. It's white – it's quite long and fitted."

Wendy: "Does she have anything around her waist?"

Maria: "No, no belt or anything like that."

Wendy: "Okay. What about the sleeves on the dress – what are they like?"

Maria: "It has long sleeves."

Wendy: "So her dress has long sleeves. What about the neckline?"

Maria: "The neckline is normal."

Wendy: "Okay. Is she wearing anything on her head?"

Maria: "No, she has a bare head."

Wendy: "Okay. Does she have anything in her hands or on her fingers?"

Maria: "There's nothing in or on her hands – there's no jewelry."

Wendy: "You're doing great really seeing the woman walking beside you now. What does she look like?"

Maria: "She looks middle-aged. She's skinny. She's wearing flat brown shoes."

Wendy: "Wonderful – that's quite descriptive. Do you know who the woman is to you?"

(pause)

Maria: *(happily)* "Why yes, I do! She's my Aunt Grace."

← →

Wendy: "That's wonderful – you're seeing your Aunt Grace really clearly. Are you happy to see her?"

Maria: "Yes, I am!"

Wendy: "Great. Let's take a moment to enjoy that reunion."

(pause)

Wendy: "I'd like you to look down at your feet now. You can now see your own body very clearly and describe your first impressions to me."

Maria: "I'm wearing white sneakers."

Wendy: "Super! Now look up your body a bit and see what clothing you might be wearing. What do you notice?"

Maria: "I'm wearing a dress. My dress is blue."

Wendy: "You're doing so well. What else do you notice about your blue dress? How long is it? How long are the sleeves?"

Maria: "My dress is knee-length, and it has short sleeves."

Wendy: "Great, so your blue dress is to your knees and has short sleeves. What else do you notice about your clothing or appearance?"

Maria: "I have a hair bow."

Wendy: "Do you like your hair bow?"

Maria: "Yes, it looks nice in my blonde hair."

Wendy: "How old are you?"

(pause)

Maria: "I'm eight years old."

Wendy: "Well thank you for taking the time to talk with me today. What's your name?"

Maria: "My name is Norma."

Wendy: "Norma is a nice name. I have an Aunt Norma. Would you like to go to the place where you live now, Norma?"

Maria *(as Norma)*: "Yes, I would."

(I helped her move to the next important scene that had healing and information for her life now.)

← →

Wendy: "What do you see, Norma? It's going to be very easy to see your house clearly and describe it to me."

145

REGRESSION HEALING II: JOE & MARILYN

Norma: *(excitedly)* "We're going to my house!"

Wendy: *(smiling)* "Yes, we are. Be there now, and tell me what it looks like, please."

Norma: "It's quite small and cozy."

Wendy: "Oh, that sounds nice. What colors do you notice? Does it look like a single story or something different?"

Norma: "It's a brown two-story. There's a garden in the front."

Wendy: "Do you see anything you recognize in the garden – is there anything in bloom?"

Norma: "I see some small yellow flowers in bloom."

Wendy: "Okay. Let's enter your home the way you normally do. Are you ready to go in?"

Norma: "Yes, I am. Aunt Grace unlocks the front door with her key."

Wendy: "What do you see when you enter your house? Are you immediately in a room or in a foyer or front hallway? Look around you – you can see very clearly now."

Norma: "We're in the front hallway. It's all very white. It's small."

Wendy: "You're visioning so well – great job! What do you see as you look around from the front hallway? What's straight ahead, and to your right and left?"

Norma: "The kitchen is straight ahead. The living room is to my right, and there's the staircase to go upstairs to my left."

Wendy: "Let's go to your favorite place in your house, Norma. Do you have a favorite place you'd like to revisit?"

Norma: "Yes, I want to go upstairs to my bedroom."

←→

Wendy: "Okay, let's do that. Be in your room now – what do you notice about your bedroom?"

Norma: "It's small. My walls are painted a bright color."

Wendy: "What color are your walls?"

Norma: "They're a bright yellow."

Wendy: "Do you like the color?"

Norma: "Yes, I do."

Wendy: "What else do you see in your bedroom – any furniture, any favorite toys or books, perhaps?"

Norma: "There's a small bed-side table next to my bed."

Wendy: "Do you see anything on the bed-side table?"

Norma: "Yes, some of my dolls are here."

Wendy: "Do you have a favorite doll you play with the most?"

Norma: "My favorite doll changes from time to time."

Wendy: "Which is your favorite doll now? Would you like to show her to me?"

Norma: "She's in a chair in the corner. She's the one with the dark hair and pale skin – the one in a dress?"

146

Wendy: "Yes, I see her. Thank you for showing me your favorite doll. What else do you notice about your room, or would you like to explore?"

Norma: *(sounding surprised)* "Oh – my room is messy! I have dolls scattered here and there – some are on the floor."

←→

Wendy: *(smiling)* "That's okay. Is there anything else on the bedside table or in your room you'd like to look at more closely?"

Norma: "There's a black and white picture of my mother on the little bedside table."

Wendy: "What does your mother look like?"

Norma: "She's not very tall. She's skinny. Her hair is reddish-brown."

Wendy: "What is your mother wearing in the picture?"

Norma: "She's wearing a dress. It's grey or white – I can't tell for sure because it's a black and white picture."

Wendy: "You're doing great. How is the picture displayed?"

Norma: "The picture is in a frame. It's round – no, it's oval-shaped."

←→

Wendy: *(gently)* "How do you feel about your mother, Norma?"

Norma: "I feel sad. Mostly sad."

Wendy: "Why do you feel sad?"

Norma: "Because I don't live with my mother. She's disturbed. I live with a friend of the family."

Wendy: "So Aunt Grace is a friend of the family, not your mother or father's sister?"

Norma: "That's right."

Wendy: "Are you ready to release that sadness? This was a long time ago. You don't need to feel sad anymore from this experience. We can heal and release the old sadness. Do you understand?"

Norma: "Yes."

Wendy: "We learned earlier today your life lesson is to release this sadness. Are you able to do that?"

Norma: "I think so."

←→

Wendy: "I have an idea. What makes you happy right now as eight-year-old Norma? Would you like to do that now?"

Norma: *(enthusiastically)* "Yes! I'd like to watch TV."

Wendy: "Great, we can do that. Where is the TV?"

Norma: "It's downstairs in the living room."

Wendy: "Are you ready to go downstairs?"

Norma: *(excitedly)* "Yes!"

Wendy: "I'd like you to get truly comfortable here, Norma. What's your favorite place to sit to watch TV?"

Norma: "Well, there's a sofa but I like to sit on the floor to watch TV."

Wendy: "Okay, why don't you sit on the floor, and I'll sit on the sofa. Is that okay?"

Norma: "Sure."

Wendy: "What do you like to watch on television?"

Norma: "I watch my favorite films!"

Wendy: "That sounds wonderful. Do you get to choose what you watch, or does Aunt Grace choose for you?"

Norma: "I get to choose what I watch."

Wendy: "When do you typically get to watch your favorite films?"

Norma: "I watch more on the weekends."

Wendy: "When you don't have school?"

Norma: "That's right."

Wendy: "Does your Aunt Grace normally watch with you?"

Norma: "Aunt Grace may or may not watch with me."

←→

Wendy: "That sounds really nice. Can you tell me more about school? What is your school like?"

Norma: "Well, during the week I have school. I walk to get to school."

Wendy: "So you walk to school on weekdays. Do you have a favorite subject or thing to do in school?"

Norma: *(enthusiastically)* "My favorite subject is English. I like to read!"

Wendy: *(smiling)* "So do I. It's one of my favorite things in life. What do you like to read?"

Norma: "I like everything – history, genres. Everything."

Wendy: "That's wonderful, Norma. I'm so glad you like reading so much and that you enjoy school. You must be a very smart girl."

Norma: "Thank you."

←→

Wendy *(gently)*: "Would it be okay if we talked a little about your mother? You don't have to if you don't want to. Your Higher Self and Guides love and support you and only want you to have a pleasant experience today during our session."

Norma: "Yes, that would be okay."

Wendy: "Good. What I'd like to know is do you ever see your mother – your birth mother?"

Norma: "Mom sometimes comes by unexpectedly to visit."

Wendy: "Oh? How do you feel about that?"

Norma: "Today she stormed in. She tried to take me with her. I felt scared – terrified, even."

Wendy: "But you're okay now. Did you or Grace tell her no?"

Norma: "Yes, we both did!"

Wendy: "This may be why we're revisiting this specific day and time – to allow you to release the old fear and terror. You're just fine now – you have a wonderful mother now, and you are safe and loved and protected. Can you feel that energy instead?"

Norma: "Yes, I can."

Wendy: "Wonderful. Is there anything more for you to learn from this time and place?"

Norma: "No, I don't think so."

Wendy: "You've done a wonderful job really exploring these memories, Norma. You can now release the old sadness, and any fear and terror as well as any feelings of abandonment and other energy that no longer serves you. Are you willing to do that?"

Norma: "Yes."

Wendy: "That's fantastic! I'm so proud of you. More importantly, you should be proud of yourself! You can let go of what other people think of you."

(pause)

Wendy: "I'd like you to move forward to another time and place, the one with the most healing and information for your life now. Be there now! Please tell me the first things you see or experience – your first impressions."

← →

Maria: "I'm going into town – I'm wearing red high-heeled shoes."

Wendy: "Your red shoes sound lovely. What do they look like? You can see them clearly in more detail now."

Maria: "They're actually straw – they're casual – they're more like a high wedge shoe."

Wendy: "That's great. You can vision very clearly now. What else are you wearing?"

Maria: "I'm wearing shorts."

Wendy: "Can you tell what the fabric is like? You can feel them as well as see them, or simply know..."

Maria: "They're jean material – denim. My top matches the shoes with red and white."

Wendy: "Very good, so you're wearing denim shorts with a top and with your red wedge shoes. Does your body feel healthy?"

Maria: "Yes, my body is healthy."

Wendy: "Do you get a sense of your age? It's okay if you don't."

Maria: "I'm young – I'm nineteen."

Wendy: "Look at your hands and wrists – are you carrying anything or wearing any jewelry?"

Maria: "I have a small leather purse on my arm. I'm not wearing any jewelry."

Wendy: "Okay. Are you wearing anything on your head?"

Maria: "No, I'm not wearing a hat."

Wendy: "Carry on your natural course. Where are you going as you head into town today?"

←→

Maria: "I'm going to the movies – I'm here now."

Wendy: "Do you meet anyone outside the theater?"

Maria: "No, I don't meet anyone outside."

Wendy: "What happens next?"

Maria: "I purchase my ticket."

Wendy: "Do you know the person who sells you your ticket or the ticket taker?"

Maria: "No, I don't know the ticket taker this time."

Wendy: "So it sounds like you may have been to this theater before – how do you feel about being here right now?"

Maria: "Yes, I've been here before. I'm comfortable and happy here – there are lots of people at the film."

Wendy: "Are you meeting anyone at the film or going on your own today?"

Maria: "I'm looking for someone – I find him over toward the left-hand side."

Wendy: "What does he look like?"

Maria: "He's male – he's quite tall – very healthy-looking."

Wendy: "What is he wearing?"

Maria: "He's nicely dressed. He's wearing a long-sleeved shirt and slacks with good leather shoes."

Wendy: "Do you get a feel for his age? It's fine if you don't."

Maria: "He's a few years older than me."

Wendy: "How do you greet him?"

Maria: "I give him a hug – I'm happy to see him."

←→

Wendy: "That's wonderful. You can clearly hear him greet you by name as you meet – what is your name?"

Maria: "My name is Norma."

Wendy: "Are you the same Norma who lived with her Aunt Grace as a little girl?"

Norma: "Yes."

Wendy: "Thank you. Do you enjoy the film and the company of your male companion?"

Norma: "I feel wonderful but disappointed I have to go right home after the film."

Wendy: "Why do you need to go right home?"

Norma: "I need to practice my audition for a film. My date gives me a ride home."

Wendy: "Oh, I see. That was considerate he gave you a ride home."

Norma: "Yes, it was."

Wendy: "Do you get a sense of his name?"
(pause)
Norma: "No, I don't remember it."
Wendy: "That's fine. Is there anything more to explore from this memory?"
Norma: "No, I don't think so."
Wendy: "Okay. I'd like you to move forward to the next important time and place – the one with the best healing and information for your life now. Please tell me the very first thing you see or sense or experience – what are your first impressions?"

← →

Norma: "The next day I take a short bus ride to my audition."
Wendy: "Is this the day immediately after you went to the movies with your date, Norma?"
(testing name to verify if same life)
Norma: "Yes."
Wendy: "What are you wearing?"
Norma: "I'm dressed up for it."
Wendy: "What part are you auditioning for?"
Norma: "It's a small comedy part in a movie."
Wendy: "Do you know if a lot of people audition for the same role?"
Norma: "A few people audition for the role."
Wendy: "What's your audition like? How are you feeling about your audition, Norma?"
Norma: "I read my lines for the two men. I'm nervous – I don't do too well."

← →

Wendy: "I'd like you to go forward in time. Do you know if you get the part?"
Norma: "No, I don't get the part."
Wendy: "That's okay. Practice makes perfect, doesn't it? Sometimes we need to learn to persevere despite momentary disappointments."
Norma: "Yes. My will – my desire – is still strong!"
Wendy: "That's wonderful. Is there anything more for you to learn from this experience?"
Norma: "No, that's it."
Wendy: "Okay. You're doing wonderfully. I'd like you to move to the next important scene in your soul's journey. I'd like you to move to the time and place with the most healing and information for your life today."
(Note: I chose to use the wording 'in your soul's journey' so Maria was free to experience a lifetime other than Norma. I believe it is crucial hypnotherapists do their best to not 'lead the witness' with suggestions, but to be as open-ended as possible with questions and supportive of any client experience, on-planet or off.)

← →

Maria: "I'm going to a photo shoot."

Wendy: "What's your name?"

Maria/ Norma: *(laughing)* "I'm still Norma!"

Wendy: "Thank you, Norma. How do you get to the photo shoot?"

Norma: "I take the bus again."

Wendy: "Is the bus more convenient for you than driving?"

Norma: "I don't have a car."

Wendy: "Oh, that makes sense. Thank you. What does the place look like where you have your photo shoot?"

Norma: "It's a home-like building with a studio down on the first floor – on the street level."

Wendy: "That's a great description, Norma. What happens next?"

Norma: "I'm speaking with the photographer now. He gives me some quick instructions as to what my poses could be. And what my expression and energy should be."

Wendy: "Great – it sounds like what a director would do in a film. What are you wearing for the photo shoot, Norma?"

←→

Norma: "Right now I'm wearing a blue and white bikini."

Wendy: "So you're wearing a blue and white bikini. Do you pose in any other outfits?"

Norma: "I also brought a red one."

Wendy: "A red bikini?"

Norma: "Yes."

Wendy *(gently)*: "Did you get an opportunity to pose in anything besides the bikinis or is this simply a swimsuit photo shoot?"

Norma: "No, not this time. I would later."

Wendy: "How are you feeling about this photo shoot, Norma?"

Norma: *(sounding wary)* "I don't feel comfortable."

←→

Wendy: "Do you remember what you were paid for this photo shoot, if you were paid?"

Norma: "I don't earn much for these photo shoots. I do them because I really need the money."

Wendy: "I understand. It's okay – there's no shame in what you did, Norma. You can hold your head high. Do you understand that or is there some energy to release?"

Norma: "I'm okay. We can move on from this photo shoot."

Wendy: *(gently)* "You're doing great. Let's move to the next scene from any lifetime that will have the most healing and information for your life now. Perhaps you'll chose to explore why money is tight. I trust your Higher Self and Guides to take you to the right time and place that's best for you."

(Note: The hair on the back of my neck was standing up. I realized I was steeling myself in case this turned into an unwanted nude photo shoot or worse. I was feeling protective of Norma/Maria and needed to rein in my emotions.

The question was whether Norma felt any trauma. There didn't need to be associated trauma from this swimsuit photo shoot, but something felt exploitive. I was working to remain neutral, especially as I wasn't certain if Marilyn had ever posed nude. Clearly, I was not up on my Marilyn history, which I think was a plus for these sessions.

I later learned Marilyn Monroe was the cover of the first Playboy magazine in December 1953. Marilyn arguably launched Hugh Hefner's tremendous career without ever agreeing to be featured in Playboy. Would that have been her choice? To my knowledge, she was not paid for her photographs beyond the initial $50 photo shoot years earlier.

It's important to understand there can be many people who've chosen to experience a life as Marilyn Monroe – or who are tapping into the Collective Consciousness. Each may have different memories and experiences. When someone may have had a potential historic, Biblical, or famous past life it's especially crucial to assume nothing. The person may have had experiences that differ from the recorded 'history.' It often conflicts.)

←→

Wendy: "What's happening now, Norma?"

Norma: "I'm not living with my Aunt Grace any longer."

Wendy: "Do you get a sense of when you moved out or why?"

Norma: "I moved out a few years ago. I have – no, I had – a new home with a guy."

Wendy: "Tell me more about that relationship, please."

Norma: "I moved out again. We're separated now. He was my husband."

←→

Wendy: "Are you living with anyone now?"

Norma: "No, I live on my own."

Wendy: "What's your life like now, Norma?"

Norma: "I visit my mother more often. My life is quite stressful. It's a struggle with paying the rent and having enough money for food and other things."

Wendy: "I understand. That sounds hard. Is there anything more you'd like to explore here – any emotions to release?"

Norma: "I'd like to be happy. I'd like to see myself truly happy."

←→

Wendy: "Yes, let's move to a wonderfully happy memory as Norma Jeane. We learned when we started your session today that it's important to help you release old sadness that doesn't serve you in your current life. Would you like to do

153

that?"

Norma: "Yes, I would!"

Wendy: "Okay, Norma, let's enjoy reliving a happy time in your life now. Be there now!"

← →

Norma: "I'm outside a house. It's quite big. It's white."

Wendy: "You're doing great, Norma. What happens next?"

Norma: "Other people will be coming."

Wendy: "How are you dressed today?"

Norma: "I'm wearing high heels – white pumps. I'm wearing a very special white dress."

Wendy: "What does your dress look like?"

Norma: "This is a dressy dress. It's quite long. It's white, but with a faint pink shimmer. It's fitted and has a mid-neckline.

Wendy: "Your dress sounds beautiful. What else do you notice about what you're wearing?"

Norma: "My dress is sleeveless. I'm wearing short white gloves."

Wendy: "Do you have anything on your head?"

Norma: "I have on a headpiece."

Wendy: "What type of headpiece?"

Norma: "It's a bride headpiece."

Wendy: "So you're the bride?"

Norma *(beaming)*: "Yes!"

← →

Wendy: "How exciting. Are you wearing any jewelry?"

Norma: "My left hand has a gold band. It's on my ring finger. We'll be married here."

Wendy: "So you can feel the gold band on your finger under your glove?"

Norma: "Yes."

Wendy: "What is your name?"

Norma: "It's now Marilyn. I go by Marilyn Monroe, now. I changed my name."

Wendy: "Who are you marrying, Marilyn?"

Marilyn: "I'm marrying Arthur!"

Wendy: *(smiling)* "How do you feel?"

Marilyn: "I'm feeling excited!"

← →

Wendy: "What is your wedding to Arthur like, Marilyn?"

Marilyn: "Arthur wanted a ceremony. Our officiant is Jewish. I needed to convert to Judaism to marry Arthur Miller. I've been studying Judaism."

Wendy: "What does your new husband look like?"

Marilyn: "Arthur wears glasses. He has on nice leather shoes. He's wearing his wedding ring with his suit."

Wendy: "That sounds wonderful, Marilyn. Are you truly

happy?"

Marilyn: "Yes!"

Wendy: "Great. I'd like you to tune into that feeling and feel it permeate your entire body, your entire aura, and to bring that feeling to your life now. Can you do that for me?"

Marilyn: "Yes!"

Wendy: "Perfect. Is there anything more to learn from your happy wedding memories?"

Marilyn: "No, we can move on now."

Wendy: "Okay, I'd like you to go forward to the most important time and place to bring healing and information to your life now. What's happening?"

← →

Marilyn: "I'm going to a very important party. I will perform a song."

Wendy: "What's your name as you get ready to perform?"

Marilyn: "I'm still Marilyn."

Wendy: "Thank you. Can you tell me more about this important party where you're to perform?"

Marilyn: "This stage is huge. There are so very many people here."

Wendy: "What song will you perform?"

Marilyn: "The birthday song."

(pause)

Wendy: *(puzzled)* "Do you mean 'Happy Birthday'?"

Marilyn: "Yes."

Wendy: "Who will you sing the birthday song to?"

Marilyn: "Why, to John."

Wendy: *(taking care not to assume)* "What's John's full name?"

Marilyn: "President John Kennedy. Jack Kennedy."

← →

Wendy: "Thank you for clarifying, Marilyn. What happens next?"

Marilyn: "I've been practicing. Preparing how to make the birthday song somehow special and new. I showed up late tonight, so I had to dress in a hurry."

Wendy: "But you're ready now, right? Take a good look at your dress – what does it look like, Marilyn?"

Marilyn: "This is a super long dress – it reaches to my ankles..."

Wendy: "Look down, you can see it very clearly now."

Marilyn: "Oh, it's even longer than I thought. It's pooling on the floor behind me a bit. It's so beautiful!"

← →

Wendy: "What are you wearing on your feet?"

Marilyn: "I'm wearing high-heeled shoes."

Wendy: "What type of high heels?"

Marilyn: "They have very thin high heels."

Wendy: "They sound beautiful, Marilyn. Are you wearing anything else with your gorgeous long dress and thin high heels?"

Marilyn: "I'm wearing a white fur jacket."

Wendy: "Do you know what type of fur? It's fine if you don't know."

Marilyn: *(thoughtfully)* "I don't know. It must have been a large animal as it's one piece of fur. It's not the type that's pieced together."

Wendy: "Yes, I understand. You're visioning so well, you're very good at this type of work. What does your dress look like in addition to being quite long and lovely?"

←→

Marilyn: "It's sort of a nude color – like a beige, but so beautiful. It's beaded with small pearls. They're crystal."

Wendy: "Do you get a sense of where the crystal pearl beading is on the dress?"

Marilyn: "They're all over the dress – they're not just in one place."

Wendy: "Your dress sounds just gorgeous. Was it custom-made for you, do you know?"

Marilyn: "I bought it but it was too large for me, so it had to be sewn in to fit properly."

Wendy: "So it was custom-fitted for you."

Marilyn: "Yes."

←→

Wendy: "How are you feeling as you get ready to perform?"

Marilyn: "I feel a little tipsy, honestly."

Wendy: "You can do this. What happens next?"

Marilyn: "It's time! I'm being introduced now."

Wendy: "By whom? Do you know who introduces you?"

Marilyn: "There's a man at the microphone. I walk over to him."

Wendy: "Okay, that's great. Do you see what type of microphone or set-up you use to perform?"

Marilyn: "It's like one of those special tables. One where you can place your speech paper so the audience doesn't see them? I think it's called a podium in English?"

Wendy: "That's exactly right, a podium. You're doing great, you're describing this so well in English for me, Marilyn. Just enjoy reliving your performance."

(Pauses to allow time for Marilyn to sign 'Happy Birthday' to President John F. Kennedy)

Wendy: "How did it go?"

Marilyn: *(excitedly)* "It went so well!"

Wendy: "That's wonderful. May I ask how old you are now?"

Marilyn: "I'm thirty-five. I'll be thirty-six quite soon."

Wendy: "How wonderful you got to give this performance and it went so smoothly. Enjoy that memory fully. Let's explore it more if that's alright with you. What happened just before you went on-stage?"

←→

Marilyn: "I met John and Bobby before I went on stage."

Wendy: "How did that go?"

Marilyn: "They were happy to see me, but I was feeling stressed as I had to go on-stage. I was so late that I downed my drink too fast."

Wendy: "But you performed well, Marilyn. Enjoy that memory and be proud of yourself. I think you made a lot of people happy with a beautiful tribute. What happened after you sang 'Happy Birthday' to the President?"

Marilyn: "I left early."

←→

Wendy: "Did you see either John or Bobby Kennedy after you sang? Was it Bobby Kennedy you're referring to – the President's brother?"

Marilyn: "Yes. I briefly saw them both after, then I needed to leave."

Wendy: "I think people often forget or don't understand that acting and performing is work, and requires preparation, effort and talent."

Marilyn: "Yes. Thank you for recognizing that."

Wendy: "You're visioning so well. I'd like you to go to the place with the most healing and information to help you now. Are you ready to explore another memory or scene?"

Marilyn: "Yes."

Wendy: "Where are you now?"

←→

Marilyn: "I'm arriving home."

Wendy: "Is this right after you sang the birthday song to President Kennedy?"

Marilyn: "Yes, it's the same night. I just got home."

Wendy: "Where do you live?"

Marilyn: "I live in Brentwood."

Wendy: "Where is Brentwood located?"

Marilyn: "It's in California."

Wendy: "Is Brentwood near Hollywood?"

Marilyn: "It's the western side of Los Angeles. It's a beautiful part of town."

Wendy: "Thank you. Are you inside or outside your Brentwood home now? You're able to see this very clearly. You're doing such great work visioning and remembering."

Marilyn: "I'm outside."

Wendy: "What does your home look like from the outside as you arrive home that night after singing the birthday song to the President?"

157

←→

Marilyn: "It's a large home."

Wendy: "Are you able to tell what color is it? I know it's nighttime, so it may be dark. Are there any lights on or do we need to turn on some lights to see better?"

Marilyn: "My home is white stucco."

Wendy: "Wonderful. What else do you notice about your home or yard?"

Marilyn: "There's a pool."

Wendy: "Where is the pool located in comparison to the house? Is it in the back yard?"

Marilyn: "No, it's rather more in front of the house."

Wendy: "It sounds lovely. Do you use the pool, Marilyn, or is it more for looks? Or was it just part of the property when you bought it?"

Marilyn: "Oh, I use it."

Wendy: "Great, that sounds so nice. Do you like to swim?"

Marilyn: "Yes, I do like to swim."

←→

Wendy: "What else do you see as you look around outside your home? Can you read the number of your house?"

Marilyn: "Let me see – there's some sort of sign."

Wendy: "Are there numbers on the sign? It's okay if you can't tell. I know I'm asking a lot of questions to help you remember."

Marilyn: "Yes, there are numbers on the sign."

Wendy: "Where is the sign in comparison to your front door? Or are the numbers located out by the street?"

Marilyn: "It's in the asphalt."

Wendy: *(confused)* "Your house numbers are in the asphalt?"

Marilyn: "Yes, the sign with the numbers was already there when I bought the house from when it was originally built. I left it the same."

Wendy: "Oh, I understand now. Thank you for explaining that to me. Would you like to go in now or to explore your yard more?"

Marilyn: "I want to go inside."

←→

Wendy: "Ok, let's go in. How do you normally enter your home?"

Marilyn: "Through my front door."

Wendy: "Great, you're going in through your front door now. Look around you and know you can see your home very clearly. How is it laid out?"

Marilyn: "We're standing in the front entry. We're in the hallway. It's an open floor plan."

Wendy: "That's sounds lovely. What's your favorite room

or spot in the house? I'd like you to go there now and describe it to me, please."

Marilyn: "Oh, I like all of it! Let me think. My favorite if I had to pick one place is the dining room and living room portion. I love my home."

Wendy: "It sounds so beautiful. You said it's an open floor plan?"

Marilyn: "Yes, there are no doors except to my bedroom and the bathroom."

Wendy: "Is it a one-story house or do you see some stairs?"

Marilyn: "Yes, I think it's a one-story house."

Wendy: "You can walk around and see it very clearly."

Marilyn: "I see it now. There are a few stairs. My bedroom is upstairs. It's a two-story at least in part."

Wendy: "You're doing such strong work, is there anything more you'd like to see or experience in your home now? You can take all the time you need to enjoy your home."

Marilyn: *(smiling)* "I'm finished exploring it for now."

Wendy: "Okay, I want you to go to the place that has the most healing and information for your life today."

(pause)

Wendy: "Where are you now?"

(There was a long pause before Marilyn replied)

(Note: Memory is an imperfect thing. I see the purpose of past life regression as releasing old energy that no longer serves us and bringing forth forgotten abilities to the present day.

Maria may have had a few details about Marilyn Monroe's Brentwood home incorrect such as the location of the pool being in the back yard and the home being a one-story hacienda. There may not have been emotional content around those details, so she simply didn't need to recall them more precisely like moments with an emotional load. It's hard to say.

As she moved to the next scene, I was surprised by how emotional I felt. I wasn't certain if it was her energy, mine, or a combination. I kept quiet to let the experience remain hers. Tears were suddenly running down my face, yet I felt incredibly happy as she began to describe what she was experiencing.)

← →

Wendy: "What's happening now? What's your name, please?"

Marilyn: *(coyly)* "Why I'm visiting with someone – it's you-know-who!"

(pause)

Marilyn: *(laughing)* "And you should know I'm Marilyn!"

Wendy: "Thanks for humoring me. It's best I don't assume. What are you experiencing now?"

Marilyn: "I'm visiting with someone."

(I had the sense she was batting her eyelashes at me.)

159

REGRESSION HEALING II: JOE & MARILYN

Wendy: "Who are you visiting?"
Marilyn: "A man!"
(sound of Marilyn giggling)
Wendy: *(smiling)* "Great, how do you feel about this man?"
Marilyn: *(a bit dreamily)* "I feel good. Really good!"
(pause)

←→

Wendy: "What's happening now?"
Marilyn: "He's just arriving to pick me up."
Wendy: "Is he going to visit with you at your home?"
Marilyn: "No, we're going for a drive and then take a walk on the beach."
Wendy: "That sounds wonderful. What time of day is it?"
Marilyn: "Lunch time. It's mid-day."
Wendy: "Great, what are you doing now?"
Marilyn: "We're walking on the beach."
Wendy: "Are you wearing anything on your feet?"
Marilyn: "No, we're in our bare feet now, carrying our shoes."
Wendy: "How do you feel?"
Marilyn: "I'm happy."
Wendy: "What do you talk about as you walk barefoot along the beach together that day?"
Marilyn "We talk about our relationship."
Wendy: "Your relationship with this man?"
Marilyn: "Why, yes."
Wendy: "What is his name, Marilyn?"
Marilyn: *(sounding coy)* "You know his name – it's you, Joe!"
Wendy: "Are you referring to Joe DiMaggio – your former husband Joe?"
Marilyn: "Yes. You know who I'm walking with on the beach, discussing our relationship. It's you back when you were Joe!"
(Note: I had to pause briefly to digest this. I needed to keep the focus on Maria's healing. This was somewhat unusual to have a client be describing a moment we'd shared together in a previous life, but it does happen as I described in my first book, 'Regression Healing I.' Other hypnotherapists experience this from time to time with their clients, too.)

←→

Wendy: "How do you feel about your relationship with Joe?"
Marilyn: "Good. Really good."
Wendy: "Do you see Joe a lot?"
Marilyn: "It's been a while."
Wendy: "Ok, so it's been a while. Were you divorced recently? From Arthur?"
Marilyn: "Yes, exactly."
Wendy: "Are you still walking?"

160

Marilyn: "We're fishing now."

Wendy: "Oh, you're fishing. Did you bring fishing gear with you do you know, or do you rent it down at the beach perhaps? It's okay if you don't know. You're doing great."

Marilyn: "Joe brought the fishing equipment for us."

Wendy: "Are you fishing from a boat or from the beach? Are you able to fish from the beach where you are, or would it be too shallow?"

Marilyn: "We're fishing from the beach."

(pause)

Marilyn: "Maybe from a little pier? That's what we're doing."

←→

Wendy: "That sounds nice. Do you like fishing or is this more something Joe enjoys?"

Marilyn: "It's good for relaxing."

Wendy: "Do you catch anything that day?"

Marilyn: "Yes, we do, but it's not edible, so we throw it back."

Wendy: "You're wonderfully detailed with your descriptions. What happens next?"

Marilyn: "We take a long walk. We say goodbye. We promise to call each other very soon. We're making our plans!"

Wendy: "You're making plans?"

Marilyn: *(giggling)* "Yes, big plans. You know – special plans!"

Wendy: *(working to keep my voice even and energy calm, despite the tears streaming down my face)* "Yes, I remember those special plans."

(Referring to their plan to remarry, but not wanting to say more and influence Maria in her memory of Marilyn.)

←→

Wendy: "What's happening now, Marilyn?"

Marilyn: "We're heading home now."

Wendy: "Are you back in Joe's car? Or did you take your car to the beach that day? Or did you more use a driver at this point?"

Marilyn: "Oh – look – I'm driving myself!"

Wendy: "You took two cars to go to the beach together?"

Marilyn: "Yes, it worked out better that way for some reason."

Wendy: "I understand. What's happening now? Have you said goodbye to Joe?"

Marilyn: "Yes. We'll see each other very soon."

Wendy: "Okay, I'd like you to go where the most healing and information is for your life today. Be there now! What do you see or experience?"

←→

Marilyn: "I'm back at my house."

Wendy: "Your home in Brentwood?"

161

Marilyn: "Yes, we're back at my house in Brentwood – in L.A."

Wendy: "Do you head right in, or do you do anything outside first?"

Marilyn: "I go right in as Eunice opens the front door for me."

Wendy: "Super. Who is Eunice?"

Marilyn: "Eunice Murray. She does the cleaning and cooking for me."

Wendy: "What happens next?"

←→

Marilyn: "We make dinner together."

Wendy: "You make it together versus her making it for you?"

Marilyn: "Yes. Eunice is a friend, too."

Wendy: "Oh, I see. What happens next?"

Marilyn: "She's cleaning up for me. It's a large house. It's really nice to have her clean."

Wendy: "That sounds great. Does anyone else live in the house with you, Marilyn?"

←→

Marilyn: "My dog lives with me."

Wendy: "Oh, you have a dog? Wonderful. What's your dog's name?"

Marilyn: "Maf."

Wendy: "Maff – like M-A-F-F?"

Marilyn: "It's spelled M-A-F, just the 3 letters. *(Giggling at the inside joke.)*

Wendy: *(not yet getting the reference, thinking maybe it had to do with the dog breed?)* "Okay. What type of dog is Maf?"

Marilyn: "Maf is a Maltese."

Wendy: "A Maltese? Remind me what a Maltese looks like."

Marilyn: "A Maltese is a small white dog."

Wendy: "Got it. Is it like a Bichon, do you know?"

Marilyn: "They look quite similar, but a Maltese is a poodle."

Wendy: "Thank you. I'm better at large dog breeds. Do you take care of Maf or does Eunice?"

Marilyn: "I do. He's my dog. I make sure he has food and water."

Wendy: "Of course. It sounds like you love Maf a lot and take great care of him. What do you want to explore now?"

←→

Marilyn: "Thank you. I'm going up to my room now."

Wendy: "Be there now and know you can see it quite clearly. What do you do usually do up in your bedroom?"

Marilyn: "I normally sleep or read."

Wendy: "What are you reading now?"

Marilyn: "It's a manuscript."

Wendy: "What is the manuscript for? You can read the cover page easily."

Marilyn: "It's for a film."

Wendy: "Great, you're seeing very clearly now. Which film?"

← → ← →

Marilyn: "*Something's Got to Give* is the name of the film."

Wendy: "Are you reading the movie manuscript in your bedroom?"

Marilyn: "Yes, I am."

Wendy: "Do you have a favorite reading chair or do you read in bed?"

Marilyn: "I like to read in bed so I can spread my papers out all over the bed. There's room for Maf, too."

Wendy: "Is Maf allowed up on your bed?"

Marilyn: "Yes, he is if I invite him up. He knows not to jump on the bed or furniture unless he's given permission to join me."

Wendy: "Maf sounds like a sweet friend for you. Did Eunice go home for the night?"

← →

Marilyn: "No, she's still downstairs cleaning up. Sometimes she stays over."

Wendy: "Is Eunice a live-in?"

Marilyn: "She does both. She lives in sometimes, but she also lives out as she has her own place."

Wendy: "Thank you for explaining that to me, Marilyn. What happens next? Are you still reading the manuscript? Is this a movie you're hoping to be cast in or do you already have a part?"

Marilyn: "Oh, I have a part in this film."

Wendy: "So you've been cast in the film, *Something's Got to Give*."

Marilyn: *(happily)* "Yes, I have."

← →

Wendy: "So what happens next? Are you still reading?"

Marilyn: "I fall asleep reading the manuscript."

Wendy: "Do you sleep through the night?"

Marilyn: "No, I wake up and take my medications. I say goodnight to my housekeeper and turn off my lights."

Wendy: "So now you're going to sleep for the night."

Marilyn: "Yes, I am."

Wendy: "May I ask how old you are, Marilyn?"

Marilyn: "I'm thirty-six. I had my birthday not too long ago."

Wendy: "Do you tend to go to sleep early or are you more of a night owl?"

Marilyn: "I'm trying to go to sleep early as I need to go

163

to the set in the morning. I'm going to be celebrating with the cast and crew."

Wendy: "Wonderful. What are you celebrating?"

(pause)

Marilyn: "I'm going to sleep now and then we'll talk about that more."

Wendy: "Okay. You can sleep now and tell me when you're ready."

(long pause)

←→

Marilyn: "We had our celebration and now I'm back home."

Wendy: "What are you doing today now that you're home?"

Marilyn: "I'm relaxing. I'm doing a little gardening."

Wendy: "Do you like to garden?"

Marilyn: "Yes, I do."

Wendy: "What type of gardening do you enjoy? Vegetables or flowers or both?"

Marilyn: "Flowers. I'm good with and really enjoy flowers."

Wendy: "Do you garden for long?"

Marilyn: "A few hours."

Wendy: "That sounds nice. What happens next?"

Marilyn: "I go back inside, and my housekeeper arrives."

Wendy: "So Eunice arrives. What do you ask her to do today, or does she just know what to do?"

Marilyn: "She's cleaning."

Wendy: "Okay, Eunice is cleaning. What happens next in your day?"

←→

Marilyn: *(sounding upset)* "I found out I'm no longer filming."

Wendy: "Why are you no longer filming? Is the film being put on hold?"

Marilyn: "No, they're trying to fire me because they claimed I wasn't sick. But I was sick when I missed all those days of filming!"

Wendy: "So that caused issues for you?"

Marilyn: "Yes. I may get my role back, though."

Wendy: "Would you still like to work on this movie?"

Marilyn: "Yes, I would."

Wendy: "What do you do after you find out it's a question if you'll still be in the film? Are there any steps you can take?"

←→

Marilyn: "I make some calls."

Wendy: "You make some phone calls?"

Marilyn: "Yes, I do."

Wendy: "May I ask who you call?"

Marilyn: "I call my friend Peter."

Wendy: "What's Peter's last name?"

Marilyn: "Lawford. Peter Lawford."

Wendy: "So you call Peter Lawford. Do you know why you call Peter Lawford? It's okay if you don't."

Marilyn: "Because I need to know what time the photographer will be coming for the photo shoot."

Wendy: "You'll be having a photo shoot?"

Marilyn: *(perking up)* "Yes, I am."

Wendy: "Do you call anyone else?"

←→

Marilyn: *(giggling)* "I call your son."

Wendy: *(surprised)* "My son?"

Marilyn: "Yes, Joe Junior."

Wendy: *(taking care not to assume)* "What's his full name?"

Marilyn: "You know, Joe DiMaggio, Junior. Your son!"

Wendy: *(a little confused)* "Why do you telephone Joe's son Joe? Do you know him personally?"

Marilyn: *(laughing)* "Yes, you remember. I was his stepmom when Joe and I were married. When we were married – when you and I were married the first time. I've known Joe for years, as well as Joe Junior."

Wendy: *(choosing to stay in her hypnotherapist role and to not speak as Joe DiMaggio)* "Oh, I see."

Marilyn: "Joe Junior has a new girlfriend. He wants my advice, so I return his call."

Wendy: "Of course. Thank you for explaining that to me, Marilyn. Can we talk more about why the studio was trying to remove you from the film 'Something's Got to Give?' "

←→

Marilyn: "Yes, I can."

Wendy: "Can you explain more why it seemed like the studio was questioning whether you were ill? Couldn't a doctor verify that fact, or didn't you see a physician?"

Marilyn: "I did see lots of doctors. A major part of why I was fired was because the studio knew I did the *Happy Birthday, Mr. President* performance during the time I was day-by-day recovering from surgery and other illnesses."

←→

Wendy: "Oh, now I can see why that became a hot issue. You did a very public performance during the time you weren't feeling well enough to film and the studio of course learned about it? Ouch. What do you think of your decision now? Was it the best one for you?"

Marilyn: *(strongly)* "I'm glad I did it! I promised to do it. I felt okay that day. It wasn't very strenuous to sing a simple song my own way. I enjoyed it!"

Wendy: "I understand. That was probably a lot easier than a long day filming."

Marilyn: "Exactly!"

Wendy: "So you made the best decision you could, and it had some fallout."

Marilyn: "Yes."

Wendy: "Is there anything else to explore with that topic?"

Marilyn: "No."

Wendy: "Do you feel complete with it?"

Marilyn: *(nodding vigorously)* "I do."

Wendy: "Great."

←→

Wendy: "What happens next on this day when you're now home and are having a dispute with the studio?"

Marilyn: "I'm taking care of Maf, which makes me think of Frank Sinatra."

Wendy: *(puzzled)* "Why does your dog make you think of Frank Sinatra?"

Marilyn: "Because Frank gave me Maf."

Wendy: *(surprised)* "Frank Sinatra the singer gave you your dog?"

Marilyn: *(giggling)* "Yes! Do you get the joke about my dog's name now?"

Wendy: *(carefully)* "I think I might, but I don't want to assume. Is it appropriate to share the joke with me? My Guides are saying, *Don't rush in where angels fear to tread,' Marilyn.'*"

Marilyn: "Maf is short for Mafia. That's all I'm going to say."

Wendy: "Okay, let's leave that alone. I'm pulling my energy back now as that's my guidance. Let's let that be. The angels say that's not our mission today to poke at that energy."

(pause)

←→

Wendy: "What happens next?"

Marilyn: "I take some meds to sleep."

Wendy: "Do you do that regularly?"

Marilyn: "Yes, I have to have medication to be able to sleep."

Wendy: "That sounds challenging."

Marilyn: "It is."

Wendy: "Do you fall right to sleep?"

Marilyn: "No, I don't. I hear Eunice still cleaning downstairs."

Wendy: "Ok, you hear Eunice cleaning. Are you able to sleep now?"

Marilyn: "I fall asleep – but something strange happens..."

Wendy: "Something strange?"

Marilyn: "Yes. My housekeeper comes up and checks if I fell asleep."

←→

Wendy: "Does she do that normally?"

Marilyn: "No."

Wendy: "How does that make you feel?"

166

Marilyn: "I get up and lock my door for privacy."
Wendy: "Okay, what happens then?"
Marilyn: "I fall asleep again."
Wendy: "Yes? And then?"
Marilyn: "I wake up again."
Wendy: *(gently)* "How do you feel now? It was an event filled day. You're planning your wedding with Joe. You're in a dispute with the studio."
(pause)
Wendy: "We can release that old dispute energy now. This was a long time ago."
Marilyn: "I feel very alone – very lonely – very scared."
Wendy: "Why do you feel scared?"
Marilyn: *(becoming agitated)* "Because I live alone – I sleep alone. I feel like something might happen to me. I'm afraid I won't wake up again *(begins to cry hard)* – I'm dying – dying..."

←→

There was a long pause. Wendy helped Maria cross over to the Light from her lifetime when she recalled being Marilyn Monroe, formerly Norma Jeane Mortenson, baptized Norma Jeane Baker.

←→

Wendy: "You're very brave! Let's release this old fear and sadness that no longer serves you. Your Guide and others will be here to greet you, to welcome you, to love you and to heal you."
(pausing for a moment to allow Maria's Higher Self to connect with her Guide)
Wendy: "What does your Guide say about how you did during your lifetime as Marilyn Monroe?"
Maria: *(smiling)* "My Guide says I did very well!"
Wendy: *(smiling in return)* "Excellent - how does that make you feel?"
Maria: "It's so nice to hear."
Wendy: "Yes, I'm sure it is. What else would your Guide like you to know about that life as Norma Jeane, who became Marilyn Monroe?"
Maria: "My Guide says because of the challenging childhood and environment I had to live in it would have been harder to do much more or to do any better than I did."
Wendy: "How do you feel about that insight?"
Maria: "It helps me."
Wendy: "Excellent. Is there more?"
Maria: *(jubilantly)* "He wants me to know it's why I was so sad this lifetime, and that I don't have to be sad any longer!"
Wendy: "That sounds amazing! What a powerful release."
Maria: *(sounding peaceful and relieved)* "Yes. Yes, it is."
(pause)

167

←→

Wendy: "Was your main mission accomplished that life?"

Maria: "No, it wasn't."

Wendy: "What was your main mission?"

Maria: "To live longer that lifetime and more happily..."

Wendy: "Can you do that this lifetime? Are you set up for success now? Is that what your Guide recommends for you."

Maria: *(beaming)* "Yes, he does."

Wendy: "Wonderful. You're young and have your whole life ahead of you now to live well, to be happy and healthy. Are you meant to focus on anything from that life that wasn't done?"

Maria: "Yes. To be happy."

Wendy: "Is this why you have such profound memories from being Marilyn that we've explored together on two separate occasions?"

Maria: "Yes, it is."

←→

Wendy: "I'd like you to know that you are so loved and supported. Your entire team of Guides and your soul family is here for you now. Is there anything else you need to have your current life go well to progress as a soul and to live your life purpose?"

Maria: "Joe being reincarnated helps me. You having been Joe – that we found each other again."

Wendy: *(choking back tears)* "Yes – it helps me, too, that we met again. And that you forgave me for the actions that I deeply regret from during our marriage."

Maria: "It's okay. It's going to be okay now."

Wendy: "Bless you for forgiving me."

Maria: "I do."

←→

Wendy: "Would you like to go to a Place of Healing now, or back to the Place of All Knowledge? We can go anywhere you want. What does your Guide suggest is best?"

Maria: "He says to go to the Place of Healing."

Maria had a private healing session which focused on her heart and eyes. She was able to envision new opportunities for her current life she had not been able to see before. It was literally 'eye-opening.'

That concluded our session.

←→

Joe DiMaggio summarizes what occurred upon Marilyn's death.

Joe: "Wendy needed tremendous healing when she fully grasped that the day Marilyn and I (as Joe DiMaggio) walked on the beach was the day we were finalizing our

168

plans to marry. We chose Wednesday, August 8th, 1962, for our wedding day.

To my great shock and dismay, Marilyn instead died the night of Sunday, August 5th. I had her body interred on August 8th with my son Joe by my side, wearing his Marine uniform. Marilyn's half-sister had agreed it would be a great relief if I would plan Marilyn's funeral.

It was a purposefully small funeral of around thirty people. I did my best to honor Marilyn's life and not have this tragedy – and her life –turned into a circus. Many people – including Hollywood's elite – were turned away at the gate. I didn't give a damn who I offended. Today was for Marilyn's memory.

Lee Strasberg, Marilyn's acting coach and friend, gave the eulogy. I could not trust myself to speak. My heart was so squeezed in my chest it was hard to breathe. I couldn't process that she was gone – how could such a bright light be extinguished while I was still alive?

What caused her death? And most haunting of all – was there anything I could have done to prevent it?"

Chapter Nine – Prince Goes Galactic

Six months had passed since Maria's extraordinary second past-life regression. I had been focused on building my business while also seeking traditional employment. Writing was temporarily on the back burner.

On February 14th, 2018, my Valentine's Day gift to myself was a past-life regression session with another Newton Institute trained friend. I had no idea what lives we might visit. I trusted that my Higher Self and Guides would share what I most needed.

My hypnotherapist set the stage with twenty-three minutes of relaxation. It was designed to show me the most beneficial past lives to help with my current life purpose and abilities. We pick up with her command to "Be there now!" in that lifetime.

←→

Hypnotherapist: "What are you wearing on your feet?"
Wendy: "Men's dress shoes."
Hypnotherapist: "What do they look like?"
Wendy: "They're leather. They're loafers – they're quite handsome. These are Italian loafers which were quite expensive. They're very comfortable as they fit me well."
Hypnotherapist: "What are you wearing?"
Wendy: "Dress slacks."
Hypnotherapist: "How would you describe them?"
Wendy: "They're brown slacks with a sharp crease down the center. They also fit me well. I'm a tall and slim male. I have on a crisp white oxford shirt with long sleeves."
Hypnotherapist: "You're doing great. How old would you estimate you are?"

←→

Wendy: "I'm an adult male. I'm in my mid-forties."

Hypnotherapist: "Very good. I want you to take a deep breath and go deeper and deeper than before as I count from one to five. One – deeper; two – deeper than before; three – deeper; four – deeper still; five – deeper than before."

(pause)

Hypnotherapist: "Tell me more about yourself. What color is your skin?"

Wendy: "I'm a Caucasian of Italian descent. My parents emigrated from Italy to the United States."

Hypnotherapist: "Can you tell me your name?"

Wendy: "It's Joe. Joe DiMaggio."

←→

Hypnotherapist: "Very good, Joe. What year is it?"

Wendy *(speaking as Joe)*: "It's the mid-sixties – 1964 or 1965."

Hypnotherapist: "Where are you, Joe?"

Joe: "I'm inside my home in Northern California."

Hypnotherapist: "That's excellent, Joe. What are you doing inside your home?"

Joe: "I'm finishing my cup of tea while I read the newspaper."

Hypnotherapist: "Very good. What do you spend your time doing, Joe, in addition to those moments relaxing with your tea while you read the paper?"

Joe: "I had the good fortune to take early retirement. I'm doing some charity work and spending time catching up with family and friends after those busy years in pro ball."

Hypnotherapist: "That sounds wonderful, Joe. I'm going to count to five again and I want you to go to a significant event in your life. Be there now!"

←→

(Sounds of repeated heavy sighing from Joe – a palpable sense he didn't want to be where he had gone.)

Hypnotherapist: "What's happening, Joe? You're going to be just fine."

Joe: *(voice tight)* "I'm at my second wife's funeral."

Hypnotherapist: "It sounds like there's some understandable emotion to release about this event."

Joe: *(tightly)* "Yes. We were only married a short time after a long friendship and courtship. She remarried after our divorce, and then divorced again."

Hypnotherapist: "What about you?"

Joe: "I didn't remarry. We were planning to remarry when – when – when– *(begins to sob)* she died unexpectedly!"

Hypnotherapist: "It sounds like you have a lot of emotions to release. What are you feeling, Joe?"

Joe: "Sadness."

(long pause)

Joe: "Self-blame."

(another long pause)

Joe: "Angst."

Hypnotherapist: "So there are a lot of emotions to release here. I'm asking your Guide to speak through you to help you process this, Joe. What would your Guide like us to know?"

←→

Guide: "He – this soul – is punishing itself too much. It's not helpful. He spent the next forty years alone."

Hypnotherapist: *(shrewdly)* "Why is this presenting now?"

Guide: "For Wendy to realize she doesn't need to do the same thing. It's been hard for her to accept that she truly lived this parallel life. It's not imprinting from the Collective."

(pause)

Guide: "She'd been asking her Guides to help her attract her new life partner. But there's been this push-pull energy going on with her life as Joe."

(pause)

Guide: "We needed to help her cut the cord with her life as Joe. It was overly influencing her life as Wendy. Joe chose to hide away as everyone wanted something from him. This was due to his sports fame and from being Marilyn's long-term confidant and husband. That was the best choice for him. It's not the best choice for Wendy."

←→

Hypnotherapist: "What would be best for Wendy?"

Guide: "She needs just a little bit of fame to allow her to be seen to do her work – to live her life purpose. We kept her cloaked until last week. We've slowly been removing the cloaking she had."

(pause)

Guide: "She felt invisible as many middle-aged or older women do. Her partner can now see her energetically. He can see her and find her energetically and then in the physical – in your 3D world. We need to get the two homebodies to meet. They will then be a great match in many ways."

Hypnotherapist: "That sounds wonderful. What else should she know?"

←→

Guide: "She's felt a lot of self-blame. She's been punishing herself in the romance department because her partners have so frequently died – both male and female partners. It's not just been in this one Joe and Marilyn timeline. It's been many lives."

(pause)

Guide: "That's true for a fair number of souls but what's

172

compounded the issue is she has such a remarkable soul memory. She recalls an unusually high number of her past and parallel lives, many of them with tremendous detail."

Hypnotherapist: "So how do we best help her now?"

Guide: "We wash away the angst."

← →

Hypnotherapist: "May I ask who I'm speaking with? Which Guide is this?"

Guide: "This is Prince. The artist formerly known as Prince, too."

(Prince laughed)

Hypnotherapist: "Very good! Prince, how do we best wash away her angst?"

← →

Prince: "I'm bringing in the Violet Flame of transmutation. She works with it regularly. We've both worked with it before. It's perfect for her."

(pause)

Prince: "I'm now going to bring in all seven of the Sacred Flames. I'm asking her to reposition herself on the bed so the flames can get to more of her body more easily. This is a powerful healing! I'm asking her to visualize the Violet Flame for one more moment."

(pause)

Prince: "I'm now bringing in the green ray of healing."

(pause)

Prince: "And now the Christ Light. I'm using it to burn away the old angst. She's carried it for many lifetimes – back to the time of Christ – even longer. This is a deep level healing."

(pause)

Prince: "Anyone who would like to read more about the sacred flames can look for Aurelia's book. Aurelia Louise Jones – *The Seven Sacred Flames.*"

← →

Hypnotherapist: "Thank you. This is amazing to witness."

Prince: "I'm calling in the Ascended Masters now, the Angels, the Ancestors – her entire team. I'm working with the crystal grid we asked her to place around her bed before this session began."

(pause)

Prince: "I'm restoring her health with the aid of the crystals at the foot of her bed, and the Buddha who is seated there. I am activating the crystals on the right-hand side of her bed for her financial abundance to be restored, and the rose quartz on the left side of her bed for a healthy romance."

Hypnotherapist: "That's wonderful. What else does she need?"

Prince: "Her root chakra has become stronger in the last few days since the two of you reconnected and began planning this session. Healing has been flowing in. Her crown is opening fully – it is quite balanced. Her root and now sacral chakra are continuing to strengthen."

←→

Hypnotherapist: "That's wonderful. What else does she need to know?"

Prince: We encourage her to begin re-reading 'The Seven Sacred Flames' meditations at night before she falls asleep, or a page or two from the accompanying prayer book. This is one path to enlightenment."

(pause)

Prince: "She's already become enlightened. But reading and rereading this book helps synch her conscious mind with her subconscious mind. She will learn all five secret rays which few are able to do. She doesn't need to know them consciously. The knowledge can be within her heart and mind."

Hypnotherapist: "Thank you. I see why that book is so important for her. Is there anything else?"

Prince: *(smiling)* "It's the book of her lifetime."

←→

Prince: "We would like her to spiritually surrender to us once a week using the MAP meditation technique. It is outlined in the MAP (*Medical Assistance Plan*) book by Machaelle Small Wright."

(pause)

Prince: "She could do this meditation weekly on Sunday evenings. This timing is merely a suggestion. We'd like her to surrender what's bothering her – what feels heavy, meaning not of the Light. She could do this regarding her health, wealth, or relationships, for example."

(pause)

Prince: "She can surrender something in each of these areas. She can choose which needs help the most – where she feels the most resistance – the least flow."

(pause)

Prince: "She flows outward to help others so automatically that we need her to pull in and help herself more for a time. Then she'll be able to serve others on a higher level once she's mastered the highest self-care first."

←→

Hypnotherapist: "It sounds like she's to discover her personal gifts and beauty more."

Prince: "That's well-put. I'll give her the simplest example now. She needs to sit up, blow her nose, and drink some water. That will show her how much better her back is feeling since we began today's session."

(pause)

Prince: "At this point staying on the highest path really is as simple for her as meditating for fifteen minutes a day. Then auto-write from us – from her Guides – for five minutes. She should do a major session like this at least once or twice a year. More often if we ask her to when it's time for major change."

←→

Hypnotherapist: "I know she's been working hard to build her client volume – to help more people every week."

Prince: "I'll be blunt. Many practitioners are too busy. They're doing twelve or so past-life regressions a week. They can't remember or up-level well from them as they're on autopilot."

(pause)

Prince: "Sessions are meant to bless both the recipient and the hypnotherapist with new information. They are stepping-stones up to the Light."

(pause)

Prince: "We're not judging those who chose to operate that sort of practice, but it's not her path. We encourage her to put aside the business coaching advice you must build to twelve sessions a week to have a viable practice. She's meant to do the comprehensive, longer sessions for fewer people – those who are the right vibrational match."

(pause)

Prince: "We needed her to move into more of a self-love and self-care vibration first before having her spiritual services become busy. Think of it as a beautiful time-out. It's not punitive. It was meant as a reward."

(pause)

Prince: "This is why her business didn't launch as she expected it to. She did everything right in the 3D world including working with a business coach. But the energy needs to be right first – the flow needs to be there."

←→

Prince: "She needs to surrender into her body more."

Hypnotherapist: "How can she do that?"

Prince: "Joe had such a comfortable, athletic, well-coordinated body. I'm going to help her tune into it to bring more of that energy into her own body now."

Hypnotherapist: "Thank you. Will that energetic adjustment help her attract her financial affluence?"

Prince: "That's a remarkably astute question. Yes, the energy body needs to be able to receive. We'd like her to surrender in this area so that her romantic partner as well as her affluence and her health flow to her easily."

(pause)

Prince: "I'd like her to picture herself stepping easily off a cliff. This is in preparation to fly, not to fall. She may dip

175

down for a moment, but we will always catch her as we fully support her. This will help her build her trust. It's a spiritual surrender so we can help her more."

Hypnotherapist: "So it's the proverbial leap of faith..."

Prince: "Yes. There are no big crashes left for either of you – for you or for Wendy. You've both had those experiences and worked through them."

(pause)

Prince: "This is important. What we invite you to do is to heal your low expectations of life. Your thoughts create your reality. It's important to dream big and to get excited about possibilities!"

← →

Hypnotherapist: "That's wonderful. She has a question if she's still meant to do philanthropy as part of her soul purpose?"

Prince: "Yes, she is. She is to trust large funding will come to her for the philanthropy areas we've outlined. It will come to her in an unexpected way. It will not come from quote – *'Working a day job'* or *'I scaled my business.'* "

(pause)

Prince: "This is unusual. She needs to trust and to let go in this area so we can do our work on her behalf. There will be multiple large inflows as we trust her to use them for the good of humanity. She knows where they may come from. That's all that needs to be said."

← →

Hypnotherapist: "Thank you. Do I sense some blocks to remove to embrace moving into this role?"

Prince: "Yes, you do. She has worked too hard this lifetime to the detriment of her health and her energy. This came from family conditioning. The grandparents lived through the Depression. Both her parents had an exceptionally strong work ethic, but it comes from poverty consciousness."

(pause)

Prince: "This lowers her vibration. She needs to rise from any shame from having been laid off from her traditional employment. It was a gift to her. It was simply time."

(pause)

Prince: "Her daughters – especially the youngest – are feeling some fear their mother is now 'unemployed.' They want their college educations to continue and need her help."

(pause)

Prince: "The truth is she is not unemployed. She is becoming self-employed, which in her case is spiritually employed. Over time the word *employed* will be outgrown, too."

(pause)

Prince: "She's simply living her Divine Right Purpose

with Spirit. But that's too woo-woo for most people to get!"
(Prince laughed heartily)

←→

Hypnotherapist: "This is very helpful. What else would you like her to know as she goes through this pivot point with her life purpose, her finances and career in the best way she can?"

Prince: "We'd like her to practice raising her vibration before she opens and pays her bills or does her on-line banking or handles any finances."
(pause)
Prince: "Don't just thoughtlessly rip open your bills with your heart in your mouth. This serves no one. Control the flow of the energy, including of money. It doesn't control you, but too many of you give your power away in this area."

←→

Hypnotherapist: "She has a delicate question should she call her daughter's counselor to request a new rate? Their services are income-based, and her income is quite different from what it was before."

Prince: "Yes, she should call them. Her daughter needs the counseling and benefits from it. We applaud her daughter for doing this challenging work."
(pause)
Prince: "Wendy should be fact-based. This is an opportunity for her to practice feeling no emotion, no shame with asking for what they need. She's always done more than her fair share of paying bills, reporting income, and paying taxes."
(pause)

←→

Prince: "This small task feels so big to her because it's triggering her back to the time period when she and her husband had both lost their jobs when she was pregnant with this same daughter. It's why the daughter is triggered, too."
(pause)
Prince: "The daughter was born into poverty, so to speak, with both parents out of work. Wendy is remembering feeling the shame of having to use the WIC coupons. This is the old food stamp energy but was from the Women, Infants & Children (WIC) program. She felt deep shame to have to pay for some of the family groceries with those vouchers as both the cashier and the other customers could see she was using food stamps – Medicaid."

Hypnotherapist: "So there's a bigger picture to this?"

←→

Prince: "Yes! This is coming up at this moment because your current President in your country – the man known

177

energetically as the *Great Dismantler* – is doing his job well and quickly. One of his first acts was to threaten to take away the food services program that she benefitted from for a few months so many years ago, and for which there was an honest need."

(pause)

Prince: "We are healing your U.S. government and many other governments it's time to smarten up to their purpose – to rise up, to remember their purpose is to SERVE THE PEOPLE! Their purpose is not to have a few long-time politicians become wealthy, and all the other abuses of power including sexual exploitations."

(pause)

Prince: "This is a powerful surrogate healing. Just give it a moment for her to heal and absorb this fully. We can then triage from her uplifted energy to all of mankind."

Hypnotherapist: "Wow! Thank you. I wasn't expecting to go there."

Prince: "This healing is so needed for this country, and many other countries."

←→

Hypnotherapist: "What else would you like her to know?"

Prince: "The floor has been pulled out from under her so she can temporarily fall to learn how to fly! We've pushed the baby bird out of the nest just like a mother bird does, with the highest expectations their offspring will fly."

Hypnotherapist: "And what about her daughters?"

Prince: "Her daughters are old enough as young adults to stay in their power. The eldest is a different case than the youngest. The eldest doesn't need anything from the mother for much longer as she will be graduating from college in three months and working full-time. She should be preparing to stand on her own two feet financially as of her graduation with no additional financial support from her mother."

(pause)

Prince: "Wendy should talk with her about this and outline for her in writing the exact cost of the bills she's paying for her. They should plan how and when the daughter will pay her own bills upon graduation. These include her health insurance and medical bills, her car insurance, her cell phone bill and the other expenses Wendy has been working so hard to pay as her daughter was a full-time student."

(pause)

Prince: "They can revisit financial support after her gap year of working full-time while she applies to veterinary school. They will decide together if Wendy will help her daughter pay for vet school."

←→

Hypnotherapist: "Very good. And her youngest daughter?"

Prince: "The younger is a different case as she is earlier in her college career. They will need to continue to have a dynamic conversation with the mother helping the daughter. The goal is for the young woman to have the confidence to stay in college to complete her Engineering degree. The girl is right where she needs to be. She's worked hard to get there!"

← →

Hypnotherapist: "Thank you. I'm sure that will be a load off Wendy's mind."

Prince: "She now knows not to push. She knows to contact potential business partners, radio show hosts and clients once or twice and to then let it go. Let it be. This is part of the trust and surrender she needs to master to fulfill her life purpose."

(pause)

Prince: "This is counter-intuitive as she was raised to try and try again and to push-push-push. That ship has sailed, meaning it no longer serves her."

(pause)

Prince: "We encourage her to try on new relationships. To plant seeds one or two times with new contacts and then let it go. If it's meant to flower, it will be met with reciprocal energy."

(pause)

Prince: "We know she felt flattened by so much apparent loss last year of not only her job but her retirement plan, her family's health insurance and so many friends and colleagues. I repeat, it was a blessing in disguise."

(pause)

Prince: "A chapter closed on an old book. It's time to write a new one! She's been feeling the void of so many friends leaving her life, including the two best friends she lost in 2017 as well as her job."

(pause)

Prince: "It's time to be gracious – to part peacefully. New people are coming. She's needed to develop her skill set with this sort of ebb and flow and is getting better."

← →

Hypnotherapist: "Anything more to know about attracting the new friends and partner?"

Prince: "Not at this time. She succeeded well in some male-dominated industries. It took a huge toll on her energy as she never fully activated her left side – her feminine receiving side. This also interfered with her romantic relationships."

(pause)

Prince: "We are helping her recapitulate it – to be able to

179

graciously receive – to be in feminine flow."
(pause)
Prince: "It's why she has a grumpy left hip and her left knee buckles. She had to wear the pants in the family when she was married. Her former husband didn't help enough."

Hypnotherapist: "Well, that's all in the past and we can only move forward from here, offering thanks and forgiveness to her ex-husband."

Prince: "Very wise. Perfectly said."

←→

Hypnotherapist: "She mentioned paying a big ongoing bill of over $1200 a month to have health insurance for herself and her daughters via COBRA insurance from her former job. She knows they could apply for AppleCare via the state. She said it makes her feel so sick to her stomach each time she tries to complete the application on-line she can't get it done. She feels there's an energy block as it's not smart to be paying so much out-of-pocket for health insurance as it's depleting her funds."

Prince: "I can explain this energy block. It's much deeper than the required on-line application being hard-to-navigate. There are some bugs in the system which require many applicants to need to call, and the phones lines are often jammed."
(pause)
Prince: "But the real reason she's giving up – the real reason she feels sick to her stomach and defeated is she's been tortured and imprisoned by various governments numerous times. She has a lot of negative associations with authority and the government and politics in general."

Hypnotherapist: "Wow, that sounds big. What do we do to help her?"

←→

Prince: "I'm transmuting the residual energy now. She's no longer a victim. She's done her work and healed that energy. It is more than appropriate for her to apply for AppleCare health insurance, given her current reality. Release the fear and shame."
(pause)
Prince: "I want her to look at her calendar and pick a morning when we'll sit down at her computer together. We will get that application done. I want her to have a nice fresh juicy apple at her computer and we'll take care of that application, bite by bite! AppleCare – get it?"
(Prince laughed merrily as his own pun)

←→

Hypnotherapist: "Very good! She has a question is she meant to continue hosting her own radio program? It was quite expensive, and she'd heard from her Guides it was to be a short-term arrangement."

Prince: "That's correct. She is meant to be on radio but does not have to be the host. She is a voice healer. It's why she works with clients via the telephone. This is appropriate for her and what's best for both Wendy and her clients."

(pause)

Prince: "We had her host her own radio program for six months to release her specific fear of public speaking where she could not see the audience. This was from multiple past lives where she was criticized, cast out, harmed, tortured, imprisoned, had her children, home and wealth torn from her or was killed for speaking the truth – for speaking her own truth from her heart. It was a deep wound from multiple lifetimes. I can't count them all."

Hypnotherapist: "Ouch."

←→

Prince: "We are proud of her for stepping to the plate and learning how to host the radio program in such a public way. She was meant to align with two actors to help end sex-trafficking. She knows who they are. We ran out of time to align all the pieces to get her connected with them as they are such well-known individuals."

(pause)

Prince: "That opportunity may come around again. The two 'stars' may only be on for five minutes. There is a soul contract for them to work together with Wendy to help end sex trafficking. They bring the star power, and Wendy brings her divine energy."

(pause)

Prince: "She's known them both in previous lives, hence the soul contracts when they were all last Home together. She is likely to work with them separately as she knew them in separate lives. The actress was at Plimoth Plantation with Wendy in the 1600s."

←→

Hypnotherapist: "What else was accomplished with her hosting the radio show or could come to fruition?"

Prince: "She learned technology, marketing, and branding skills as well as public speaking. The radio hosting is now over for a time. We agree with her thinking if she doesn't soon attract a radio advertising partner that she should back-burner her program."

(pause)

Prince: "She would do well as a guest on many programs and podcasts. Having released her fear of public speaking on radio or TV is priceless! She's right where we need her to be."

Hypnotherapist: "That's fantastic. Thank you. Anything else on that topic?"

Prince: "We've had her focus on building her new business for the last six months. Becoming a part of the radio network she joined gave her street credibility quickly in a new field. That's invaluable. Some branding occurred, too, which is at first invisible but is crucial for long-term foundational success."

(pause)

Prince: "We've been setting the table for her to serve the most gorgeous meal of her life. She should enjoy we're selecting the best cutlery, linens, and flowers for her."

(pause)

Prince: "She had no concept of divine flow or divine timing. She can't see the progress as it's off-stage from what she can discern. I trust my analogy will reassure her."

←→

Hypnotherapist: "Thank you. Is there more on this topic?"

Prince: "She deserves flow. You both deserve flow. Make sure you demand it, by your choices of who you spend time with. This is how you honor yourself. Give yourself time and room to attract better energetic fits."

(pause)

Prince: "Wendy has now mastered parting peacefully. Few on Earth can do this. She can now fully master this and teach it. This is part of why there have been so many leaving her life."

Hypnotherapist: "I see. Thank you. Is there more learning here?"

Prince: "Yes. She didn't understand there may be a reason or a season for a relationship or a romance. They're not all meant for a lifetime. She was overly conditioned to have only lifetime relationships. She's outgrown that conditioning and needs to live her life as it's intended, meaning for herself – not for others view of it. She needs to set herself free."

←→

Hypnotherapist: "Should she consider holding some group teleconferences or video conferencing versus being in-person with potential clients? She's already done a lot with in-person workshops, and it hasn't scaled."

Prince: "Yes, this is a fantastic fit. We are keeping her face a bit hidden on purpose. She knows why. It's for a good reason – there's nothing duplicitous about it. She's not a criminal."

(Prince laughs)

←→

Hypnotherapist: "Which book should she complete next?"

Prince: "*Regression Healing II, regarding Joe & Marilyn.*

The reason is it has the most energy for her to release. She may get a bit of criticism because of the famous names – so be it. She needs the energy release, like she did with the two previous books in the order they came."

(pause)

Prince: "This isn't about seeking fame or fortune. She needs to be open to this energy as some degree of it is needed to fulfill her life purpose. Focus on the life purpose – that's the key! Put the rest aside as simply being tools or a vehicle."

Hypnotherapist: "Thank you. Is it to be presented as non-fiction?"

Prince: "Yes, it is. The exact title will come later when more is written."

←→

Hypnotherapist: "I'm noticing the specificity of the information she's getting in this session is really on-point today. What's the best way for her to get information from you and her other Guides daily?"

Prince: "She already does. Her clairaudience – her ability to hear her Guides – and her auto-writing accuracy would make most people squeal with joy. She should simply continue these practices. They will continue to improve."

←→

Hypnotherapist: "That's wonderful. Thank you. She has questions if she's to include both the Marilyn client sessions in their entirety?"

Prince: "She's to include both in full. They have energetic releases not only for Wendy, but for the Marilyn client as well as for that client's mother. They will for some readers, too."

(pause)

Prince: "There hasn't been only one Marilyn Monroe. The timelines have some differences. We encourage Wendy to stay in her power and to include them as intended."

(pause)

Prince: "There was some angst leftover from Joe and Marilyn's marriage. That's the energy she's feeling and why she's asking the question. Joe's going to work it through from Home."

←→

Hypnotherapist: "We appreciate the clarity for her. She has a question as to what is the best way to write the Magdalen story?"

Prince: "It's to be the third book in *The Flow* series just as she has it currently drafted. She may write it later as non-fiction, too, as a Book of Love."

(pause)

Prince: "The memories and experiences are all there.

It's that simple. She knows what she needs to know, and no more needs to be spoken of at this time. She is to use her name as the author. That book is her gift to the world."

Hypnotherapist: "Thank you. I respect the limit of what we're to learn as this is in her best interests."

Prince: "Exactly. We appreciate your maturity in facilitating for her. How else may I help?"

←→

Hypnotherapist: "She feels very drawn to help with a certain dog rescue. She's sensing this is important soul contract work May we know more?"

Prince: "She has strong separate contracts with both the founder of the rescue and with the founder's husband. Let's call them Jamie and Jack for their privacy."

(pause)

Prince: "Animal rescue is physically and emotionally draining work. It has a high rate of burnout. The benefit for Wendy is it is wonderfully grounding for her. She needs that as she works with her Guides, the Angels and Ascended Masters so much and that's high vibrational work. One needs to be extremely grounded to be operating at that high vibrational level and still be functional on Earth."

(pause)

Prince: "She is likely to give this dog rescue major funding. Jamie and Jack are high-functioning individuals. They are hard workers with big hearts and a strong sense of ethics and of community."

Hypnotherapist: "So that's why the contracts – they're a good vibrational match?"

←→

Prince: "Exactly. She will help Jamie and Jack get to the next level. Perhaps she will help them attract or retain more fosters as this is a foster-based rescue. Just as examples, she may help them buy a ranch or farm or get a dog café going. What's most needed will be determined over time."

(pause)

Prince: "She's had many lives with Jamie. They've been siblings several times as well as mother and daughter. Jamie helps Wendy get in her body by her physicality, and Wendy helps Jamie stay heart centered."

(pause)

Prince: "Dog rescue in Seattle attracts a lot of young women. It is very physical work. This rescue is going to grow and grow. It is fully on track."

←→

Hypnotherapist: "How does Jack fit in? You said that was a separate soul agreement?"

Prince: "Yes. Jack and Wendy have been married to one another in other lifetimes. Wendy recognized him and

enjoys his company in a platonic way. She greatly respects his marriage with Jamie, as well as the institution of marriage."
(pause)
Hypnotherapist: "So there won't be any issues?"
Prince: "Exactly. She is a different generation than Jack and Jamie. There won't be any issue with untoward energy from their previous marriages. Wendy has her timelines straight and Jamie and Jack aren't consciously aware of the shared past lives and the soul contracts. They don't need to be."
(pause)
Prince: "All is well in this arena, other than Jamie is over-working. The rescue work is heart-rending. If she doesn't accept a dog into the rescue as she has no place to foster it, that dog is likely to be killed."
(pause)
Prince: "Most people don't understand the reality that an estimated 5,500 dogs a day are killed in the United States alone through no fault of their own. There simply aren't enough loving, responsible homes for them."
(pause)
Prince: "This must change – the animals and the Earth must be cared for by humans in much more responsible ways. The current trajectory is unsustainable."

←→

Hypnotherapist: "Yes. I think many of us are aware of the critical nature of the changes that are needed. May Wendy know more about her new life partner?"
Prince: "They are coming closer to their time to meet in-person. She feels it in both her hips. We've been working with her to unlock her hips. There was so much difficult, stuck energy there."
(pause)
Prince: "Jack as a male friend is helping her attract her new partner. She's been in an all-female world for a long time. She may literally meet her new man through Jack or through the rescue."
(pause)
Prince: "She's now uncloaked her energy and men can see her again. She's gathering platonic new male friends and going new places as a start."

←→

Hypnotherapist: "Thank you. Why did so many people leave her life over the last year or two?"
Prince: "The lessons were complete. She was to master parting peacefully. Few have this skill as I said earlier. She's to teach it, so we've drilled her on it hard."
(pause)
Prince: "Her former spiritual teacher, her husband and
185

the Shaman they all worked with could have done better when they stopped working together as a team."

(pause)

Prince: "The teacher's husband chose to vilify Wendy when it didn't make sense. She's had to work hard to recover from his verbal and more importantly his energetic attacks."

(pause)

Prince: "He actively cursed her multiple times. That is not to be taken lightly. She handled it with a maturity he does not possess. She'll be fine. She's strong, and lessons and skills were learned. We can move on."

←→

Hypnotherapist: "Thank you. What about the best friend who disappeared without an explanation? What happened there – lessons complete?"

Prince: "That one hurt the most as there was no explanation. She 'ghosted' Wendy as young people like to say today. Her excuses of being 'too tired or too busy' to get together were not truthful. She wasn't able to speak her truth."

(pause)

Prince: "They were meant to be lifetime friends. They have been sisters and more so many times. They are both angelic, incredible women."

Hypnotherapist: "So what happened?"

Prince: "Wendy triggered the other woman's self-worth issues in a way we didn't anticipate. She came across as stronger, more confident, even brash at times by comparison as her friend has such a gentle energy. The other woman didn't know how to part peacefully, so she ghosted a true friend of the heart."

(pause)

←→

Prince: "Wendy meditated and talked with her friend Higher Self to Higher Self to learn what I'm describing. She unraveled what was not said. That takes skill."

(pause)

Prince: "She honored her dear friend was incapable of being friends any longer. Wendy shed her tears privately. There have been a lot of tears for several years. It was a deep cut."

Hypnotherapist: "That sounds very hard."

Prince: "It was. We confirmed that was the way it needed to be by having them run into one another at a workshop. The other woman's boyfriend was delighted to see Wendy as he didn't know what had happened. Her friend couldn't even speak of it to her boyfriend."

(pause)

Prince: "When her former best friend gave her a stiff-armed A-frame hug, she knew it was over. Her friend wasn't capable of straight talk with Wendy. She let it be, and simply sent her love to honor the many times they'd been best friends and sisters. She cried many tears that night to release the difficult energy."

(pause)

←→

Prince: "Shortly thereafter, just before Christmas she received a package in the mail from the other woman. Her heart leapt that perhaps she had begun to heal her self-worth issues?"

(pause)

Prince: "All that was in the package was Wendy's MP3 recorder. She left it by mistake at her friend's home. There was no simple note with it – no Christmas greetings. She knew the friendship was complete. She closed it out once again with love in her heart via meditation."

(pause)

Prince: "Her cat Midnight loves this friend dearly as she hears him well. He will continue to talk with her directly if he needs to."

Hypnotherapist: "Thank you for so much detail. Closure can be a big deal."

Prince: "Yes, it certainly can. Learning how to gain peaceful closure on your own is a necessary skill. What else may we assist with?"

←→

Hypnotherapist: "Wendy doesn't understand why she was asked by her Guides to purchase a hypnotherapy course from a local teacher she doesn't feel an affinity for. Is she supposed to be Wendy's teacher or is there another type of relationship planned?"

Prince: "No, there is not. Her instinct was correct from the beginning there is no vibrational alignment between them. This teacher is struggling. She's lost her faith in the Divine. She is denying Guides exist and exhibiting poor energy practices that concerned Wendy. Wendy appropriately distanced herself."

(pause)

Prince: "The fee for the course was simply 'fair for the fare' – for what was being offered. This is the reason we guided her to work with the teacher's assistant to complete the coursework."

Hypnotherapist: "Thank you. Was there any other reason?"

Prince: "Wendy owed her some money from a past life. We're clearing all her debts to set her completely free. Is that clear?"

←→

Hypnotherapist: "Yes, thank you. Why is Simon – her former boyfriend – back in Wendy's life again? Do they have more lessons to complete?"

Prince: "Yes, they do. They are both managing the energy between them well. He is to be another male platonic friend for a time. I stress for a time – remember our conversation about relationships being for a reason or a season?"

Hypnotherapist: "Yes. She needed to learn it's not always meant to be for a lifetime as well as how to part peacefully."

Prince: "Exactly. We are amazed by them both. They have come so far! We'd like to offer kudos and congratulations to them."

(pause)

Prince: "If he moves back into his lower vibrational energy, she will distance herself and end it if necessary. We agree with her decision to keep their occasional coffee dates or meals in a restaurant private. They are single adults, and she has firm control of her heart. He no longer has the key to it."

(pause)

Prince: "Their communication is no one's business. They are accomplishing important spiritual work together. They are trading tips on how to continue their writing and publishing that we have tasked them both with and where they have a soul contract."

(pause)

Prince: "It's a tremendous accomplishment to be truly cordial like this with an ex-husband. Let's not forget she has been married to him six times in their many lifetimes together."

←→

Hypnotherapist: "Oh my goodness – that is a lot of energy to manage!"

Prince: "Yes. Nineteen lives in total. She practiced parting peacefully from him and walked away before writing her first book, with his blessing. He's the client in the book. She had his full backing to do so and carefully blinded his identity."

(pause)

Prince: "She gave him the opportunity to read the book before she published it. He told her he trusted her and to move forward. That fulfilled one of their contracts to write about spirituality together."

(pause)

Prince: "Once it was published, we surprised her. We encouraged her to contact him to see if he was interested in having coffee or lunch. We saw another growth opportunity so had her reach out. She gave him an autographed copy with her true gratitude for helping her become a published author."

←→

Hypnotherapist: "How did that go?"

Prince: "Extremely well. We saw this as a teachable moment for them both. They were to rebuild on higher ground and to see each other in a new light where romance was permanently off the table. There would be no physical or emotional affair again."

(pause)

Prince: "They are not to be lovers again as it becomes toxic for her – toxic for them both. They parted peacefully after that meeting. Because it went so well, they meet sporadically from time to time. It is rare to know and love someone so well at the soul level and to remember it in human form, but their values do not align this lifetime."

(pause)

Prince: "She's not good at spontaneity or at surprises. Nor at surrendering, or at releasing the control illusion. These are areas in which he excels. She excels at planning and getting things accomplished. Therefore, they balance one another out now that they've learned they must stay out of the bedroom, despite their shared astrology. It provides a lot of physical and emotional desire for one another."

Hypnotherapist: "But that's truly complete in a healthy way?"

Prince: "There was a wonderful time and place for a special physical relationship neither of them will forget. Both know it is complete. They have learned to look back on that chapter with great fondness, without wishing for more. That is the definition of closing things out peacefully."

←→

Hypnotherapist: "Thank you. She'd appreciate feedback how she's doing as a single mother?"

Prince: "She should continue to build a loving structure for her daughters, yet make sure not to tip over into being a 'control freak.' Let them live their lives as they're intended to while being there fully for them is the best path."

(pause)

Prince: "Who said the two most important things to give to our children are wings to fly and roots to come back to? This is a big part of how Joe DiMaggio excelled."

←→

Hypnotherapist: "Thank you. Should Wendy encourage her daughter to visit Paris? Her daughter has been feeling the pull to visit Paris again – possibly to even live there."

Prince: "It would be wonderful for her to go to Paris! It would benefit her health. She should make her own decision, of course, without too much parental influence."

(pause)

Prince: "The young woman is an extremely old soul. She's had a profound memory wipe of who she is as a soul, therefore her mother's beliefs and work perturb her deeply. That's a major piece of the estrangement between them."
(pause)
Hypnotherapist: "So what's really happening with the daughter?"
Prince: "The daughter's soul is trying to make a mid-course correction from the girl falling apart not only physically and mentally but energetically – at the soul level – in the current human form."
(pause)
Prince: "She expects many services from her mother, friends and others, but then often rejects them. This victim energy is not an easy part of the personality to deal with."
(pause)
Prince: "The mother would be wise to encourage her to continue to build her own coping strategies. Both the girl and the mother are doing what they need to do. It's remarkably hard for the girl to genuinely ask for help, and to graciously receive it. This is her life lesson. She's struggling with it."

←→

Hypnotherapist: "That's extremely helpful. Is there anything else Wendy should know?"
Prince: "It's important the mother not molly-coddle her. This is a challenge with a daughter that can be seriously ill at times – even suicidal. She is to mother her, not to smother her or to be a so-called helicopter Mom as that will only clip the girl's wings – her planned growth."
(pause)
Prince: "It would be best for Wendy to ask her daughter, 'What do you need from me?' That will allow the young lady to practice asking and receiving. It's crucial the mother does not go into healer mode. That would be a form of unbalanced ego on Wendy's part and cause more resentment from her daughter."
(pause)
Prince: "It would deprive her daughter's soul of her experiences, particularly as she is an experiential learner. She needs to thrash about at times. She needs to have experiences to learn. This is the reason souls incarnate."
(pause)
Prince: "She should gently share with her daughter the costs of her medical bills that Wendy is paying as the father is not participating. They are extensive as she needs to self-pay the first five thousand dollars each year herself and to pay twenty percent as a co-pay of certain services. There was an expensive GI scope and an MRI and much more."

(pause)
Prince: "Wendy can practice being fact-based with no emotional load about money. There have been years of high medical costs for her daughter with no helpful Western medical diagnosis or treatment plan."
Hypnotherapist: "Why is there no helpful diagnosis?"

← →

Prince: "Because it's the soul that needs to heal! It's energy medicine that's needed, but the daughter won't agree to it, hence the estrangement."
(pause)
Prince: "The daughter is not currently capable of holding a part-time job with her demanding college load and challenging health. Just help her get through college and be supportive if it takes a bit longer than four years. She had to drop back to part-time for a period when she was so ill. Frankly, she's done well to stay on planet and to not leave early – to not suicide."

← →

Hypnotherapist: "Thank you, that's reassuring. It's hard to see our children struggling but you've helped explain the purpose and the bigger picture. Wendy would like to know if you have any meditation tips for her at this time?"
Prince: "She should hold her wand during meditation, and call me in. She can ask for an off-planet message – one at a time. She can ask for more clarity when needed."
(pause)
Prince: "We'll start simple – which planet – which message? This will help her left ear-ringing greatly. We know she suffered significant hearing loss in this ear from all the galactic clamors. We've worked with her to restore some of her hearing and will restore more. We know she needs excellent hearing for her profession – for her life purpose."

← →

Hypnotherapist: "Thank you. May she know more about the Purple Planet?"
Prince: "It's premature to know much more other than it's a very loving, beneficial place. The energy is much like Venus – the planet of love. The Purple Planet runs Violet Flame energy to Earth."
(pause)
Prince: "My song *Purple Rain* is to do with a Purple Flame – the Violet Flame is the association as I mentioned before. *Purple Rain* is the energy signature for the planet. It energetically calls the souls who work with the Purple or Violet Flame to work with Saint Germaine and the Violet Flame he created, although they may not be consciously aware of it. They can just enjoy the song on a surface level."
(pause)

191

Prince: "You don't have to know everything consciously when in human form – it would be exhausting! There's good reason for you to have a subconscious. Many reasons."

←→

Hypnotherapist: "Thank you. May we know the reason the planet hasn't been discovered by scientists?"

Prince: "It wasn't time for the planet to be found so it was cloaked. It was kept etheric – energetic – so it was not discovered by astronomers or by the low vibration energy we were cloaking it from."

(pause)

Prince: "I dropped my body and went Home in part to strengthen the ties between Venus, the Purple Planet and Earth to help Earth prepare for what is to come. I say this not to provoke a fear response – quite the opposite. It's important when you feel fear to stop, to take a moment and take a breath and open your heart to love. Love is the antidote to fear."

Hypnotherapist: "That's wonderful. Anything else along this vein?"

←→

Prince: "It was an amazing gift from Birdie – Wendy's former spiritual teacher – to tell Wendy the planet existed once I went Home and showed the Purple Planet to Birdie. Wendy then put the pieces of the puzzle together as to how it pertained to her. She has strong abilities in that area."

Hypnotherapist: "Yes, she clearly does, based on her questions today. Is there anything more on this subject?"

Prince: "Wendy has learned to be highly discerning without being distrustful or a skeptic. There's a fine line. Discernment is a critical skill. It's often hard to master. She knows to validate everything in her heart – how does it make her feel? Is it right for her?"

(pause)

Prince: "This can make her opt-in or opt-out from surprising things. When you are discerning from the heart, it gets the heart pulsing in a beneficial way. It helps one ground in the physical human body. She can begin to teach others to do this."

←→

Hypnotherapist: "She's been struggling with concentrated urine. That can be caused by multiple things. Can you tell us how she can improve this?"

Prince: "Her pelvic floor is good. She's turned that around nicely. She's going through an energy upgrade currently which is presenting as concentrated urine. This is a big piece of why we brought you ladies together today for this session."

Hypnotherapist: "Oh, so this is a big deal."

Prince: "Yes. The reason for the concentrated urine is she's feeling energetically pissed off. This energy is like a bladder or UTI (urinary tract infection), but she is right she doesn't have either. It wouldn't help her to go to a Western medicine practitioner. It would likely cause more issues."

←→

Hypnotherapist: "So what does she need to resolve this?"

Prince: "She needs to balance up her masculine and feminine energies. That's the current energy upgrade. That's the 'I feel pissed off!' struggle."

(pause)

Prince: "We'd like her to work to balance these two aspects of her energy – these two parts of her physical body – by drinking seventy-five to eighty ounces of water a day. She should fill her blue glass pitcher and add a small piece of fresh lemon to each glass. The lemon will help her balance up her system."

(pause)

Prince: "The blue pitcher with the yellow lemon creates a high vibrational beauty. She's working from home now so follow this practice most days. She can carry a refillable water bottle with her when she's away from home."

←→

Hypnotherapist: "Thank you. Did you say she's releasing anger – the concentrated urine? Can you speak more to that?"

Prince: "Yes, you are correct she needs to find constructive ways to acknowledge anger to then release it. She's been feeling anger with her body it's been so hard to work with this lifetime. There have been so many health challenges."

(pause)

Prince: "We're going to call in a new Over lighting Deva of her Health for her right now. But first let's give thanks to the outgoing Deva of her Health – it's been a hard job! The new Deva is a bit like the Green Man energy if you're familiar with him? But this one is feminine. She's associated with the green drinks and detox products Wendy has been using."

(pause)

Prince: "She wants to encourage Wendy to let go of the pissed off energy by first acknowledging she has every right to feel it! It's been a tricky, challenging body to work with. She was too quick to acknowledge she chose it. It was spiritual bypass to not feel the 'pissed off!' energy first before releasing it."

(pause)

Prince: "This is what spiritual bypass is. You need to 'feel it to heal it.' We want her to truly feel and acknowledge how hard this body has been while we hold sacred space for her with you. She just needs to truly feel the anger, the disappointment, the frustration, and the upset for a mere sixty to ninety seconds and we can then heal it for her. We can fix it. We can then upgrade her energy."

←→

Hypnotherapist: "Very good. Can we do that now and you tell me when it's complete?"

Prince: "Yes – beginning now. I want her to feel the anger and the other emotions fully. It's time. Get ready – clock begins now..."

(there was a long pause)

Prince: "It's complete. She released a big bolus of anger and welcomed in the new Deva of her Health. We upgraded her energy. She'll see big improvements within a few days. She can't process more quickly than that."

←→

Hypnotherapist: "Thank you, that's fantastic! You said her pelvic floor is good now?"

Prince: "Yes, the daily pelvic floor exercises are perfect. They take her no time to do now that she worked with a Physical Therapist and had a biofeedback device to learn how to isolate the muscles to properly do the exercises. This is quite beneficial for many women to learn correctly, particularly after childbearing. Their partners will thank them for it, too!"

(Prince winked)

Hypnotherapist: *(laughing)* "That's great – thank you, Prince."

Prince: "The pelvic floor exercises are helping her strengthen her root and sacral chakras. She should visualize a strong pelvic floor with the affirmation of "I'm so supported!" She'll have one in no time."

(pause)

Prince: "Her blood sugar decreasing, getting enough water as I described, letting go of the angry energy, having the new Health Deva, adding cinnamon and using less salt will support her kidneys. We like her using the Himalayan salt grinder to add a touch of salt to taste. This is a much better practice than pouring salt into boiling water like she was taught to cook, or to sprinkle it from a shaker onto her meal before even tasting it."

←→

Hypnotherapist: "She was told there's an issue with her two front teeth and they're likely to fracture?"

Prince: "This was a well-intentioned comment from her dentist. It was not helpful. We want her to let go of the worry, all the regimens. Just be guided if she's to take silica in her water or to do oil-pulling."

(pause)

Prince: "She has been treating her health as broken – as an annoyance – as upsetting and hard to fix. These were clues it was time to ask if she should call in a new Over lighting Deva of her health. She knows how to do this for herself and for others, but she missed the clue."

(pause)

Prince: "The worry became fear. There was a negative energy associated with 'fixing' her health issues that by the Law of Attraction attracted more and more issues to fix. She mistakenly broadcast the signal – 'I'm broken, I have health issues' – so the Universe thought that was what she wanted."

(pause)

Prince: "This is manifestation, but it was manifesting what she didn't want. It's a common error. Visualize what you do want. Spend as little time as you can in the other lower vibration energy. When it pops up from time to time, acknowledge it, thank it, learn from it, feel the emotions, and visualize what's more in alignment with your life purpose and what you need to fulfill it. Don't do spiritual bypass. Do you understand?"

←→

Hypnotherapist: "Yes, I do. Does Wendy?"

Prince: "Yes, she has it now or she will when she listens to her recording and transcribes it. She's somnambulistic – I don't mean she sleep-walks. She moves quickly and easily into the deepest level of trance so won't recall much of this session afterwards. It's why we are quite particular who she does sessions with as both the client and the practitioner, and always have her sessions recorded. Thank you for working with her today."

Hypnotherapist: "I'm having a great time! Thank you."

Prince: "To summarize, if she has health challenges in the future, she should keep her energy as free and easy as possible. She will hear us well and should just try to enjoy the many ways to be well."

(pause)

Prince: "She's been trying too hard. Surrendering more to us would be the most helpful approach as I mentioned. The weekly MAP meditation is one technique that consistently gets strong results for her."

←→

Hypnotherapist: "She had a question if she's been making progress with de-aging?"

Prince: "Yes, she certainly has. Several individuals have commented positively on this to affirm Wendy is on the right track. This will be another module she can teach as she's learned it so well herself. It took time and effort."

(pause)

Prince: "We give her a gold star in this area. It's part of why she was laid off. We need her to focus on improving her health by getting eight hours of sleep a night and changing her food and drink and exercise regimens."

←→

Hypnotherapist: "Is she meant to be a walk-in?"

Prince: "Again, yes, if this would be enjoyable for her. Experiencing things as being light and fun is the best way to keep your vibration high, and then everything has the best possible divine flow to it."

(pause)

Prince: "She is highly adept at being a walk-in soul. It is always by agreement of both the outgoing soul and the incoming soul. A healthy body is taken over by a soul that still has a big life purpose to fulfill and isn't guided to take the time to go Home and be reborn as a newborn."

(pause)

Prince: "I want to reassure her we kept her off-camera and energetically veiled for a time to leave the door open for her to stay for an unusually long time in one healthy body. This is what she jokingly calls the 'Saint Germaine Plan.' I hinted at this earlier?"

Hypnotherapist: "Yes. What does she mean by the Saint Germaine Plan?"

←→

Prince: "The Count Saint Germain lived his last life on Earth for several hundred years before becoming Ascended Master Saint Germain – creator of the Violet Flame of transmutation."

(pause)

Prince: "We had her watch the film 'The Age of Adaline' twice. It's related to the concept of staying the same age in a healthy body for a long time."

Hypnotherapist: "What was she to learn from that?"

Prince: "We wanted her to understand she has multiple options – all good. She can de-age and stay in her current body for a long time. She can begin to teach others how to do this."

(pause)

Prince: "In the film the main character Adaline – played by Blake Lively – learns she needs to change her name and identity every decade or so and to move. Otherwise, the government could become overly interested in studying someone with such a unique ability as not aging."

(pause)

Prince: "It's why we originally kept Wendy off-camera and a bit cloaked. But times have changed, thankfully. More people will be able to do this – it will be a non-issue. It will be another free will choice. Don't forget the Lemurians lived thousands of years in the same healthy body. She remembers some of her lives in Lemuria."

Hypnotherapist: "Fascinating. What else would it help her to know? It sounds like it may have felt both exciting and kicked off some concerns or even fear."

←→

Prince: "Exactly. We'd like her to know she won't be incredibly lonely and isolated like Adaline became in the film as everyone else around her aged – quote 'normally' – but all this will be changing."
(pause)
Prince: "Adaline's daughter in the movie becomes an elderly woman while Adaline is still young and beautiful, so no one can know their relationship. Adaline doesn't allow herself to have a romantic partner as she knows the aging – not aging dichotomy will distance them over time. She therefore denies herself years of happiness and a romance with Harrison Ford's character."
(pause)
Prince: "Adaline passes on a relationship with Harrison Ford – who would do that?"
(There was the sound of Prince's rich, ribald laughter)
Prince: "We used this simple movie as a teaching tool with Wendy. Rather than the outcome of the film, she knows she can teach her new partner to de-age, if he is interested."
(pause)

←→

Prince: "She knows she has the option to work with another soul to plan a walk-in if that soul wants to go Home and it's a more compatible body for Wendy. Being a walk-in is not going to be as traumatic as it used to be with months if not years of disorientation. There was also frequent rejection by the family and friends as they sense the massive energy change but can't comprehend it."
(pause)
Prince: "I don't mean for these important soul-level and energy decisions to sound trite – only achievable. These are wonderful possibilities for her which she can teach others. All options are good!"

←→

Hypnotherapist: "Thank you. That's a lot of food for thought. She'd like to understand more why she feels guided to astral travel to specific places?"
Prince: "That's easy. Because she has an incredible ability to do so. She's not being fanciful she can easily sit and meditate to consciously astral travel anywhere we ask her to go. She has good clear intent and excellent ethics around it. This isn't playing with fire like is sometimes done with government spies who are remote viewing."
Hypnotherapist: "Can you give an example of how this

works for her?"

Prince: "Certainly. She knows she's meant to travel to the Egyptian Temple of Isis at Philae but hasn't been able to physically go to Egypt yet. As an interim step she astral traveled to Philae to remember more of her past life in that temple two thousand years ago."

←→

Hypnotherapist: "Was it beneficial?"

Prince: "Very much so. This allowed her to bring forth forgotten abilities from her former Mystery School training that will benefit mankind. The Mystery School knowledge is being reintroduced on the planet at this time. It's appropriate to do so once again as Earth's vibration is rising, as is much of mankind's."

(pause)

Prince: "She could astral travel to Glastonbury, England. It would benefit her greatly. She needs specific healing that can best be attained at Glastonbury where two of her three key past lives intersect – Magdalen and Guinevere."

(pause)

Prince: "We want her to make Glastonbury her top priority for overseas travel, but astral travel will help with the healing she needs in the interim. Think of astral travel as a free plane ticket to any place and time you want to visit!"

(pause)

Prince: "The limits you place on your minds are just baggage, so to speak. You can start to unpack some of that baggage and free your mind and your energy by working in concert with the Divine."

(pause)

Prince: "I'm going to table further discussion about astral traveling for another time as she's beginning to tire, and you must be too. She's been channeling me for a good three hours. Let's begin to wrap up for today. She has astral travel down to a fine art. She can teach this, too."

←→

Hypnotherapist: "Absolutely. Your timing is perfect as her last question was whether Wendy and I have ever had past lives together? Is there anything we need to clear or can enjoy knowing about consciously?"

Prince: "You've had several past lives together that were positive and friendly. There's nothing to clear. You were sisters once, and good friends another time. There's no shared biology between you now. There were no romances together."

(pause)

Prince: "You've been friends, sisters, and have had good business relationships. You may focus your energy on the latter this lifetime to build on your shared energy. You can gently help hold one another accountable in your shared careers as Past-Life Regression healers."

← →

Hypnotherapist: "Prince, I can't thank you enough. This has been an amazing conversation! We're truly grateful for the insights you've shared as a Guide."
(pause)
Hypnotherapist: "May I summarize today's session for Wendy as to continue to surrender to the Divine; to have fun; that only the good stuff is to come; and she needs to simply trust?"
Prince: "I couldn't have said it better myself."

← →

The hypnotherapist closed out our remarkable three-and-a half-hour session. I was grateful for the healing, the insights, the energy releases, and the specificity of the information.

It was reassuring to know all options were good at this point in my life. That made what happened six weeks later even more shocking. I was suddenly spinning wildly in my car, blinded by multiple airbags, unable to get my foot on the brake...

Chapter Ten – The Angels Allow a Crash

On April 20th, 2018, I had a powerful two-and-a-half-hour past-life regression with a hypnotherapist who is also a trained medium. We jumped straight into planning my session as we spoke for the first time.

←→

Hypnotherapist: "What's your purpose and best outcome for today's session, Wendy?"

Wendy: "I'd so appreciate help attracting the resources to live my life purpose. The financial resources, being healthy with plenty of energy, and having a happy, healthy romance with a life partner."

(Pause – Wendy laughs)

Wendy: "Can we do all that in two and a half hours – I know could I make that a bit bigger?"

(both women laughed)

Hypnotherapist: "Easy peasy – no problem! Let's heal the world while we're at it."

Wendy: "Perfect. I'm all about world peace."

←→

Hypnotherapist: "Tell me more about your practice."

Wendy: "I love it! My past-life regression practice was part-time for several years while I continued working my full-time day job. I'm now offering healing sessions on a full-time basis along with writing and public speaking."

Hypnotherapist: "How did you make the decision to go full-time?"

Wendy *(ruefully)*: "The Universe helped me out with something called a layoff. I know that's frequent. The timing is interesting. I'm really getting to practice my trust and heal my financial abundance as both my daughters are in college."

Hypnotherapist: "So how's it going?"

Wendy: "I'm working to attract more ease and grace to this transition. The human part of me would have waited until my girls were out of college to quit my job. I'm able to feel delighted most of the time, but the business hasn't really launched."

(pause)

←→

Hypnotherapist: "What did you do?

Wendy: "I was guided to host my own radio program. It was a fantastic opportunity to be a part of the top-rated alternative talk radio program in Seattle. But my program didn't monetize. It didn't result in any business for me."

Hypnotherapist: "How did you feel at that point?"

Wendy: "I have no regrets. I was guided to invest in that exact radio program for many reasons. I know I've been doing this type of healing work for eons – not just in this lifetime. I have an MBA in Marketing, but that knowledge hasn't scaled well to becoming a solopreneur more than thirty years later."

Hypnotherapist: "What did you do next?"

Wendy: "I was sensing internal blocks and self-limiting beliefs that I was struggling to resolve on my own. Therefore, I hired a business coach and signed up for a six-month group coaching program."

Hypnotherapist: "How's that going?"

Wendy: "It feels like the pieces are starting to come together. I'm changing my service offerings from single sessions to packages and addressing why my prices were too low to be sustainable."

←→

Hypnotherapist: "What's the bigger picture for what you feel you have to offer?"

Wendy: "I know I'm to be in a role of financial stewardship – to do philanthropy. I know that deep in my bones and my Guides talk about it regularly. I can sense there will be large sums to help others, after taking care of myself and my family first."

Hypnotherapist: "That sounds exciting. Do you know what types of areas you'll be helping with?"

Wendy: "Yes. There are three focus areas. My legacy work is to help the animals; to help mankind and Earth via some sort of clean, affordable water project; and to help end sex trafficking and slavery."

Hypnotherapist: "Wow, that is big! Have you been able to start this work?"

Wendy: "Yes. I started by volunteering with a dog rescue.

It's a true labor of love. I can just show up and do the work. No money is required although I am making small donations, too."

←→

Hypnotherapist: "Is the dog rescue already launched?"

Wendy: "Yes – about eighteen months ago. The energy of it feels great. I'm happy to donate to the rescue. Each time I donate I visualize it turning into larger sums by blessing the funds. I pray daily for more dogs to find their homes. This week we were able to save fifteen dogs from the kill shelters."

Hypnotherapist: "You talked about what financial abundance looks like for you. Your being comfortable and able to easily take care of both yourself and others. What does the disconnect look like? I'm feeling it, too."

Wendy: "I feel like I still need to fully restore my trust so it's automatic – not so much work. There's some sort of hitch in my giddy-up. I doubt too often. I don't easily trust that the Universe has my back."

Hypnotherapist: "What else?"

Wendy: "I catch myself automatically saying or thinking, 'Oh, I don't have enough money for that' without getting the facts first. I know this is an old energy loop I'm stuck in. Are you able to tune into what my blocks might be so we can release them?"

←→

Hypnotherapist: "Yes. This feels both intellectual and energetic with you. Let's take a moment and visualize what it would really feel like to celebrate, "Oh, cool, ten thousand dollars came in this month – isn't that wonderful! It's going to take you more work to heal your lack of trust regarding abundance flow."

Wendy: "I agree."

Hypnotherapist "It feels like you've had lots of lifetimes of poverty. We've all had them. It's time to let go of them. There's more than enough financial flow for everyone on this planet. Don't buy into the top one percenter story and 'the middle class is dead' rhetoric."

(pause)

Hypnotherapist: "Stop yourself immediately if you're fussing with that energy. It's not your job to fix it – it's not your monkey."

Wendy: "Exactly. I've been working hard to let that go, but I don't know how to easily receive."

(pause)

Wendy: "My sense is that hasn't happened for me many times in the past. Perhaps we'll find those types of lives – we can superimpose the energy imprint from those positive, easy abundance flow lives over my life now..."

Wendy (*sounding surprised*): "I have no idea why I said that – my Guides are speaking through me? Clearly, we're ready to go!"
(both women laughed)

←→

Hypnotherapist: "But there have been some real challenges, too?"

Wendy: "Absolutely. I've been having more interesting wake-up calls. I had a collision recently on March 31st. My car was totaled. I chose to buy a new car yesterday and it felt a little weird."
(pause)

Wendy: "I made that decision carefully with my Guides after looking at a lot of alternatives. I asked my Guides why this happened. I burned through savings to buy a car when I was happy with my twelve-year-old CRV."

←→

Hypnotherapist: "How did the accident occur?"

Wendy: "That's what was odd. I was highly cognizant of my driving that day, where I parked, and how I pulled out into traffic. But I was hit so hard three of my six airbags went off. It was quite the explosion in my face. I was really spun around and shaken up, but thankfully there were no serious injuries."
(pause)

Wendy: "I was petrified I was going to hit a pedestrian or a dog as there were lots of people on the sidewalk walking their dogs. There were also people eating at the outdoor dining area in the parking lot. I was spun back over the sidewalk and into the lot. I didn't know how close I was to the entrance or to the dining area."
(pause)

Wendy: "It was terrifying as I couldn't get my foot on the brake, and I couldn't see a thing as the airbags blocked my view. My car was totaled, the car that hit me was totaled, and the driver that hit me so hard also took a second hit as she careened into a parked car."

Hypnotherapist: "Wow. What did your Guides say?"

Wendy: "My Guides are saying to let this be. They'll work with me directly if I have more questions about the collision. They'd like us to work on attracting my life partner."

←→

Hypnotherapist: "Okay. What's going on there? Can you bring me up to speed?"

Wendy: "I had an intriguing reading a few days ago. There was old energy around trauma – specifically difficulties with romantic relationships. I've been working to clear that romantic trauma out – again it all comes down to trust."
(pause)

Wendy: "I know there's a fantastic new partner for me soon. If feels like it's as soon as within a couple months. We've been working to meet one another for the last six months or so."

Hypnotherapist: "How are you feeling the connection?"

Wendy: "It's an energetic connection. It's telepathy. We haven't yet met in the physical. Other people see his energy around me, too."

(pause)

←→

Hypnotherapist: "Okay. Let's go through your questions. Have you and I met before? How do I release any remaining fear to live my destiny? What does it mean to be an Incarnate? Have I balanced my energy to be here now as Wendy Rose Williams? Am I fully embracing prosperity consciousness? Is there new information regarding becoming a philanthropist. How do I restore my trust as some of my past romantic relationships destroyed my trust? How do I restore my confidence in driving? Is everything energetically aligned for me to have a wonderful time training with Dr. Weiss in July."

Hypnotherapist: "That's awesome you'll be training with Brian Weiss. I've done that program four or five times. It's amazing for personal experience – it may not teach you much for technique."

Wendy: "I have the coursework from another hypnotherapist that's all technique. I don't relate to her personally, but my Guides urged me to purchase her course."

←→

Hypnotherapist: "I'm skimming your other questions. Am I healing the dogs in the best ways possible? Am I meant to help with a friend's father's prostate cancer? Does my oldest daughter need anything from me as she goes through her gap year before applying to vet school? Will my youngest accept a surrogate healing today for various mental and physical challenges?"

(pause)

Hypnotherapist: "What are those, specifically? It feels like there's a lot of energy there to move – to release."

←→

Wendy: *(becoming upset)* "She's been diagnosed with so many things. Anxiety, depression, panic attacks, possibly bi-polar disease. I believe she has PTSD, but it hasn't been diagnosed. It's been hard to get her medications at a therapeutic level. It's hard for her to eat as she has so many food sensitivities and allergies; it's hard for her to sleep..."

(pause)

Hypnotherapist: *(gently)* "Is there more?"

Wendy: "She's carrying such a heavy load she's considered suicide. I'd like to ask her Higher Self and Guides can that load be lightened or is it not appropriate to do so? We're burning through a lot of my savings with Western medicine testing. I don't feel any of it helps her. Now we're being told to do a brain MRI and a sleep study. She had a GI scope. I just want her to get an accurate diagnosis and some relief, but I don't think we're accomplishing anything."

←→

Hypnotherapist: "Has she done a past-life regression?"

Wendy: "No. She is petrified of anything to do with metaphysics and energy. It totally freaks her out and she moves into more panic attacks. I was able to get her to try sensory deprivation floating and she said she relaxed and fell asleep but refuses to go again. Occasionally she'll agree to a massage. She went to my energy chiropractor once and refuses to go again as said as soon as she fell asleep the gongs would startle her and wake her up, whereas I just sleep through them. I sleep like the dead – it's one of my gifts."

(Wendy laughs)

Hypnotherapist: "She's a high vibrational spirit. That's what she's having trouble with – an MRI isn't going to help."

Wendy: "I couldn't agree more. But having an MRI was written on her medical record as the next step. We're going against medical advice if we don't do it and then I'm the bad guy. I'll need to pay about $1,000 toward it as my co-pay and the real issue is I don't think it's going to help her. It's a tough one."

(pause)

←→

Wendy: "A friend went to Egypt and brought back some amazing essential oils. I offered my daughter some and she accepted them graciously. That's a first. She usually says, 'My skin is too sensitive' and refuses even high-quality hypoallergenic products. She was interested in what each of the oils were used for."

(pause)

Wendy: "I think she's ticked off by the container – by her body."

Hypnotherapist: "Yes, I agree. I see this a lot. People are diagnosed as bipolar because Western medicine doesn't understand vibrational levels."

Wendy: "It's not a useful diagnosis. How does this not make the person feel worse about themselves? It doesn't offer them help or hope."

Hypnotherapist: "You're correct. High vibrational individuals often have anxiety and PTSD. They can be suicidal because they don't want to be in a body. They don't feel at home in it – they don't feel like they're at Home."

Wendy: "Thank you for saying that. I'm glad you have other experiences with this. I've had to work hard to become as dispassionate as I can to stay strong for her and for myself. I can't be knocked off my feet every time my child has a panic attack or is so depressed that she's considering suicide..."

(Wendy began crying)

Wendy: "I can't help her. It's awful. I'd just like to know how I can best support my daughter!"

← →

Hypnotherapist: "I know it's super stressful. I have family members like this. My best advice is to try to see her and tell her she's bright, strong, and resourceful – she can do this!"

Wendy: "Yes, I'm trying to reframe as it's her lens that matters, not mine or any of her doctors. I see and hear what she says and how she looks like she's in a bad place, but she corrects me and says, 'I'm okay right now.' She corrects me and says, 'Mom, my dark humor is a coping strategy I need to use.'"

Hypnotherapist: "Can you give me an example?"

← →

Wendy: "Yesterday we drove past the location where my car was totaled. My daughter said, 'Mom, wouldn't it be ironic if you had another accident here in the rental car right now?' "

(pause)

Wendy: "I was stunned. I whipped my head over to look at her and said sharply, 'You need to watch your Law of Attraction! I worked hard to energetically clear this accident scene.' "

(pause)

Wendy: "She became angry with me and replied, 'Mom, you're all rainbows and unicorns and don't live in the real world.' "

(pause)

Hypnotherapist: "What did you respond?"

Wendy: "I told her my head isn't in the sand. I'm working hard to manage my energy well – I'm not in denial."

(pause)

Wendy: "It was a genuine conversation – one that we're not usually capable of. I agree with her there are people doing spiritual bypass. I don't believe I am, but I think that's how she sees it."

(pause)

Wendy: *(sadly)* "It's hard for her to even smile. It's hard to look at her as she's so sad and depressed."

← →

Hypnotherapist: "She's so empathic. She jumps timelines and isn't in the present moment. She went back to when you had the accident and she picked up on your biggest fear. You cleared it – but she doesn't know how to clear it. You moved forward, but she doesn't know how to, so she accuses you of spiritual bypass."

Wendy: " That's so insightful! That helps me understand why we're seeing things so differently."

(pause)

Wendy: "It feels like she's digging for the deepest fear and pain and then doesn't know what to do with it?"

Hypnotherapist: "Yes, because she hasn't learned empowerment yet. That would drain the power of the anxiety over her. This is her power – what you do with it is your choice. Her empathy can become a gift, but right now it's a huge wrecking ball. She doesn't know it's her super-power! She's being told it is dysfunction."

(pause)

Hypnotherapist: "I do this work with clients often – when she sees her empathy as a power or as a gift it changes everything."

←→

Wendy: "She's starting to understand she's an Empath. Her senior year in high school I was able to experience one of her panic attacks first-hand for the first time. We were in the mall. The mall was almost empty, yet she had to run outside to ground her energy, which was a smart thing to do. When I caught up to her outside, she had found some little twig of a tree to hold onto."

(pause)

Wendy: "It was almost all cement outside in the parking lot, but she was touching this tiny tree. I showed her how to crouch down and put her hands on the Earth, too, along with her feet. She calmed down quickly. I was impressed and told her so."

(pause)

Wendy: "Once she was calm, I asked her if she knew what happened. She said, 'Yes, I realized I was picking up on the energy of every single person in the mall.'"

(pause)

Wendy: "I was so happy because I knew that we could then work with it. She can ask herself is this my energy, someone else's, or a combination?"

Hypnotherapist: "Good!"

Wendy: "I need to teach her that piece next, if she's willing. Learning to clear energy that isn't mine, is a combination or doesn't serve me has helped me so much."

Hypnotherapist: "This could help your daughter transform her PTSD, too."

←→

Wendy: "Thank you. My Guides want me to know I am trying to do too much because I don't one hundred percent trust. That's what we're here to change today. I'm to learn to say this is too big for me. I trust the outcome. I give this over to the Divine. I don't want to know specific outcomes anymore. I ask for the most loving outcome for all."

(pause)

Wendy: "I don't ask for specifics unless I'm guided to. I know that can be an ego thing. When I surrender to the Divine, I like to say it's above my pay rate!"

Hypnotherapist: "Yes, but that's tough to do when it's our children."

Wendy: "It certainly is. There are lessons there for us, too."

Hypnotherapist: "It's incredibly difficult to not want to fix it for them."

Wendy: "Which is why I prefaced this by saying if her Higher Self is willing and if her Guides recommend that she receive some healing and assistance today."

Hypnotherapist: "Her Higher Self is so wise and old. You need to look at her as this full being, even though she's suffering."

Wendy: "Absolutely."

(We discussed what worked best for me in hypnotherapy. I requested a short induction as knew everything was aligned. I felt like a race car pushing against the starting block - go, go, go!)

← →

Hypnotherapist: "Okay, let's get started. Feel the peace and relaxation – just letting go."

(The rest of the induction is not included here)

Hypnotherapist: "Are you deep enough to continue on?"

(Wendy begins speaking as her Higher Self)

Higher Self: "Yes."

Hypnotherapist: "What colors are pumping into your system?"

Higher Self: "Purple and green and some gold. The gold is the Christ Light but it's primarily the purple and the green."

Hypnotherapist: "Any thoughts in particular what it's working on?"

Higher Self: "The upgrade is primarily to her musculo-skeletal system – the bones and joints. Her nervous system is looking remarkably good from the work of the last few years."

(pause)

Higher Self: "She primarily needs her bones and joints upgraded from the body changing so much. The body container is not able to hold all the divine energy she has and that she moves for others. The result is pain."

Hypnotherapist: "Who am I speaking to? You're referring to her in the third person."

Higher Self: "The Higher Self – the eternal soul."

←→

Hypnotherapist: "Thank you. Are you able to bring in healing specialists for Wendy's body for what you described?"

Higher Self: "Yes, Dr. Lorphan is here. Also Dr. Usui and his higher consciousness Confucius are immediately presenting, along with Isis, Serapis Bey, Yeshua, Mary Magdalen, Mother Mary, Father Joseph, Archangel Michael, and Archangel Gabriel."

(pause)

Higher Self: "The whole team is here for her. We are so glad you are both doing this session."

Hypnotherapist: "Why?"

Higher Self: "Because she needs the physical healing. It's hard to trust. It's hard to launch the new career. It's hard to fully energetically attract and hold the large amount of funds we are sending her way as well as the new partner when the basics – the bones and joints - need this upgrade."

←→

Hypnotherapist: "Excellent. May we ask the Higher Self to go deeper than Wendy has experienced? Is there another level is what I'm asking?"

Higher Self: "Yes, we're integrating more fully into her heart."

Hypnotherapist: "Thank you. I was shown earlier the removal of a bullet fragment or two?"

Higher Self: "Yes. We're working on her upper back. It was being shot through the heart, but from the back. It's her upper back but toward the center – it's opening and closing the heart."

Hypnotherapist: "You said this is partially opening and closing the heart. Has that made it harder to manifest the right partner?"

Higher Self: "Yes. She worked diligently her whole life to repair her heart. Last August, we had her remove her own heart chakra and replace it. This was an excellent move."

(pause)

Higher Self: "Many things can be repaired. Other times you need to replace it – to make it new – just like the example we shared earlier of her car energetically needing to be replaced."

Hypnotherapist: "Yes. They showed me that heart chakra replacement and how beautiful it was. I'm also seeing shrapnel in her aura – like being shot from a shotgun? This to me represents she may have experienced a psychic attack by a male?"

←→

Higher Self: "There have been innumerable psychic attacks. We are not going to count them. Instead, we are

209

going to bring in the Violet Flame and the green ray of healing. There have been so many of these problems – so much vitriol thrown her way."

(pause)

Higher Self: "It's been a lot of work to replace that old victim and martyr energy. We want her to know it's done! Congratulations. That is a huge uplift as the incarnate of Mary Magdalen."

(pause)

Higher Self: "You're quite right there are fragments presenting. Let's move those out. Who wants to attract a new partner when they're flinching and in pain? That's not a productive way to do this."

(pause)

Higher Self: "She grew up in a domestic violence household. Congratulations to her for having survived that well in many ways. She carefully selected her partner so she would never be in that situation. She was crystal clear with her boundaries in that area. That was her mother's deal – not hers. She broke the cycle."

Hypnotherapist: "Yes – now it's about lifting the trauma."

← →

Hypnotherapist: "I was told in my own quest to find my own partner that the only true way to protect one's heart is to open it fully all three hundred and sixty degrees. You then stand in the center with it fully wide open. The only protection you need is yourself. You find your center as needed. You know that you can come back to your own center if anything happens in a human or physical way."

Higher Self: "Wonderful. That resonates for her highly. She's willing to give her love fully to a man who deserves it and who earns it."

(pause)

Higher Self: "She knows not to give her heart away again. That was the mistake she made with the primary soul mate. She had a traumatic relationship with him. She learned to give her love fully to the right man – but never her heart – and so many other things with him."

(Wendy suddenly began sneezing and coughing hard)

← →

Hypnotherapist: "They are saying he still has a part of her essence. He's still trying to pull on her, to own a piece of her heart."

Higher Self: *(strongly)* "No, that is not permitted! She is sovereign. She owns her heart and all her own energy."

Hypnotherapist: "We can be gentle with this. She has the power to pull that part of herself back to herself. She doesn't need to be scared or upset by this."

Higher Self: "She's angry. This is dirty pool on his part

210

to reject her and then to try to hold onto her heart."

Hypnotherapist: "Let's call back all her energy from all time and space all the way back into her body. Others who need energy can have their own energy from Spirit. She doesn't have to give it to them – that will allow him to let go. He's struggling to let go of her."

Higher Self: "Yes, he is. We can continue to do this work in the background. She is doing extremely well with this release."

Hypnotherapist: "Normally I would take her to a past life at this point. Does she need to do that?"

←→

Higher Self: "No, she does not. She's explored all nineteen past lives with him quite thoroughly to free herself through all space and time."

(pause)

Higher Self: "She doesn't need to see any more past lives with him. She's had her fill of them. It's done."

(pause)

Higher Self: "She knows to allow the past lives with him if there's energy to release. She doesn't have a charge around those lives at this point. She's been feeling them resolve over the last few weeks."

(pause)

Higher Self: "She had a big clearing last night in the middle of the night with lifetimes where she was burned – where there were fires. She woke up coughing and choking. She sat up and drank a lot of water and we helped her clear them all."

←→

Hypnotherapist: "May I ask if there any place you would like to take her that has a higher vibration than where we are now?"

Higher Self: "We'd love to. We'd like to go to the twelfth dimension – 12D - with the Ascended Masters and Archangels and Nature Spirits. That's a lovely place for her to be. Let's stabilize there and then she can go up to the thirty-second dimension."

Hypnotherapist: "Does her Higher Self ever need healing?

Higher Self: "Yes."

Hypnotherapist: "Can any Higher Self healing happen as well?"

Higher Self: "Yes. We're going to leave that to the Archangels."

Hypnotherapist: "Can that happen in the background of the other healing?"

(There was a long pause - Wendy's Higher Self began crying)

Higher Self: *(tearfully)* "Yes. It's never been requested for me before. It's a wonderful question."

Hypnotherapist: "You are loved."

Higher Self: "They're asking us to be quiet for a moment

while they work."
(long pause)

←→

Hypnotherapist: "Is there anything you'd like to share for the recording?"
Higher Self: "There is a beautiful technique to request healing for the Higher Self if needed. She is to go to a crystal bed. All manner of crystalline energy was used to heal her Higher Self."
Hypnotherapist: "Do you have awareness of what was healed?"
Higher Self: "It boils down to lack of trust. There's some small degree of impatience, frustration, and anger, particularly regarding the starts and stops with finances – with her easy abundance. Her perceived lack of traction with the romantic partner."
(pause)
Higher Self: "I just want to comment everyone is laughing sweetly. Her Guides are saying, 'We just got you new wheels! You have traction now – you just don't know it yet. Her new car symbolizes her new wheels in life."

←→

Hypnotherapist: "Wonderful. Is there anything that she needs to be made consciously aware of regarding where that anger or resentment came from? Sometimes we need to consciously understand something to release it."
Higher Self: "No – to just know they were quite valid. It's been an important part of learning to stand up for herself – to be in her power in an appropriate way, without abusing it. That's what her former boyfriend slammed home in such a challenging way."
(pause)
Higher Self: "Her boundaries were too soft – too weak. There were too many requests of her. Too many psychic attacks. Too many implants that didn't serve her."
(pause)
Higher Self: "It's been a lot of beautiful work over the last few years to clean all that up. Today is a wonderful culmination of that re-set."

←→

Hypnotherapist: "Good. What about her business?"
Higher Self: "We've been up leveling her business. She'll need to go through the full six months with the business coach. They've worked together before as have you with her, so there is lots of good sister energy. Best friend and supporter energy. A good feeling of sisterhood – the Divine Feminine."
(pause)
Higher Self: "There is more power coming to bat for

212

her. Joe DiMaggio will help her as they're one. They are the same soul."

(pause)

Higher Self: "The Mystery School knowledge is returning to her more consciously. She knows when to share it. It's not about secrets any longer – it's sacred knowledge to share."

(pause)

Higher Self: "Much of it will fall on deaf ears. She knows with whom and when to share it. Many don't need to hear the term 'Mystery School.' Just share the nugget. Others will be ready for her books – her talks – her radio programs to learn more."

←→

Hypnotherapist: "Speaking of radio, it sounds like she was disappointed with her radio host experience. Do you have any info about that experience?"

Higher Self: "There was some human disappointment. We pushed her hard to do the program. She made a significant investment. It was hard to bootstrap the forty-five hundred dollars needed. She thought her radio program would attract some ideal clients. She didn't fully realize it wasn't for clients."

Hypnotherapist: "What was it for?"

Higher Self: "We were healing her fear of public speaking and of being seen. To be willing to show up and to talk with such a large audience when she couldn't see anyone."

(pause)

Higher Self: "That's what led to so many attacks in the past. That's what we were really healing."

(pause)

Higher Self: "It was so worth that amount of money and effort. That's what it was truly about. She went more to the business place. 'Why don't I get inquires to my website from the show? Why am I not able to convert clients from it?' "

←→

Hypnotherapist: "Excellent. Anything else to understand about the radio host experience?"

Higher Self: "She heard us well; it was a highly positive contract with the woman she did the radio program with. It was an honor to work with her directly as she hosts the number one alternative talk radio program in the Seattle market."

(pause)

Higher Self: "It truly was a big deal. The program wasn't only heard in Seattle. There was a large media buy of ninety stations, plus it's archived for permanent download."

(pause)

Higher Self: "Her money, time and effort were well-spent. She understood it would be an intense learning and a short-term relationship. She parted from that radio network on great terms and left the door appropriately open for possible future projects."

(pause)

Higher Self: "We've placed radio on the back burner for a bit. We'll come back to it later in her timeline."

Hypnotherapist: "Thank you. I appreciate that."

Higher Self: "Certainly."

←→

Hypnotherapist: "There are many questions on her list."

Higher Self: "Please just go through them. Go to the Place of All Knowledge. We'll answer from the galaxy. The answers will flow quickly and easily."

Hypnotherapist: "Have we met before?"

Higher Self: "Yes. Your experiences have all been positive. There's nothing to release. You've been sisters. You have served together in the Mystery Schools. Just enjoy and be happy you've met again."

←→

Hypnotherapist: "How is she to best receive galactic info without left- ear ringing?"

Higher Self: "The fact that you had her ground into her favorite planet was huge. She never thought to do that. She should continue to do that daily, along with meditation and auto-writing."

(pause)

Higher Self: "Prince should triage for her as her galactic guide. She can simply say, 'Please give me a message from my galactic family.' Prince can choose which of the three planets we discussed with her in previous sessions. This will be a helpful boundary because the ear-ringing has been so loud – so distracting – such a clamor."

(pause)

Higher Self: "She should continue to ask her Guide Prince to bring her the most important message from Venus, the Purple Planet, or from the Pleiades – the Seven Sisters."

Hypnotherapist: "And what about the hearing loss?"

←→

Higher Self: "She's had to heal a lot of hearing loss from that clamor – too much energy and noise was directed her way. We're working to balance it up for her."

(pause)

Higher Self: "The moment she had her car collision she was spun hard almost 360 degrees. Her human self was frightened and confused as the impact was so large and sudden. Three air bags exploded in her face across the entire front windshield and driver's window. She had no way to see. She couldn't get her foot on the brake due to the

centrifugal force of the spin."
(pause)
Higher Self: "At the moment of impact, her soul forcefully declared, 'It's time to clean up everything in my life – I'm going to go up and up and up from this experience! Her right ear began ringing to balance it up. It also laid the groundwork for her to raise her vibration to a higher dimension when the time is right."

←→

Hypnotherapist: "So that was a powerful soul declaration."
Higher Self: "Yes, it was. That's an excellent explanation. You likely know you don't hear through your ears. You hear through your heart."
(pause)
Higher Self: "She's to place her hand on her heart and it will resolve the buzz in her ears. That loud buzz is not needed. We have her full attention. She is to ask to ground – to expand her energy field. She can now ask to ground not only to Earth but to her home planets to really get centered."
Hypnotherapist: "I love the hand on the heart."

←→

Hypnotherapist: "Is there anything the physical body needs to release from that car accident?"
Higher Self: "She needs to release the whack – the impact."
Hypnotherapist: "Where is it stored?"
Higher Self: "The heart and hips."
Hypnotherapist: "What color is it?"
Higher Self: "It's black. It's quite low vibration energy. It's not beneficial. Let's bring in White Light for her. Also, the Violet Flame and the green ray of healing like where we began today's session."

←→

Hypnotherapist: "Does she need anything else?"
Higher Self: "She's already done two of the three pieces we asked her to do to clear this energy. We recommended she get a Saint Christopher medal for her car and enjoy his protection for travelers. She purchased it as a visor clip."
(pause)
Higher Self: "We guided her to take her old car keys and title and place them on her altar. The energy of the old car is moving to the new car. It doesn't have a soul yet – it's reincarnating."
Hypnotherapist: "It's reinCARnating!"
(Both women giggled)
Higher Self: "How perfect is that?"

←→

Hypnotherapist: "When you remove the black energy does that help her?"

215

Higher Self: "Removing it lightened her up. The black energy was fear – a lack of confidence. It made her heart happy again and her hips. She hadn't realized she was storing fear there."

Hypnotherapist *(gently)*: "Did she do anything wrong?"

Higher Self: "No, she did not. I would not classify a mistake as doing something wrong. She's a careful driver. She always drives with the angels because she knows she can be floaty – up above her body. She carefully grounds and connects with her car and angels before driving. We discuss where she's to go and how she'll get there."

Hypnotherapist: "Yes?"

Higher Self: "That's why she was taken aback at first because she had specifically asked, 'Should I park here?', referring to the place in the lot. She heard a clear yes, so parked in the one remaining place in the lot. When she was leaving the parking lot, she asked twice 'Should I pull out now?' She asked for help because it was hard to see through the parked cars along the street."

(pause)

Higher Self: "She asked us, 'Is it safe to pull out?' We told her yes, and she was immediately hit. That threw her off until she meditated."

←→

Hypnotherapist: "What was the purpose of her car being hit?"

Higher Self: "The 3D reason was to have her buy a new car. This is part of the full upgrade of her life. She would not have purchased a new car otherwise."

(pause)

Higher Self: "The more important reason was to heal her fear of authority. She easily called the police. We were proud of her. She knew she would be judged at-fault as she was pulling out of the lot while the other cars were in motion. She knew questions would be raised regarding any alcohol consumption as she was leaving a dog rescue event that was held at a microbrewery."

Hypnotherapist: "What happened when she called the police?"

Higher Self: "She listened well to us despite the smacks she took not only from the serious collision but from three air bags deploying. That experience energetically was three explosions in her face in an enclosed space. That's a big deal both in the here-and-now physical and due to PTSD from past life war time and other explosions."

(pause)

←→

Higher Self: "We told her to not approach the other driver – to not speak with her. Bystanders were attending

216

the other driver. Several men immediately entered the street and began directing traffic to prevent additional collisions and to preserve the accident scene."

(pause)

Higher Self: "This was a serious collision with injuries as well as multiple vehicles involved. We told her let the police sort it out. We guided her to call the police and have them collect the insurance information from the other drivers as well as her own."

(pause)

Higher Self: "People came running to her car to offer aid and to assess if 911 needed to be called. The first man to arrive told her to turn off her engine as it was still running. She was too stunned to do so immediately on her own."

(pause)

Higher Self: "Several of her friends who'd been at the same event found her outside and offered their assistance. They got her water to drink as she was trying to drink from an empty water bottle. It was another teachable moment to let go of what others think and to graciously receive."

Hypnotherapist: "How did calling the police go?"

Higher Self: "Extremely well. She called the police and was questioned if she had consumed any alcohol before the accident. The policeman was thorough but caring. She called a tow truck. The driver was extremely kind and helped her get what she needed from her car. She was ticketed by mail and stood up for herself and received a reduced ticket from traffic court and was allowed to make her statement via email rather than driving into downtown Seattle to go to traffic court. She's doing everything right! We are so proud of her."

←→

Hypnotherapist: "Did this accomplish what it needed to regarding her issues with authority?"

Higher Self: "Yes, that, and more. She feels for the first-time things can go well after a challenging situation. To her surprise she found out she had accident forgiveness on her driver's insurance policy. Her rates won't go up. This is her first at-fault ever. This is important as she also insures her two daughters on her policy and it's expensive."

(pause)

Higher Self: "She realized with a lot of relief and even joy, 'This is so easy!' She was concerned, 'I'm buying a new car and am used to insuring a twelve-year old car with two young drivers on my policy. She asked us before calling her insurance agent, 'Can you help me with any increase?' She was so happy to find due to safety updates on the new model her insurance would only cost a hundred dollars more for the year."

Hypnotherapist: "So this had a lot of silver linings to it."

Higher Self: "Very much so. We're healing her belief that things need to be hard, she can't afford it and they will be expensive. We're unwiring that old wiring and helping her attain more flow in life. We're helping her become more open-minded, as well as fact-based. She was too often knee-jerking to the worst-case scenario – her empathic daughter's specialty, as you mentioned."

← →

Hypnotherapist: "Can we go to the deeper issue?"

Higher Self: "The deeper issue was the wounding of no longer trusting the Divine. That is what we are healing."

Hypnotherapist: "Yes."

Higher Self: "The lack of trust in authority was the subset. The fear – the anger. The real issue is she lost her trust two thousand years ago when she witnessed the crucifixion. It's been a deep wound to heal. She needed the new heart to heal it."

(pause)

Higher Self: "This is meant to be a wonderful reward life. It can and will be! We've told her it's written in the stars, but she doesn't understand that yet. She will with time. Let's let that be."

← →

Hypnotherapist: "Thank you. Can she now trust again based on our work today?"

Higher Self: "Yes."

Hypnotherapist: "Will it be easy?"

Higher Self: "She needs to now make it a habit. Positive affirmations such as 'The Universe always has my back!' would help. She can write them on a sticky note and place them on her bathroom mirror and computer screen. She can update them as needed."

(pause)

Higher Self: "That would be helpful. That's really all that's needed."

Hypnotherapist: "Excellent. She's like to know, 'What's my best protocol to release the last of the fear and to fully live my destiny?' "

Higher Self: "We've already covered it. She can more consciously partner with Isis. Isis is here. She'd like Wendy to call on her more regularly. She can do some special meditations with Isis. They will be both profound and enjoyable."

Hypnotherapist: "Would Isis like to say anything now?"

Higher Self: "Yes, she would. Isis is saying, 'Welcome home, welcome back. You can connect with me on a deeper level via the Egyptian oils your friend brought back from Egypt. The fact that your daughter accepted them from you shows

you are both moving into your power in benevolent ways."
(Midnight began meowing loudly)
Isis: "The cat would like to be acknowledged. He was an Egyptian cat with her in my Temple at Philae."
Hypnotherapist: *(laughing)* "I hear him – I knew what he was asking."

←→

Hypnotherapist: "What does it mean to be an incarnate?"
Isis: "She is running that pure essence – that pure energy from Magdalen. Ascended Master Mary Magdalen has given one percent of her Ascended Master energy to Wendy to be Mary Magdalen incarnated on Earth."
(pause)
Isis: "This is not information Wendy enjoys sharing. It's hard for her to accept and deal with because the mere thought invited a lot of attacks. It felt incredibly presumptuous and like an unbalanced ego."
(pause)
Isis: "She had to learn how to move out of the victim and martyrdom energy. She had to learn how to bolster her own energy as well as to be self-confident in her own truth. This is an important piece for her to complete her lesson to 'let go of what other people think.'"
(pause)
Isis: "It's why we delayed the Mary Magdalen book several times. She needed to be ready for it. We asked her to speak her truth she recalls that past life and many others do, too – to leave it open."
(pause)
Isis: "It's not about the ego or getting kudos. There are currently several other Magdalen incarnates on the planet. Being an incarnate is more than having lived that past life. It's the pure essence of the Ascended Master."
Hypnotherapist: "What is the purpose for her being an incarnate – for herself and for others?"

←→

Isis: "For Wendy it's to learn the lessons I just outlined. She is also to make it safe and acceptable for others to explore these sorts of possibilities as well as the potential historic, Biblical, and famous – or infamous – past lives."
(pause)
Isis: "If she keeps skirting this reality of being Magdalen's incarnate, she's not in full integrity of owning who she is. It's the same with Joe DiMaggio. Since she's stepping to the plate today, we will now make it easy, fun, and pleasurable to finish the next book and publish it."

←→

Hypnotherapist: "Thank you. What's going on with her business coach? I sense some push-pull energy."

219

Isis: "She is right to occasionally push back at her coach. This is teaching Wendy to stand in her power fully, without abusing it. The coach is knowledgeable but strong-willed, domineering and has a blind spot."

(pause)

Isis: "You can't know someone else's truth. Her ego is not balanced in this area. She thinks she knows better. She's taking too heavy a hand at times."

(pause)

Isis: "The coach supposedly has twenty friends who are authors who are not yet making money from their writing. That may or may not be reality. More importantly, don't project that onto Wendy. Also don't feel it's always about money. It may or may not be about money."

(pause)

Isis: "Her first few books may or may not make much money. We leave that open. She's learning to write, to publish and to create audiobooks. She is also helping others by the books being available for them to read or listen to."

← →

Hypnotherapist: "So how is Wendy handling this?"

Isis: "When the coach says something that's not for her, she knows not to comment. She hears her Guides clearly tell her to disregard that one point. But don't throw the baby out with the bathwater – she is learning other things from the coach that are both practical as well as energetic."

(pause)

Isis: "When the coach pushes her personal agenda about writing not being worthwhile a second-third-fourth time and challenges Wendy for spending time writing, Wendy appropriately says, 'I hear you and I respect your right to your opinion, but that is not my path. I am meant to be an author of many books. It's a key part of my life purpose.' "

(pause)

Isis: "The coach eventually stops. She'll have to do that with her a few times to establish her boundaries."

(pause)

Isis: "What's really going on is the coach's blocks around writing her own book. That's the real issue. That's why she told Wendy the cover on Wendy's first book scared her. It's the fact that the coach is not writing her own book that's scaring her."

(pause)

Isis: "Wendy's book cover is perfect for the content. The book cover is not meant to match Wendy's website and to be all soft lavender and light greens. That makes no sense. The book cover is to make the book come alive to attract its best audience!"

(pause)
Isis: "It's like your disclaimer on your website and instructions when we began today – always respect your own Higher Self guidance the most of all."
Hypnotherapist: "Absolutely!"

←→

Hypnotherapist: "Continuing with her list of questions – 'Have I balanced my energy to be here now as Wendy?' "
Isis: "That was accomplished profoundly in the last year or two. It was done at a deeper, higher level today by grounding into her other planets."
Hypnotherapist: "Am I fully embracing prosperity consciousness and receiving at the highest level?"
Isis: "Let's make this like a school grade, for simplicity. We'll give her a ninety-eight percent on that. Now make it a habit. Expect the best – use the affirmations. Soon she won't bobble in her beliefs about her plentiful abundance."
(pause)
Isis: "Then the large resources will come. She and her partner will excel with their business backgrounds and energetic guidance combined with their hearts. They'll form charities and endowments. They will hire attorneys, accountants and advisors as needed. The money will replenish itself. It will spread itself to multiply and multiply and multiply again, giving her seeds to plant for humanity."

←→

Hypnotherapist: "Wonderful. How do I best heal from romantic relationships and restore my trust in that area?"
Isis: "It's already done."
Hypnotherapist: "I know. But what does she need to know to relax?"
Isis: "I appreciate you called out that blind spot with the former primary soul mate. He has such huge energy he had a tentacle on her that you called out appropriately. She reached out her hand and took his hand off her and gave it back to him. He was being an octopus with her. He tries this with all his former girlfriends to build his large, yet fragile ego. It's annoying but all can learn from it."
(pause)
Isis: "I'm going to step back now that I'm well-connected with this Magdalen – with Wendy – and invite her Higher Self back in to answer the remaining questions. This is empowering for the soul. Your own Higher Self is your best Guide although it is wonderful for your Higher Self to coordinate with other Guides, too."

←→

Hypnotherapist: "Thank you. She wrote, *How does my now full-time Regression Healing business feel energetically?*"
Higher Self: "It's a bit of a fledgling bird coming out of

the nest. It's okay for her to use the business coach as a bird mother for a bit."

(long pause)

Higher Self: "This is a tortured analogy – please go with it anyway!"

(Both women laughed)

Higher Self: "She's doing what she should be doing to get amazing on-track business information from her business coach. She should continue to take it in. She can also enjoy the daylights out of the Dr. Brian Weiss training. By next fall the clients will really start to come."

(pause)

Higher Self: "We pushed her hard to exhibit tomorrow at a Mind-Body-Spirit Fair. She's not ready. It's just practice. A dress rehearsal."

(pause)

← →

Higher Self: "The banners she ordered will either show up or they won't. We'd like to take this opportunity to address her number dyslexia. We'd like to fix that right now because she gave the wrong address for her banner for the show."

(pause)

Higher Self: "She looked at the address carefully before ordering but she can't see the numbers being transposed. The compensatory strategy is to read the address aloud. That will help her know it was wrong."

(pause)

Higher Self: "The company she was ordering from had hard-wired the wrong zip code for her address. She knew that would likely cause a delay. She got so fixated on calling the company to fix the zip code that she then transposed two of the digits in her own house number."

(pause)

Higher Self: "We're working to fix that as it's not fun or easy for her to get the right phone number or the right credit card number or address. We're working to fix that now."

← →

Hypnotherapist: "What's causing the issue?"

Higher Self: "It's a left brain – right brain – center brain connection issue. She's extremely fluid through all of them. This is a gift and part of how she does her work so well. But she needs the precision for numbers in the left brain to be a bit more fixed."

Hypnotherapist: "I understand. I have it, too. It allows us to be broad-minded and not judgmental as well as to move quickly to connect the dots when we're speaking and working with clients."

Higher Self: "You have it exactly right. But we need to fix

222

it for her now that she's a solopreneur and running her own books. This is the reason she so disliked spreadsheet work and couldn't do a lot of it, which was surprising for an MBA. It tired her out."

(pause)

Higher Self: "Her new partner is an accountant. He's a finance guy – numbers and spreadsheets and taxes are fun, fast and easy for him. They'll be a nice blend of skills."

← →

Hypnotherapist: "Wonderful. Can we pull a typical client of hers in front of her – Wendy's ideal client?"

Higher Self: "Yes."

Hypnotherapist: "The Guides would like to show her that she can ask that client where and how they want to be reached. This is to be for Wendy's highest good. As she and the people she works with transition to a higher vibration, those client preferences can change as well."

Higher Self: "That's beautiful. That makes perfect sense. She's been visioning her ideal clients with her business coach. This will help her move toward her full abundance. She'll be able to choose which are her ideal clients. You don't have to scrape for them nor accept all comers."

Hypnotherapist: "Exactly."

Higher Self: "Her ideal client is –"

Hypnotherapist *(interrupting):* "Give her a visual please so she can talk to them."

Higher Self: "She works primarily with women and a few wonderful men. Many are middle aged or older, but she attracts a few who are college age or even in high school. She relates to them well due to her daughters being in college."

(pause)

Higher Self: "They are high vibrational souls. That's the main component in common. They are high vibration, on a spiritual path and have been for lifetimes. She is not meant to work with newbies. She already knows this."

Hypnotherapist: "Please give her a visual. An embodiment to talk with that will be an example of her highest and best fit client."

Higher Self: "A representative is stepping forward."

← →

Hypnotherapist: "What does she see?"

Higher Self: "She sees an attractive woman in her forties stepping forward. This woman is educated – motivated – engaged – grateful. She is grateful to be working with Wendy."

Hypnotherapist: "What is her name?"

Higher Self: "Mary Ann."

Hypnotherapist: "She can call on Mary Ann as the conglo-meration of the highest and best client, correct?"

Higher Self: "Mary Ann said yes. She will be the point

person. This is a brilliant strategy. Wendy had not gotten this far with visioning her ideal client. Mary Ann is to sit next to her when she updates her website. She will help her know what language to use to reach her ideal clients."

Hypnotherapist: "Thank you. That feels powerful for her."

←→

Hypnotherapist: "She'd like to know if she is to help heal a friend's father who's been diagnosed with cancer?"

Higher Self: "We recommend she sit and focus to send love to him and to his family. She can do specific meditations on his behalf. The healing will not be in-person as his belief system doesn't align well enough with hers."

(pause)

Higher Self: "The wife is earning an advanced degree by studying the Universe. But metaphysics and energy healing are not part of his belief system, nor his daughter's. Wendy stretches her friend's materialist beliefs hard all the time."

(pause)

Higher Self: "She and her friend are in a good place. Their contract together is being upheld. They're both growing from it. It's not the most comfortable relationship for either of them. There's a lot of push-pull energy as they're so different. But behind the scenes they are each encouraging the other soul in a good way."

←→

Hypnotherapist: "Is there anything she should be helping her oldest with?"

Higher Self: "Her eldest daughter is sailing along beautifully. She's right where she should be. She just needs to feel her mother's love and backing. The mother needs to keep the communications flowing."

(pause)

Higher Self: "The young lady is incredibly busy and hard-working partly because of the box she put herself in financially by choosing such an expensive school so far from home. Lessons learned."

(pause)

Higher Self: "She needs to feel her mother's love and support. The daughter is so amazing, so delightful! She is well-balanced. She will go far in life as she's so on her intended path. So is her boyfriend – they will go far. Full steam ahead!"

←→

Hypnotherapist: "Her other daughter we've already discussed. We appreciate any additional insights."

Higher Self: "She should go ahead with the brain MRI for her younger daughter. It's not going to show any abnormality or useful information. Her physician has rightly raised the question could there be a brain tumor with so

224

many health challenges? Unfortunately, we can't yet do an imaging study of the girl's energy."

(pause)

Higher Self: "She should also help her daughter get the sleep study. There is value in rule-outs in medicine. We know you ladies know what's really going on."

Hypnotherapist: "Absolutely."

Higher Self: "Western medicine is essentially rule out - medicate – rule out – medicate. It's quite limited. It's often most helpful in the areas of Emergency Medicine and emergency surgeries. We look forward to the day when medicine is more integrated and includes Reiki energy healing, Chinese medicine and so much more."

←→

Hypnotherapist: "Let's stay at the twelfth dimension – will her daughter's Higher Self please meet us there? (Name deleted), please join us at 12D."

(pause)

Higher Self: "She's here."

Hypnotherapist: "Is there anything she wants her mother to know?"

Daughter's Higher Self: "Mom, don't give up on me. I understand why you need to pull back and not enable me. Let's just keep having the real conversations."

(pause)

Daughter's Higher Self: "Thank you for being that safe landing spot when I need to come home from the dorms to crash for a couple days and for not trying to pull me back in when I don't want to communicate. You love to talk, and I hate it as it drains me. Sometimes I need to go to Dad's for a few days and I don't tell you what's going on. Sometimes I go to Grandmom's – sometimes I go to my boyfriend's parents' house."

(pause)

Daughter's Higher Self: "I'm getting better at asking for help. I ask for help from different people at different times. It's why I've created all this crap for myself – the physical and mental health issues – so I can learn my life lesson, which is to be able to ask for help."

←→

Hypnotherapist: "Is there anything Wendy would like to say to her daughter?"

Wendy's Higher Self: "*(name deleted)*, I love you. I support you. I feel we're making progress in having the real conversations even though we are so different. I'm so glad to have you as my daughter!"

(pause)

Wendy's Higher Self: "I see you as well. I see you happy. I see you moving through all these tough challenges quickly."

Hypnotherapist: "Is that helpful for her daughter for her mother to see her as healthy?"

Higher Self: "Yes."

Hypnotherapist: (shrewdly) "Is the daughter saying that?"

Higher Self: "She's nodding. She doesn't want to say yes. She's stubborn – but she's nodding."

Hypnotherapist: "Ok, good. Anything more to learn from that?"

Higher Self: "What you consider stubborn can be a strength as long as it has flexibility. They both have strength and flexibility – the mother and the daughter. This portion is complete."

←→

Hypnotherapist: "How is her kitty doing?"

Higher Self: "Midnight is doing great. He's aging gracefully. The vet is correct his thyroid is a bit fast, but he doesn't need medication. It's why he's so food driven. He's hungry."

(pause)

Higher Self: "We know she's been wondering why he's yowling so loudly after he eats and uses his box. It's not a medical issue – he's establishing his dominion over the home, property and neighborhood.

(pause)

Higher Self: "Actually over the entire galaxy. He's like a lion roaring. Midnight has huge energy! He's a jungle animal. Just let him be himself. Don't try to stop him from roaring – he's like a lion roaring or a gorilla beating his chest."

(pause)

Higher Self: "He's clearing the property exceptionally well with his yowls and roars and fast runs. Wendy knows that. It's his job. She's not to help him with it or take his job away from him. It's their soul agreement so she can do her energy work in peace. She can simply say thank you and praise him."

←→

Hypnotherapist: "Excellent. It's time to end. Is there anything else as a parting message?"

Higher Self: "To know how delightful and beautiful everything already is now. To 'be here now' in the moment. To know the correction is complete with the former boyfriend with the big energy. He will no longer be in her energy field in a dominating way."

←→

Hypnotherapist: "Do you have a gift for Wendy?"

Higher Self: "We are restoring her fully to herself, meaning the fear no longer serves her. It no longer can reside in her world. We'd like her to know she is achieving her life lesson of self-acceptance beautifully. It's more and more

226

comfortable for her to publish and speak publicly about her experiences. Her books are highly personal and open-hearted. It will become easier."

Hypnotherapist: "I see the angels handing her a package. She can go ahead and open it."

Higher Self: "She did. It's the full abundance – and it's the romantic partner."

Hypnotherapist: "Are those energetic beings – is it energy in the box?"

Higher Self: "The partner is filling in for her what he looks like – his soul essence. He's walking closer to her now that her trust is restored. He couldn't move closer before due to her trust issues."

(pause)

Higher Self: "Her abundance presents as water – rivers – oceans – waterfalls – divine flow."

←→

Hypnotherapist: "Thank you. To close out the session, I'm asking to pull all of Wendy's energy across all time and space back into her. To have it fully restored back into her body. For her to have her own pure energy healed and to know she can connect any time with the crystalline grid of Earth. I'm asking for her other world experiences to all continue healing in a gentle, easy way over the next few days – weeks – hours – minutes. To have it be easy, easy, gentle, gentle to come back to the here and now."

←→

Higher Self: "Her cat left just before you said it was time to end. His timing is impeccable."

(Both women laughed)

Hypnotherapist: "He's awesome."

Higher Self: "Thank you for the assist today. Her upper back feels so much better. She's also resolving the last of the fear and trust issues."

←→

Our wonderful two-and-a-half-hour session ended. Two months later my youngest moved out for the second time. She chose to become increasingly estranged. I could feel the weight of challenging past life energy between us. I couldn't find the lifetime of origin to heal it. She had drawn her line in the sand which I knew she needed for her own health.

I put a lot of energy into my business for the next eighteen months. I began public speaking. A fellow student of my business coach introduced me to the wonderful Wisdom Soup community. I became a teacher on the Wisdom Soup app which matches spiritual seekers with spiritual teachers.

I worked with a talented dream interpreter to learn to recall and interpret my dreams. I recognized him as my older brother in a past life. I learned how to lucid dream – to be aware I was dreaming and to create the most positive outcomes. I learned that anyone in your dreams who has a title – whether they were a hotel clerk or an Uber driver – were Guides, and to pay particular attention to what they said and did.

I did a lot of dog rescue volunteering and published my second book, "The Flow I: Plimoth Plantation," the prequel. It felt fantastic to have it complete after working on it on and off for five years!

Weekends were especially busy as a lot of clients preferred a Saturday or Sunday past-life regression as they worked weekdays. I was juggling running two past-life regression weekend workshops and two enjoyable dog funcraiser events each month as Airbnb Experiences.

I thoroughly enjoyed co-hosting a monthly podcast with a wonderful friend and fellow spiritual teacher.

← →

In July of 2019 an incredible opportunity came up to attend an independent writer's conference – at a castle in Edinburgh, Scotland.

The moment I saw the conference advertised I could sense my Guides arranging the trip.

I asked them to help me find the best editor for my work. We met immediately by sharing a cab from the airport to the conference. This was what it meant to be in flow with the Universe!

I traveled solo internationally for the first time. I spent two weeks in London, Glastonbury, and Edinburgh. I had been to the United Kingdom once before as a child. Amazingly, that trip was exactly fifty years earlier as I knew I'd been there for my birthday and we'd watched the first American astronaut walk on the moon.

I finally made it to Glastonbury, England where two of my key past lives intersected and where my Guides had been asking me to travel for a good five years or so. I received an incredible healing for my left foot and leg when I waded in the cold red spring waters of the Chalice Well Gardens in Glastonbury.

My left leg and food had been energetically missing since they were blown off in World War II when I was an American soldier sent to Berlin. This made it difficult to receive as the left side of the body represents the feminine receiving side and the right side the masculine giving side.

The War Dog, my short story about fostering a female German Shepherd mix named Berlin was published in a multi-author collaboration. Berlin was my war dog in World War II and had saved my life. Now I was able to save hers.

All proceeds from *Heaven Sent: True Stories of Pets That Have Touched Our Hearts in Miraculous Ways* are donated to veteran's and animal charities.

← →

My eldest daughter graduated from college. We had a fantastic time renting an Airbnb floating home in San Diego Harbor and hosted Tara's graduation party on the large rooftop deck. She took a gap year to work full-time in a vet office while applying to veterinary colleges.

Tara became engaged and she and her fiancé relocated from San Diego to Pullman, Washington for Tara to attend vet school! It is more difficult to be accepted to vet school than medical or dental school, but Tara was on her life path just as I'd heard in readings for years.

My talented youngest daughter's health issues escalated. She was losing her vision along with other serious issues. No one could tell us why. I wondered what it was that she didn't want to see? A naturopathic, functional medicine physician found that her iron stores were severely depleted.

Friends and family scrambled to help her study as she could no longer read most things on the computer or in her textbooks, nor could she drive. Teachers administered her final exams orally as she couldn't read the questions or write her answers.

Her therapist recommended she get a white vision impairment cane. We were all concerned about her crossing the busy downtown streets in Seattle's University District to attend classes. Her boyfriend and roommate walked her as many places as they could. We discovered the hard way she couldn't fly alone as she couldn't see well enough to find her gate at the airport. She had an eye exam and again there were no answers or useful diagnosis.

I wondered again what it was my daughter didn't want to see? This was such a tough way to learn her soul lesson of being willing to ask for help. I wished I could do more for her, but she would so seldom speak with me.

Since my youngest remained estranged and my new partner had not presented, I was open to assistance via another past-life regression. Six months later I found the perfect hypnotherapist.

Chapter Eleven – Guinevere's Round Table

On December 10th, 2019, I had an incredible past-life regression with a talented hypnotherapist who is also a psychic medium and published author.

The energy felt 'off' as we began the session. Our call dropped several times, which is unusual. My hypnotherapist wasted no time sharing her impressions once we established a stable connection.

←→

Hypnotherapist: "I sense your daughter is with us today. The discordant energy with your youngest appears to relate to your ectopic pregnancies. It's like there's an aspect of yourself stuck in a continuous loop. Your daughter is highly empathic but doesn't understand this gift or how to handle it. Part of her is blaming you. You've had past lives together where you had similar energy."

(pause)

Hypnotherapist: "As a young child she experienced a lot of anger she didn't know how to handle. It's why she's now choosing to be estranged. I am asking to go to the first cause of the estrangement – the lifetime of origin."

Wendy: "Thank you. That would be so helpful. I haven't been able to find that lifetime to heal it."

←→

Hypnotherapist: "I'm seeing the two of you in a primitive setting. It looks like Mongolia. This is the original source of the Native Americans. It's tribal times when human sacrifices were still given. I see your daughter being carried away – her arms are reaching out for you. She is crying out, 'How can you do this to me?' It is heart-wrenching."

(Wendy began sobbing)

Hypnotherapist: "It is the way of the tribe – it's the cultural conditioning. People didn't know any better. She's sacrificed on a raft – the raging waters turn to tame waters. People believe this will help the crops so they can survive. It's all very primitive."

(pause)

Hypnotherapist: "There is rage in her heart. The cords are entangled in both your hearts. She's still angry with you but doesn't understand why. That makes her even more angry as she doesn't understand herself or her emotions."

(pause)

←→

Wendy: "This breaks my heart! So how can I best help her?"

Hypnotherapist: "You need to be the Wise Woman. She's ready to start to heal or she wouldn't have come forward today. Her Higher Self crashed our phone connection several times to get our attention. I've healed tremendous anger with my own mother. Let's see if she'll come forward from the other side to help this situation."

Wendy: "Thank you."

Hypnotherapist: "She's saying to you both, 'I honor you – I bless you – I thank you for all these experiences together. You can now say that to one another and forgive one another across time. You can wipe the slate clean down to present time."

Wendy: "That's fantastic – how wonderful."

Hypnotherapist: "Let's now repeat, 'I bless you – I thank you – I forgive you – I love you' – let's manifest this in your cells, Wendy. See your daughter doing the same so she can heal and grow into divine love."

(long pause)

Wendy: "I feel the energy shifting. It's a bit lighter."

←→

Hypnotherapist: "Your mother abandoning you in this lifetime was to trigger you to remember when you were pressed into abandoning your child previously. Let's tell your mother, 'I honor you – I see you – I thank you – I forgive you – I love you, Mom.'"

(There was a long pause)

Wendy: "That was hard to do, honestly. But I know it's the path to freedom."

Hypnotherapist: "Exactly. Your sacral root is now getting freed up. Your financial body will now be able to flow. The energies around you of not feeling safe – of not trusting your physical body – not trusting the Universe and your Guides – that energy is now clearing."

Wendy: "That's amazing! My- daughter and I have a deeper connection than I knew."

Hypnotherapist: "Yes. And it can be a healthy one now, over time."

←→

Hypnotherapist: "I'd like you to now imagine the most sumptuous walk-in closet that you can. Go ahead and enter and put on anything you want."
(pause)
Hypnotherapist: "What are you wearing?"
Guinevere: "I'm wearing a long velvet green dress."
Hypnotherapist: "Do you notice anything else about it?"
Guinevere: "Yes. It has some white on it for contrast. There's gold lacing down the sides. This allows it to be pulled tight for a perfect fit and to accentuate one's figure."
Hypnotherapist: "Wonderful. What does your hair look like?"
Guinevere: "I have long red hair. It's still down loose as I'm preparing for the day. One of my ladies-in-waiting will finishing brushing my hair and put it up for me. It's hard to do it myself as my hair is past my waist."
Hypnotherapist: "Do you know how old you are, approximately, and where you might be located geographically?"
Guinevere: "Yes. I'm in my early twenties in England. I'm at Camelot in Glastonbury."
Hypnotherapist: "Okay. What's on your agenda for today? You said you were preparing for your day."

←→

Guinevere: "I'm going to the Round Table."
Hypnotherapist: "Why are you going to the Round Table? Do you have a sense of your name – of who you are.?"
Guinevere: "Why, certainly I do. My name is Guinevere. My husband is away, so I will be sitting in his place at the Round Table."
Hypnotherapist: "How do you feel about that?"
Guinevere: "I feel wonderful about it at this point. It's appropriate I be there. I have earned my place at the table, quite literally."
(Guinevere laughed sweetly)
Hypnotherapist: "How do the others who sit at the table feel about your being there?"
Guinevere: "Some of them have grown to respect me in my own right. Most of them are used to my presence at the table by now."

←→

Hypnotherapist: "What will be discussed today? What's most important on your mind?"
Guinevere: "How to accomplish peace for all lands is on my mind. Ironically, peace needs to be established via military strategy. Peace is all that interests me."

Hypnotherapist: "Do the men at the table with you understand the goal? Are they all men? I shouldn't assume."

Guinevere: "Yes, it's all men at the table with me. There are no other women. Only a Queen could be here in her husband's place – in King Arthur's place – in my time."

(pause)

Guinevere: "Most of the men at the table are younger souls. They are interested in what they see as the glory of battle – showing their chops. That's what they see as honor and bravery."

Hypnotherapist: "So then how do you work toward peace?"

Guinevere: "There are a few older, wiser souls at the table with me, but not many. I'm primarily working with Merlin. The Merlin of Great Britain."

(pause)

Guinevere: "He's my best friend. He is my mentor – my teacher – my protector."

Hypnotherapist: "Wasn't Merlin Arthur's teacher, too?"

Guinevere: "Yes, he was."

←→

Hypnotherapist: "How would you describe your relationship with your husband Arthur? Are you good mates?"

Guinevere: "Yes and no. Arthur is thirty years older than me. We have no children. I've made my peace I was married off to him – another war prize to keep the peace!"

(Guinevere sighs heavily)

Guinevere: "We've become sympatico in many ways, but I am tired of his playing war games. They are ridiculous at his age! He's holding to his old standard where he used to excel. He doesn't know how to reinvent himself."

(pause)

Guinevere: "He's gone from Camelot too much – for up to a year at a time. I don't appreciate the abandonment. There is much work to be done here. Important work to lay the groundwork toward peace."

←→

Hypnotherapist: "Are you saying Arthur's predominant energy is warring and yours is peace? Yet you have the same teacher in Merlin?"

Guinevere: "Yes."

Hypnotherapist: "How does Merlin feel about this major difference between you? And what about Arthur being gone so often?"

Guinevere: "Merlin doesn't take sides. He honors us both equally. He works with us separately to do our soul contract work that we incarnated to do on this planet."

←→

Hypnotherapist: "What's the primary energy as you

233

look around you at the men at the Round Table?"

Guinevere: *(sounding emotional)* "Most of them just want to raise their swords! They don't understand Excalibur has been transmuted – had its energy raised – to be a sword of peace."

Hypnotherapist: "So how can you help them understand the benefits of peace?"

Guinevere: "I'm trying to make it relatable in day-to-day terms. There will be enough food, shelter, safety, and freedom for their families and loved ones when we accomplish peace. We will be able to care for not only for Camelot – but for our village – our country – our region."

(pause)

Guinevere: "I am working to show them what can be accomplished in peace. I am an accomplished orator as well as military strategist, having been trained by my father from an early age. I can speak their language, but still..."

Hypnotherapist: "What's their reaction when you talk about peace?"

Guinevere: *(sighing heavily)* "Most of them look like peacocks shaking their tail feathers! Most of them just don't get it. I can only work to plant the seeds so that they may get it in their next lifetime or the one after that."

←→

Hypnotherapist: "Let's take a different approach, Guinevere. It doesn't sound like you're getting through to enough of them."

Guinevere: *(flatly)* "I'm not. What do you suggest?"

Hypnotherapist: "Why don't you call for a break and have everyone leave the Round Table? You and you alone are then to reconvene everyone back to the table. They can't sit until you've been seated, right?"

Guinevere: "They need to remain standing until I am seated."

Hypnotherapist: "Perfect. When you return to the Round Table, remain standing. Stand up tall – be fully in your power, Guinevere. Stand longer than the men are comfortable standing. Hold your power – hold your peace energy – and then transmit it to each of them as you look them fully in the eye, one by one. You may then be seated now that you have their full attention that today is going to be different."

←→

Guinevere: *(happily)* "That's brilliant! Now what?"

Hypnotherapist: "You'll want to have a basket with you with enough writing implements for each man at the table. Have them each take a quill and inkwell. You are now going to teach them the power of the pen versus the sword. Ask them – no, inspire them – men can and want to be inspired by women – to write what they most want in this lifetime."

234

(pause)
Hypnotherapist: "Ask them to be descriptive – to really feel the emotions – to be brave enough to be vulnerable to be fully truthful."
(pause)
Hypnotherapist: "You are asking them what they most desire. You should do this too, while you hold the energy of peace in your heart as an example for them."

← →

Guinevere: "We're going to need a few scribes as well as the Merlin to help the men who can't read or write. Arthur changed history in that not only men noble-born could serve as Knights of the Round Table – it was one of his greatest accomplishments. He changed the system from an aristocracy to a meritocracy."
(pause)
Guinevere: "Some of the men did not receive a formal education and cannot read or write. We are diplomatically helping them write what they most want in this lifetime."
Hypnotherapist: "Yes. Merlin can use a little magic, so the information remains confidential. The men can now roll up their scrolls or even burn them. Their wishes will burn in their hearts. You can now give them the power of permission. No one has said this to them before. They can share if they wish, but are not judged for not doing so."

← →

Guinevere: "I understand. I'll take it from here and am now addressing my men. 'Gentlemen – Knights of the Round Table – Camelot's highest advisors – thank you for all that you sacrifice for Camelot! Thank you for your courage in writing what you most want in this lifetime. You may keep this to yourself, or bravely share it aloud now. Will anyone share?'"
(long silence)
Lancelot: "I most want respect. I want to be free to express myself and to be respected for my position."
Guinevere: "Thank you, Sir Lancelot – know that we do respect you because you respect yourself. Is there anyone else who will speak?"
(pause)
Gawain: "I want to be known for my loyalty to my King."
Guinevere: "Wonderful, Sir Gawain. It takes courage to be truly loyal. Know that we deeply appreciate your great heart and your service."

← →

The sharing continued until the Merlin of Great Britain asked Guinevere if she was willing to share what she had written. She nodded and replied, "I wish to have effective communication as I give and receive love without judgment – I do so in the form of peace for mankind."

Guinevere, the Merlin and other Beings of Light then blessed the men for their courage. They held the energy during a silent prayer as they helped them manifest what their souls desired – their life purpose.

Guinevere explained that the first step to peace was to become peaceful within oneself. She told a story illustrating how we all have both Divine Masculine energy and Divine Feminine energy within us in each lifetime, and that balancing these forces was the path to peace and to freedom.

Some were confused and even appalled to hear that they might have feminine energy. Many did not fully understand Guinevere's story. But the seeds were planted for their Higher Selves and Guides to continue to work with them.

Small gifts were distributed as Guinevere wanted to celebrate each of the men for participating with as open a heart as he could muster. The powerful meeting was adjourned from the Round Table that had been part of Guinevere's dowry when she married Arthur. On that day it truly was Guinevere's Round Table.

←→

Hypnotherapist: "I'd like you to go to the next time of significance in this lifetime."

Guinevere: *(hesitating)* "This is quite challenging."

Hypnotherapist: "Where are you? What's happening."

Guinevere: "I'm learning to be peaceful in the nunnery after Arthur banished me. I'm learning to be useful at the same time as I release my anger and rage with him over what happened."

Hypnotherapist: "How long did that take?"

Guinevere: "About two years. There was deep grief under the rage. Anger is a secondary emotion that typically masks grief."

Hypnotherapist: "Very good. What did you learn as you released the anger, rage, and grief?"

←→

Guinevere: "Eventually I had to accept I would never see Arthur again. Nor anyone else that I had known at Camelot or in my life."

(pause)

Guinevere: "I did not know that Arthur died a broken man not long after he banished me to save my life. No one told me what happened to him. I didn't learn what befell him for another 1,600 years or so until a current day friend of Wendy's who was in the Camelot life told her what happened. My soul then knew the truth."

(pause)

236

Guinevere: "The prophecy from Avalon that few knew of came true. Arthur was killed by his son Mordred in battle. Both father and son died from their injuries soon after the battle at Camlann in Cornwall."
(pause)
Hypnotherapist: "Why were you banished to a nunnery?"
Guinevere: "I committed adultery. That broke the law, but more importantly it destroyed Arthur's heart and spirit."
Hypnotherapist: "Yes. Were you able to accept that you never saw anyone again that you'd known and loved?"
Guinevere: "Yes, with time and a lot of work on myself."
Hypnotherapist: "Were there any pluses to being in the nunnery? Anything you learned to enjoy?"
Guinevere *(laughing ruefully)*: "God, yes! I did not miss all the political posturing and resultant over-thinking. All the strategy required to be Queen. I did not miss that at all. Life is so much simpler in the nunnery. I was treated fairly, but finally an equal with everyone else. What a blessed relief instead of the constant eyes and judging and gossip."

←→

Hypnotherapist: "Very good! Let's go back in time before Guinevere met Arthur. I'd like you to return to your student days with Merlin. What other options could you have taken? Really be in your power – set yourself free."
Guinevere: "Oh my, I so loved pretending to be a dragon! It was incredibly enjoyable – so powerful."
Hypnotherapist: "What did you look like as a dragon?"
Guinevere: "I was a red with gold dragon."
Hypnotherapist: "What did you like about being a dragon?"
Guinevere: "I'm able to help humanity without all that bother of a human brain. It is so freeing to not have that bothersome ego. I feel so free!"
Hypnotherapist: "Wonderful! Look around you carefully. Do you see any other dragons?"

←→

Guinevere: "Yes, I do. There's a male dragon – a big green one."
Hypnotherapist: "Remind me what was Arthur's last name?"
(long pause)
Guinevere: "Why, it was Pendragon. Pen Dragon – the pen is mightier than the sword, just like we practiced with the Knights at the Round Table. Uther was Arthur's father – Uther Pendragon."
(pause)
Guinevere: "I see it now – Arthur is the other dragon! We could have chosen a different life together. Perhaps we had a parallel life in another dimension?"
Hypnotherapist: "Exactly. I'd like you to call on that

playful, powerful red dragon energy. Embody it now – really BE it now in every cell of your being. Do so with unconditional love and acceptance for yourself – it will help balance up your seriousness."

Guinevere: *(nodding happily)* "Yes, I can do that."

← →

Hypnotherapist: "I'd like you to be that powerful dragon and fly yourself out to the desert. What does the desert look like?"

Guinevere: "There's lots of water. I see palm trees. It's an oasis. There are several of them."

Hypnotherapist: "There's going to be an object like a cube that comes to you. What do you notice about it?"

Guinevere: "It's a gold-hinged box. There's light beaming from it. There's so much light!"

Hypnotherapist: "Where was the box located?"

Guinevere: "By the first oasis."

Hypnotherapist: "Okay. I'd like you to see a ladder. Where does it go? Can you describe it."

Guinevere: "It's a long sturdy wooden ladder? It's propped up against the palm tree. We use it to get coconuts."

← →

Hypnotherapist: "Great. There's another energy being coming toward you. What is it?"

Guinevere: "It's so white! I see a large, healthy white unicorn."

Hypnotherapist: "Which direction did the unicorn come from?"

Guinevere: "It flew in from the Northwest. With me facing twelve o'clock, it came in from ten o'clock."

Hypnotherapist: "What happens next?"

Guinevere: "The unicorn is wonderfully playful. He's play bowing to me like a dog does when it wants another dog to play with it? There's a small sandstorm at two o'clock in the Northeast. I hear it's the winds of change."

← →

Hypnotherapist: "What do you do?"

Guinevere: "It's easy for me to shelter. The storm came to change the energy. I'm grateful for it. There's a beautiful calm afterwards."

Hypnotherapist: "I'd like you to vision some flowers around you. What do they look like?"

Guinevere: "I see flowers all around me. There's even that special cactus that only blooms once a year for a single day. I see purple flowers – blue – orange – yellow – every color. I see colors that are not seen on Earth."

Hypnotherapist: "Beautiful. What happens next?"

← →

(Guinevere takes a step back to allow Wendy to speak)

Wendy: "My new partner for my current life comes forward with a gold box."

Hypnotherapist: "What does he look like? What do you notice about him?"

Wendy: "He's in his fifties – perhaps early to mid-fifties? He's nice-looking. He's tall – around six feet. He can seem grouchy. It's a façade I see through right away. I'm not bothered by it as I understand it's only an outward appearance. He uses it as a shield when needed."

(pause)

Wendy: "He has blue eyes. I see a pure heart – integrity – a gentleness about him. There's some wounding, but he's healing it well. He helps heal other's hearts during the dream time. He's doing his own work. We'll each do our own work when we're together and work with one another, too. We won't be co-dependent in any way."

←→

Hypnotherapist: "Excellent. The desert image is now shrinking. You can return to your sanctuary we started from. Where are you?"

Wendy: "I'm in my own home, by my rose quartz crystal. The desert images are dissolving into my crystal. The crystal is helping me meet my new partner in current time in the physical."

Hypnotherapist: "What else do you see?"

Wendy *(laughing)*: "A big marquee sign that says, 'LET IT GO!' I can now release energy and forgive other people as well as myself easily and effortlessly. Elsa from Frozen is singing, 'Let It Go!' to help bring home the point. That's so funny."

Hypnotherapist: "What else does 'let it go' symbolize?"

Wendy: "I can now let go of everything that doesn't serve my highest good. I can now easily manifest all that is for my highest good for me and to serve humanity."

Hypnotherapist: "Fantastic! I'd like you to now see a spinning coil with your best health, your writing, your new romantic partner, other healthy relationships, your work, joy, and playfulness. Now allow that spinning coil to completely enter your energy field. Let it become one with you."

Wendy: "Got it. Wow – that's powerful! Thank you."

←→

Hypnotherapist: "Would you like to know what the symbols stood for in the desert exercise?"

Wendy: "Absolutely."

Hypnotherapist: "The cube represented you. The Light was the gold box. The dragon stood for your soul, and the ladder your helpers for prosperity. You can call on them to help you. You've got a big purpose – you need significant resources. Ask for them."

(pause)

Hypnotherapist: "The horse was a unicorn, which is a horse in its higher vibration. This is your new partner. It's a magical, playful relationship. He's going to help you not be so serious, but he truly does honor you just as you are. It's why he bowed to you. I see you bowing to him also. Neither of you will try to change the other. This is a healthy relationship."

←→

Hypnotherapist: "Let's turn now to your questions you wrote before the session and see which weren't already answered. You mentioned feeling hurt because you're hosting Christmas Eve for the family, and your daughter stated via email she is only going to attend for one hour. No church – no meal – she'll only join in for the family stocking party."

Wendy: "Yes. Why is this so difficult?"

Hypnotherapist: "She's an Empath. She's not yet grounded, so she absorbs so much energy it makes her ill. My recommendation is you respect her clearly stated boundaries. Keep holding the vision of there being more ease and effortlessness with her in the future. It may take a long time."

(pause)

Hypnotherapist: "In the meantime, say the Ho'oponopono forgiveness prayer to her once a day in relation to that lifetime of origin we found at the beginning of today's session. The one when she was made a human sacrifice and blamed you. Can you see a different outcome for that choice?"

←→

Wendy: "Oh my God yes! I wish I had grabbed her in my arms, and we had run – left that community. I don't care that we would have likely died. It would have been on our terms."

Hypnotherapist: "Exactly. Ask her to orient to the current day and time with you when you pray the forgiveness prayer. She's stuck in the past but doesn't know any of this consciously. It's why she's so angry with you, and then gets increasingly angry because she doesn't know why she's angry, as we discussed before."

(pause)

Hypnotherapist: "But that's in the past. We've released that lifetime of origin for you both."

←→

Wendy: "Thank you. This helps me tremendously. How do I resolve the angst I've felt around famous, historic, and

240

Biblical past lives?"

Hypnotherapist: "Remember that your intention magnetizes setting up the best experiences. Why don't you contact Walter Semkiw about your significant Joe DiMaggio memories?"

(pause)

Hypnotherapist: "Joe's been here for the entire session as has Mary Magdalen and Guinevere. They're not only your past lives – they're your Guides – they're you!"

(pause)

Hypnotherapist: "Contacting Walter would be a good exercise for you in coming out of the closet spiritually regarding one of your own famous past lives."

←→

Wendy: "Yes, I can do that. I'll reach out via his website. I've looked at it before. I know to let go of the outcome."

Hypnotherapist: "Yes, but first set your intention. I have two famous past lives of my own. I had to sit with one of them for thirty years before I was willing to speak about it publicly, where appropriate, as the fear of ridicule can be powerful."

(pause)

Hypnotherapist: "But we need to stand in our own truth, without asking others to believe it – to feel strong enough to share our own experiences. This takes you full circle to your 'let go of what other people think' life lesson, doesn't it?"

Wendy: *(slowly)* "Yes, it does. You're right. Thank you."

←→

Hypnotherapist: "Let's look at what happened when you were Mary Magdalen. Your youngest daughter S'rah Tamar was kidnapped by ETs when Matthias was full of ego while channeling. He didn't listen to you and didn't help you protect everyone from the sudden attack."

(pause)

Hypnotherapist: "This energy of your youngest daughter being kidnapped – ripped right out of your arms – her feeling that you failed to protect her leads to her current anxiety and feelings that you didn't take care of her. It compounds the human sacrifice experience in Mongolia – the lifetime of origin. We're healing both now."

Wendy: *(shrewdly)* "Will she accept the healing?"

Hypnotherapist: "It will be up to her Higher Self whether to accept the healing. She's approaching cautiously. It will take time. Keep praying the daily Ho'oponopono forgiveness prayer for her."

(pause)

←→

Hypnotherapist: "I'm still seeing the beautiful coil all

241

around you – there are lilacs. It's turned to lilac in color. It's gorgeous and powerful. It is manifesting for you in the physical, not just the etheric now. You will have lots of heavenly guidance. We've resolved all the trip wires that were around you. That residual energy that doesn't serve you has been cleaned up."

Wendy: "That's fantastic. Things don't feel so loaded now – your comment about trip wires is right on."

Hypnotherapist: "Like Guinevere, you just transformed to a dragon. When she so desired peace, it had a heavy feel to it as she was trying to lift a heavy load essentially on her own."

(pause)

Hypnotherapist: "But when she became a dragon and brought in the peace energy it became light and fun. You should follow her example as you have so much Guinevere energy. Look for alternate realities where your 'work' – even if it's world peace – is light and fun. This will free you up to manifest it in the physical in the present day and time."

Wendy: "That's a fantastic idea. Thank you."

Hypnotherapist: "You truly have the 'Wisdom of Avalon' energy. Keep working with Guinevere and you'll become one with her."

Wendy: "I will."

←→

Hypnotherapist: "You had a question about the official Joe DiMaggio books that were published as part of a baseball series. I agree they're likely heavily edited – professionally written."

(pause)

Hypnotherapist: "I think you're right he had a series of conversations with a ghostwriter who wasn't credited. They were likely published under DiMaggio's name as the author, as Joe was the brand. The contrast of his own voice coming through in your books accomplishes a powerful soul retrieval."

Wendy: *(laughing)* "Yes. It's Joe stepping to the plate – pun intended!"

Hypnotherapist: "Exactly. When you publish your first Joe book, your right foot that you injured as DiMaggio will fully heal. It doesn't serve us to carry past life injuries forward in time, although it does happen."

Wendy: "That's extremely helpful. I've noticed my hands are feeling so much better since we started this session. The stuck energy is flowing again."

Hypnotherapist: "Super. I'm hearing we can now wrap up and any questions you wrote before your session you'll be able to answer on your own via meditation. You're welcome to use and share the Persian future-telling exercise we did with the journey to the desert."

Wendy: "I can't thank you enough you found the lifetime of origin causing my daughter's estrangement."

←→

Our session was concluded. My follow-up meditations were especially powerful and insightful. I received future book advice and learned why my hands don't heat up as do many practitioners when I channel Reiki energy – I use color to heal, not heat.

A few days after this session I had the privilege to attend a large in-person Mother Mary blessing on December 14th, 2019. My Mary Magdalen identity was again confirmed without my asking. Mother Mary's main message was that 2020 was the year magic would return to the planet.

I felt Merlin's presence especially keenly from my Queen Guinevere past life. He'd been my friend, protector, and teacher. Magic is returning, but may not be what people expect. Time shifting and time travel is more and more possible. The ability to de-age with the Fountain of Youth energy is amplifying.

I didn't understand that magic is messy. Amazingly powerful, but sometimes confusing and chaotic until we learned to turn inward to achieve clarity and peace. Peace had to come from within, and the energy needed to be light and flowy to move freely as intended.

I was asked to speak for larger audiences including my first out-of-state engagement. It was for the prestigious IANDS (International Association of Near-Death Studies) group. I began publicly sharing my NDE (Near-Death Experience) from 1997 after not having spoken about it for almost twenty years - it took that long to digest.

I began studying NDEs as there was an amazing richness to mine with information that can't normally be accessed. I was not only able to connect with angels during my NDE but had a 'preview of coming attractions' regarding my life. What if I could help others access this type of powerful information during future life progressions? Would it help them live their life purpose and to have a happier, healthier life?

Chapter Twelve – The Midas Touch!

Two months later my Valentine's Day gift to myself was an amazing past-life regression trade with a new friend. We used light and warmth to align my pelvis, hips and back; brought peace and calm to my challenging digestive system; and flushed old issues from my bloodstream on February 14th, 2020.

The hypnotherapist suggested I move into a Hall of Doors. I was drawn to go through a purple door with an arch at the top. I immediately began recalling one of my many past lives as a nun.

←→

Hypnotherapist: "Why are you viewing a past life as a nun?"

Higher Self: "It's symbolic of a long line of lives where she took vows of poverty and experienced communal living."

Hypnotherapist: "But we now live in a capitalistic society."
(This irritated me greatly and I began to cry with frustration)

Hypnotherapist: "Why do you want to avoid the energy of the present reality? What's your name, please?"
(I switched from my Higher Self to the past life persona)

Maude: "My name is Maude."

Hypnotherapist: "Maude, where are you feeling the irritation and frustration in your body?"

Maude: "It's primarily in my heart and lungs."

Hypnotherapist: "What's needed to resolve the irritation? What do we need to adjust?"

←→

Adjustments were made to my energy body. I was now able to see that regardless if a client paid for their session with a credit card or merchant processing system like Square or PayPal that they are beautiful transactions entered into thoughtfully. They are meant to honor one another as an energy exchange.

We released religious conditioning snobbery about money. We balanced my ego. I released some 'holier than thou' energy of my distaste for money I had not been consciously aware of. I had not wanted 'to dirty my hands with money.' I released hearing my grandfather joke about 'filthy lucre' as I'd taken that literally as a child.

We laughed as we balanced my financial ego from having been a nun, a monk, and so many other lifetimes where I was expected to take a vow of poverty. That energy was now in direct conflict with my current life purpose to help others via philanthropy. No wonder I had felt so frustrated and burst into tears at the start of the session when the hypnotherapist said the word *capitalism!*

←→

Hypnotherapist: "Do you know where you are or have an idea of the time period when you were Maude?"

Wendy *(speaking as Maude)*: "Yes. I'm in France again. It feels like the 1200s."

Hypnotherapist: "What do you love about your nunnery? Are there things you enjoy?"

Maude: "Well, it's not a silent monastery. I find those exhausting. I've done my time in those and am glad that cycle is complete. I love the gardens – the land itself – the sun – the lush geography. Most of all I enjoy tending to the animals."

←→

Hypnotherapist: "What types of animals do you tend?"

Maude: "I tend the sheep. They're gentle, but not always the brightest creatures. They do better with a leader – with a caretaker."

Hypnotherapist: "I see. Do you look after them on your own?"

Maude: "No, I have a dog to help keep them safe together as a flock. He also helps me move them from pasture to pasture when we need to."

Hypnotherapist: "Do the sheep contribute in some way to the convent?"

←→

Maude: "Very much so. We shear them at the appropriate time and knit apparel and other items. We make what you'd now call textiles, I think, as we also weave."

Hypnotherapists: "What do you do with these products? Are they used just by those at the convent – at the nunnery?"

Maude: "No, we're able to both sell and trade what we

make. This is the main way we support our convent. We're quite a resourceful group."

(Midnight, Wendy's cat, began meowing loudly in the background)

Hypnotherapist: "Tell me more about your sheep dog? What is your dog like?"

Maude: "You'd likely call her a cattle dog now. She's a black and white female. Normally she gently herds the sheep together, but she can be forceful and fast if there's a ravine or cliff to keep them away from. She's a smart dog who knows how to work the herd."

Hypnotherapist: "Do you recognize this dog in your life now?"

Maude: "Oh! Look at that. She's Wendy's cat Midnight now. Her name was Benoit back then."

Hypnotherapist: "Excellent. So, kitty was meowing to get your attention to recognize him?"in

Maude: "Yes. He's a smart cat – more accurately, a smart, experienced soul. We've been together many times."

←→

Hypnotherapist: "Wonderful. I'd like you to move forward in time to when you're sharing a meal. What is that like?"

Maude: "It's just after Vespers. We're only to eat after evening prayers. There's one long table for all of us. It symbolizes community."

Hypnotherapist: "How many people are there, approximately?

Maude: "Hmm, let me count. It looks like there are about twenty-five to thirty of us in total."

Hypnotherapist: "Do you eat all your meals together?"

Maude: "We normally eat our mid-day and evening meals together. If we're out working in the fields, we carry our mid-day portions with us. It's a personal choice whether to have nourishment in the morning. That would be done on our own, often as we worked."

←→

Hypnotherapist: "I'm hearing you may wish to look for more communal feeling and experiences in your life now. You may wish to be open to different new communities."

(The Higher Self began speaking)

Higher Self: "Yes, she's open to new like-minded communities. Particularly as so many close friends have departed as there are no longer aligned interests."

Hypnotherapist: "Good. I'm hearing you should try new groups at least two to three times as there are likely to be different attendees. You may also want to round out your networking with at least one non-spiritual group."

Higher Self: "Yes, she does that via volunteering with the Dog Gone Seattle Rescue. That helps keep her grounded in

her body, among other benefits."
Hypnotherapist: "Excellent."

←→

Hypnotherapist: "Let's go ahead and share some love from Maude and her sisters to Wendy. I want her to feel very supported in her mission and to know that she is allowed some individuality just like she experienced as Maude. It feels like she's been going through some isolation that may not be ideal. Why is that – I'd like the Higher Self to comment, please."

Higher Self: "You are correct she's become quite isolated beyond the fact that she's a solopreneur working from home and lives alone. We needed things to become unstructured for her for a time to free up her energy. She's been so structured in so many of her previous lives as well as in this lifetime until recently."

(pause)
Higher Self: "But beyond that, the true cause of the isolation is she had such a tremendous belief system change that few could understand it or catch up to her rise in vibration – her level of consciousness – as she went up so fast."

(pause)
Higher Self: "Few friends remained aligned with her through the major spirituality downloads that she received over the last few years. She tried to share it with friends, but it became 'TMI' (Too Much Information) for them."

(pause)
Higher Self: "She now knows how to temper it. She was overenthusiastic for people that weren't necessarily interested or ready."

Hypnotherapist: "So what do you see as we look ahead?"

←→

Higher Self: "Her community will come. It won't be her family, which is fine, although that was a tough transition for them all. Her mother is primarily bewildered by the extreme change although she did her best to be supportive. That showed growth on the mother's part."

(pause)
Higher Self: "Her father and stepmother are uncomfortable and don't want to discuss Wendy's career, beliefs, metaphysics, or energy. Her eldest daughter and her fiancé can tolerate a small amount of discussion only because they are extremely kind and respectful individuals."

(pause)
Higher Self: "But they can't relate. Her youngest daughter is a no go – a hard stop as has been discussed in earlier sessions."

Hypnotherapist: "So how is she feeling about these current circumstances? Can any of this energy be shifted to be more supportive for her."

Higher Self: "She's worked through it in large part. She's mostly in a good place with it. She knows doors close when they're meant to but didn't expect it to be so long for new ones to open."

(pause)

Higher Self: "She's fortunate to live on the West Coast of the United States. It's a spiritually open place with little organized religion and Native American, Wiccan, Pagan and New Age practitioners. It's a good place for her to be, which is why we led her here."

←→

Hypnotherapist: "Thank you. I'd like Maude to dial into one special friend – one sister of the heart she may have shared a special bond with when they lived in the convent. Is there anyone from the life in France who's in her life now?"

Maude: "No, there's not. She's fine with that."

Hypnotherapist: "Okay. Let's look at your finances and abundance in a different way. You mentioned issues with pelvic misalignment and back and hip pain. Can the Higher Self improve the blood flow and strengthen the lower chakras?"

(pause)

Maude: "Yes, that's been done."

Hypnotherapist: "Excellent! Maude, let's return to the nunnery and I'd like you to move forward to a day that had a pleasant surprise – something that will help your current day life."

(pause)

←→

Maude: *(enthusiastically)* "Oh, this is so interesting! I see now our convent was not really supported by the Church. We were all encouraged to self-support to make the money go further, but few accomplished it. We did so – quite handily."

Hypnotherapist: "Excellent! How did you do it?"

Maude: "This nunnery life is such a wonderful contrast to a more recent nun life where she was starved and beaten by the Mother Superior. This is such a lovely, pleasant balance."

(pause)

Maude: "There was a male patriarchy, but it's not overly authoritative especially given our time period."

Hypnotherapist: "Tell me more – you said your convent was quite resourceful?"

Maude: "Yes. Our convent functioned well on our own with the local villagers as well as with the Church. We earned financial freedom with our clever work, and our trade and sales efforts. We had our pulse on the marketplace of what would sell or be a good trade. Our goods were high quality and practical as well as beautifully made."

Hypnotherapist: "Fantastic. I'd like you to breath that financial freedom into Wendy in her current life today – let's reignite it!"

←→

Higher Self: "Yes. We're helping her release her limited thinking that only traditional employment with a 401k and health plan for the family can support her well. We're showing her so many other possibilities. They're endless!"

(pause)

Higher Self: "She flourished in a convent in France in the thirteenth century. They had the intelligence to be self-sufficient, which is quite remarkable for that small a nunnery."

Hypnotherapist: "That's amazing. Maude, what was your specific role?"

Maude: "I've had lots of lives as a successful merchant. It's an archetype. I was able to sort through the many ideas and enthusiasm that the sisters and I had and then match up the few best products and services that there was a strong demand for. Something there was a true need and desire for. Something people would pay for or trade well for."

(pause)

Maude: "I was able to find the unmet needs – the perfect niches for us. The riches are in the niches, so to speak."

Hypnotherapist: "That's wonderful. What else?"

←→

Maude: "I kept us away from offering items that were well-supplied. Products or services where there was a race to the bottom with constant price-cutting. I assessed whether the item or service would scale at the right size for what we could produce, and whether we'd enjoy producing it."

(pause)

Maude: "That was the key. Would it be made with love and pleasure? People sense that energy and will pay more for a well-made product. What we did is similar energy to Etsy now."

(pause)

Maude: "We were not the cheapest. That was not our goal. We were simply the best with our few products and services."

Hypnotherapist: "Can you make this clear how it applies to Wendy's life now?"

←→

Maude: "Certainly. We want her to offer her products – in her case, her books – and her energy healing services based on assessing the need. She can feel into the marketplace demand and match that with whether it will support her well. She can work with her specific Guides on this, including Joe DiMaggio, Guinevere, and Mary Magdalen."

(pause)

Maude: "She's been trying to do this for years with Master Hilarion and Fortunata, but with the disconnects from capitalism it hasn't worked."

(pause)

Maude: "There's a reason her Guides pushed her hard to earn an MBA degree so young this lifetime. She earned that degree by the time she was twenty-two years old. She needed the Master's in Business Administration to balance her spiritual ego not liking money."

(pause)

Maude: "She'll now fully embrace money isn't good or bad. It's simply a tool to be used wisely. She needs financial resources to fulfill her purpose of philanthropy to help others. It's part of why she was so heartbroken when she and the boyfriend she had so many lives with broke up. They were meant to do philanthropy together this lifetime. They were a great team as philanthropists in previous lives."

(pause)

Maude: "So now she'll accomplish it first on her own, and then with a new partner instead. Full steam ahead!"

← →

Hypnotherapist: "Wonderful. I'd like you to now go to the last day of your life, Maude. Your 'death' – knowing the soul is eternal and doesn't die. What is your death like?"

Maude: "I'm happy to go Home to the Light. It's easy and peaceful. I'm in my early sixties. I'm simply done with what I came to do. I'm well-satisfied."

(pause)

Maude: "There are people to help me cross over – friends sit with me. You'd call them death doulas or death midwives now. I consider it a happy death. I feel great contentment."

Hypnotherapist: "Perfect! Let's stay there for a moment and really let that contentment sink in. You can feel that in your life now."

Maude: "Yes. Good idea."

Hypnotherapist: "What else do you experience as you cross over during this happy death?"

Maude: "There's so much light – so much ease and grace. This helps balance out so many warrior lives. So many lives filled with lack. So much exhaustion from working so hard to make life on Earth work. She's very tired, you know – her soul is incredibly tired."

Hypnotherapist: "What's your last thought?"

Maude: "My last thought is 'Yippee! I'm going Home!'"

←→

Hypnotherapist: "You've now crossed over to the Light. Just rise up. You're welcome to go where you want at Home. Where do you go?"

Maude: "I'm so tired as I try to rise to the Light. I catch a ride on a cloud."

Hypnotherapist: "Wonderful. Would you like to go to a place of rest and relaxation?"

Maude: "Absolutely. I'm going to my favorite rose garden. It was known as the Garden of Gethsemane in Jerusalem."

Hypnotherapist: "Notice if you need any TLC for yourself – for your soul."

Maude: "I recently dropped my heart wall. I'd appreciate my heart being strengthened."

(pause)

Maude: "Oh! That's being applauded. My Guides are coming in. They're telling me it will become easy to live and love again without a heart wall for protection. This will become fully automatic for my soul as Wendy as my trust is returning."

(pause)

Maude: "I'm fully trusting once again that the Divine – the Universe – always has my back. That is the most critical decision a person can make that will impact their life on Earth. The reason is your thoughts – your expectations – manifest into reality."

←→

Hypnotherapist: "Fantastic. What else?"

Maude: "The few times that Wendy lapses back into what I'll call 'stinking thinking,' she immediately stops it. This is critical. An example of this is she is overly independent, which can be a form of not fully loving yourself – of not receiving. It's a trauma response."

(pause)

Maude: "Someone will offer her money in the simplest way. For example, a friend will offer to pick up the bill at lunch. Wendy will knee-jerk into turning it down as she was conditioned too strongly 'to pay her own way.' This is an old tape."

(pause)

Maude: "After her session today we want her to throw out her old manual can opener in her kitchen. That will help stop this type of old tape reaction. It's time for a new can opener – it will symbolize more ease and grace for her."

Hypnotherapist: "Anything else on that topic?"

Maude: "Rejuvenation in the garden will continue in the background. It's becoming second nature for her to love and honor herself first – she's not quite there yet. Today will help."

←→

Hypnotherapist: "Wonderful. I'd now like to address her soul – her Higher Self – with the questions she wrote before today's session."

Higher Self: "The Higher Self is here."

Hypnotherapist: "Fantastic. How can she improve her overall health – the back and hip pain – the leg length difference?"

Higher Self: "We have much to say here. Are you recording for her? She doesn't remember her sessions well as she's deep in trance."

Hypnotherapist: "Yes."

Higher Self: "Perfect. She should visualize bringing in additional light to heal her back and hips. This will help her get more active. She's tried so hard to do thirty-minute walks but gets defeated by the pain."

(pause)

Higher Self: "Over time she will be able to return to work with a trainer at the gym to set up a specific plan for her. Step by step she will then be able to lose twenty pounds which will address her cholesterol and hemoglobin A1C levels being high."

(pause)

Higher Self: "She needs to visualize her bloodstream moving faster – she's now released the old fears and can flow her bloodstream."

(pause)

Higher Self: "Her Guides will help her walk. She is to call on an Angel and ask who will walk with her that day. There's not one specific Angel. It will change from day-to-day. When it is rainy or cold out, she can walk indoors on the stair-steppers. Those are one of the exercises she can do with her many exercise limits."

(pause)

Higher Self: "She is not to do heavy or free weights. Her wrists can't handle it since the wrist surgeries. They also take heavy use from the keyboarding as she writes."

(pause)

Higher Self: "We will make sure she meets with the right trainer. Many of them will not understand her specific needs with the scoliosis and fully fused spine and the injury limits."

Hypnotherapist: "We appreciate the specificity. Is there more?"

←→

Higher Self: "Yes. We prefer her walking outside. Being in nature is so helpful to clear her energy and ground her.

She should schedule a thirty-minute walk on her calendar three times a week. If it's pouring outside or too cold, then she should go to the gym."

(pause)

Higher Self: "She is to continue with the Feldenkrais exercises as a form of rehabilitation until we nudge her to stop. Currently she still needs the energetic chiropractor. Sensory deprivation floating as well as massage are quite helpful. She needs it all. You can start to see why she feels some despair regarding the amount of maintenance that is required to restore her health?"

Hypnotherapist: "Yes. Is there more info on this topic?"

Higher Self: "Yes. She will lose weight by walking and her energy will come back. She is eating cleaner and cleaner but does need calories. We do not want her to go on an ultra-low-calorie diet to lose weight. That would not suit her energy requirements."

(pause)

Higher Self: "Healthy weight will be attained and maintained by healing the physical pain response to allow her to up her activity levels. She is not to do chair yoga. Yoga has not been found to be useful for her."

(pause)

Higher Self: "That is all regarding her physical health."

← →

Hypnotherapist: "Thank you. She's noticing energy challenges with attending social activities that she enjoys. What's going on?"

Higher Self: "We've pulled her back from these events temporarily as she was doing too much clearing work. It was depleting her energy in an unneeded way."

Hypnotherapist: "What should she do instead? We talked about the need for community and for socialization given that she works from home and lives alone."

Higher Self: "Let's look at the dog rescue events as an example. She should ask Saint Francis and the Angels to go to these events before she arrives. They can clear the space, the dogs and the people more efficiently than she can without having their energy depleted."

(pause)

Higher Self: "This will stop her over-working. This is the reason we had to temporarily roadblock her attending events. It was for her own good. She can resolve this now that she understands it consciously from today's work."

← →

Hypnotherapist: "Excellent. How's her nutrition looking?"

Higher Self: "It is stellar. We are so proud of her. She needs to make sure she gets sixty-four ounces of quality water a day is my only recommendation."

(pause)
Higher Self: "Not drinking alcohol is perfect for her. It's too much sugar for her current bloodstream. No one notices when she hosts the dog rescue event at a microbrewery and doesn't have a beer herself as the host. It's not necessary. We've asked her to drink water at these events."

←→

Hypnotherapist: "Great. What about her manifesting? She had a broken heart for many lifetimes. Did this interfere?"
Higher Self: "Yes, it certainly did. Her heart is now open. She's manifesting from a healthy, loving heart versus from a broken heart. There hasn't been enough time to see the change from manifesting from her heart versus trying to manifest from her root chakra."

(pause)
Higher Self: "She hadn't known to manifest from her heart. It was tremendous work to try to manifest from her root. She had to rebuild her root as she was born without one. That made life quite challenging."

←→

Hypnotherapist: "Why didn't she have a root chakra?"
Higher Self: "Because her powerful energy was being stolen. She had to learn how to be fully sovereign in her energy and not have her power taken without her permission."

(pause)
Higher Self: "She had shut down her root in previous lifetimes. She chose to be born without a root chakra this lifetime to address her boundaries and to be sovereign. She had to rebuild her root and replace her heart and sacral chakras."

(pause)
Higher Self: "It's been a tremendous amount of work, but it broke the cycle of her energy being stolen. The root is now fully functional. She has rebuilt or replaced all her chakras. This is a major accomplishment! It's why we guided her to become a Reiki Master. She also uses Reiki healing in her sessions to serve clients."

←→

Hypnotherapist: "Thank you. She'd like to confirm is she still on the Saint Germaine plan for longevity? I'm not sure what that means. What can you tell us?"
Higher Self: "Yes, she is. The movie *The Age of Adaline* starring Blake Lively, and Harrison Ford has that energy. Certain individuals who have a large life purpose may choose the Saint Germaine plan, as one example. You remain in one healthy human body for several hundred years to assist humanity and fulfill a large life purpose."

(pause)

Higher Self: "Step number one is to fully align with Divine Will and Divine Right Purpose. You then resolve any health challenges one-by-one. You choose the age when you felt happiest and healthiest to de-age to that time energetically and physically using the Fountain of Youth energy and other techniques."

Hypnotherapist: "So this really is possible here and now?"

←→

Higher Self: "Yes, it is. It's not new. The Lemurians lived for thousands of years because they knew how to be their light body while here on Earth. It's simply returning to the Light while still in a healthy human body. It's healing your inner child and embracing your shadow if you want to use all that modern jargon. You also begin to integrate the conscious mind with the unconscious mind and the sub-conscious. They no longer need to be so compartmentalized."

Hypnotherapist: "This is fascinating. Why is it called the Saint Germaine Plan?"

Higher Self: *(laughing)* "It's not. Wendy made that term up! She needs to trademark it. She calls it that when she talks with us about this. It makes us all laugh, which is de-aging."

(pause)

Higher Self: "Here's the history. Le Comte de Saint Germain (The Count of Saint Germain) lived for hundreds of years in France during his last life on Earth. He was born in Bavaria. He ascended to become Ascended Master Saint Germaine, keeper of the Violet Flame of transmutation."

(pause)

Higher Self: "The Violet Flame is Wendy's primary flame this lifetime. Everyone has one of the seven flames as their primary flame."

(pause)

Higher Self: "She's known Saint Germaine in multiple lifetimes. Her cat Midnight is Saint Germaine's black panther. The moment she saw the film *The Age of Adaline*, she saw the opportunity and began exploring it."

(pause)

Higher Self: "I'd like to encourage everyone to follow their intuitive hunches, no matter how outlandish they may seem. This is so important. This is how magic is woven! This is how miracles land on Earth. This is how the Heaven on Earth energy is brought forth."

←→

Hypnotherapist: "Thank you. Anything more on that topic?"

Higher Self: "Yes. Wendy is to be a teacher on this topic. Clients can work with her in this area if their Higher Self and Guides suggest they consider the Saint Germaine Plan. The right intention and purpose are required. It's not to be undertaken due to a fear of dying. That won't work."

Hypnotherapist: "Yes, I can see that."

Higher Self: "Good. Wendy had a reading from a talented palm-reader. This is a field that has attracted many charlatans, but she saw a heart-centered, gifted palm reader."

(pause)

Higher Self: "He remarked how long her lifeline is. Most lifelines end on the palm. Hers wraps all the way around the thumb and wrist. This is an indicator that the Saint Germaine Plan might be an option for someone. They've preplanned the possibility. It's a choice open to them."

(pause)

Higher Self: "The question to ask yourself before you embark on that plan is whether your life is fun – is it delightful? If yes – keep going. If not, watch for the next off-ramp – the next exit point. The soul knows when to go Home. The soul chooses."

(pause)

Higher Self: "Wendy has already chosen not to take any of her five planned exit points. She'll know what to do at the right time to go Home with ease and grace."

←→

Hypnotherapist: "Thank you. So much food for thought. She'd like to confirm did her soul drop the body recently in a parallel life. She had a specific dream where she was shown that information. Can this help with her energy challenge?"

Higher Self: "Yes, we can confirm her dreams are quite important. She should ask for spiritual guidance in her dreams and write them down."

(pause)

Higher Self: "Her Guides will then interpret them with her. She no longer needs to work with a dream interpreter. 'To thine own self be true,' as Shakespeare wrote in *Hamlet*. She's to interpret her own dreams going forward."

←→

Hypnotherapist: "Thank you. Does she need more energy? Is there an opportunity to have more energy knowing she dropped her body in a parallel life?"

Higher Self: "We are going to allow her to draw more energy from the Higher Self that's at Home with the Light, not directly from the other simultaneous life. That is not a good practice. You want your energy to be from as pure a source as possible."

Hypnotherapist: "Is it true she incarnated with only twenty percent of her total energy? If so, why did she make that choice?"

←→

Higher Self: "Yes, it's true she only brought twenty percent of her energy to this life. The purpose was to learn to be as efficient as possible with her energy. She also chose multiple parallel lives beginning in the 1800s through the 1900s right up to current day."
(pause)
Higher Self: "Her soul has now dropped three parallel lives to her current incarnation. There is plenty of energy now back at Home for her to download. Her past/ parallel life as Joe DiMaggio has ended; her parallel life as the Twin-Flame who was a male attorney has ended; and her transgender life she just dreamed about has ended."
(pause)
Higher Self: "She can now bring in ten percent more energy. That may not sound like a lot, but it is a fifty percent increase in her energy since she only has twenty percent of her soul incarnated as Wendy."
(pause)
Higher Self: "We're going to allow this download from Source as her life purpose has become so expansive. This isn't done often. She's maxed her efficiency with the existing energy."
(pause)
Higher Self: "The new energy will allow her to become healthy. It is fresh energy from Source that has not endured so many traumas and surgeries that she's had this life. We are sending the new energy in a focused manner especially to her back, hips, her wrists, and right foot."

←→

Hypnotherapist: "Thank you, that's wonderful. What do you recommend for the best self-care?"
Higher Self: "To make every single day Valentine's Day! To love and take care of herself first."
(pause)
Higher Self: "We'd like her to notice the time. It is 4:44 PM Pacific Time. 444 is a powerful Angel number indicating it is time to fully honor her intuition and inner wisdom. It is time to fully embrace her divine life purpose and to know she will be fully backed to do so. The Angels are working especially closely with her."

←→

Hypnotherapist: "Beautiful. Are there any other past lives with financial blocks in addition to the life as Maude? Are there any more lives with vows of poverty or lack she should release?"
Higher Self: "Yes. There are many Native American, First People and aborigine – now called indigenous people –

257

lives where this soul was a healer. It was a privilege to be a healer. It was viewed as a gift from God or the Goddess. Healers were not to be paid for their gifts."

(pause)

Higher Self: "This outdated energy doesn't serve her. It's going to take her just a bit more time to heal these lives. We will do so during her meditations and dream time. It won't take any effort on her part. This discussion completes it."

(pause)

Higher Self: "There is a brass band coming in for her now. They're marching down the street and there is so much cheering! It's like what happens regularly in New Orleans. The brass band is saying her clearing up this old energy is huge – this should be celebrated!"

←→

Hypnotherapist: "That's amazing. Does she have any off planet lives to resolve? She's a Star seed who's incarnated on other planets. Are there any off-world contracts to resolve?"

Higher Self: "She's done all the cleansing and purging needed in those areas. She's all clear. The challenges have been met and cleared. We want her physical body to hear the resounding cry of 'All clear!' "

(pause)

Higher Self: "We're bringing in a rose from above to fill her entire system so she can enjoy the fragrant scent of the 'all clear' signal. She should use the Resurrection Flame more. Read that meditation from Aurelia Louise Jones *Seven Sacred Flames* book before bed to build her confidence after so many challenges."

(pause)

Higher Self: "This is now complete. I'm dusting my hands off to symbolize it's complete! I'm clapping my hands. Her heart is opening like a lotus flower with relief. She really needed that energy increase. Her adrenals are exhausted, and her Vitamin D levels have tanked. She's addressing these needs with blood work and high-quality supplements via a naturopathic physician."

←→

Hypnotherapist: "I'm sure she'll be so grateful. Are there particular affluent lives or lives when money and support went well that she should work with?"

Higher Self: "Yes, there are three. She should tune back into the lifetime as Mary Magdalen to visualize how well she handled that family money. It was quite brilliant how she helped finance Jesus' ministry and more."

Hypnotherapist: "And the second?"

Higher Self: "She should continue working with her success as Guinevere. Queen Guinevere of Camelot. Born to wealth and power and married to the same. She worked

hard to broker and to finance peace for all the lands. This time it will be achieved. And Guinevere won't have to be a dragon about it unless she chooses to!"
(laughs heartily)

←→

Hypnotherapist: "And the third life that would help her in this area?"

Higher Self: "Joe DiMaggio for his raw talent and his ability to create himself as a valuable brand. He was a forerunner in that area and did a lot of good with his money."
(pause)

Higher Self: "When it was time for DiMaggio to create wealth for a special project such as a children's hospital, he simply made an appearance and signed items like baseballs and baseball bats. This could generate two million dollars or more in a few hours because he knew not to overdo it. He didn't saturate his brand."
(pause)

Higher Self: "We encourage her to have fun with visualizing and creating the future endowments, charities, and philanthropic projects. She needs to then feel the emotions. We'd like her to create her destiny in this area for 2020 and beyond."

←→

Hypnotherapist: "Thank you. She wanted confirmation did her Twin-Flame pass on recently. I believe you referred to that earlier."

Higher Self: "Yes, he did. She didn't really notice it as she had already said her goodbyes with him and cut the cords."
(pause)

Higher Self: "She had already made her peace with him after doing everything possible for several years to try to help him heal. It was selfless, powerful work that helped her heal herself especially as they were Twins."
(pause)

Higher Self: "It would have been more heartbreak for her if they did reunite. He would have died suddenly from a massive heart attack six to twelve months later."

←→

Hypnotherapist: "We hear a lot about Twin souls at Home being Guides for the Twin that's living on Earth. Would this be beneficial for her?"

Higher Self: "He hasn't rejuvenated enough yet. He's still in what you would consider an energy hospital or place of healing at Home. He is the soul who was Yeshua ben Joseph when she was Magdalen. He needs to fully heal, and then he will help her. Let him come to her. She'll know when he does."

Hypnotherapist: "Thank you. You mentioned she was successful at cutting the cords with him before he passed on. Many people believe Twin-Flames can't cut the cords between them – there's always a connection to the other half of their soul?"

Higher Self: "Let's not generalize. The Twin-Flame journey is to heal and become complete in oneself. To become fully sovereign. That means no cords of attachment."

← →

Hypnotherapist: "Thank you. What about her Twin-Ray that she was to meet? Is that energy all squared away."

Higher Self: "She did everything possible for her Twin-Ray. When they were no longer an appropriate match, she ended it before they met in the physical. This was wise and an act of self-love on her part. He told her via telepathy he'd decided it would be 'fun to play the field.' She greatly appreciated his honesty. She opted out."

(pause)

Higher Self: "The runner-chaser energy between Twins will end as Earth's vibration continues to rise. The harsh life reviews of oneself can end, too. It's certainly not an all-loving Mother/ Father God sitting in judgement of you, nor any of your Guides and Elders. They're to help enlighten you and lift you up."

(pause)

← →

Higher Self: "Her work with the Daily OM's twenty-one-day meditation to 'Break the Grip of Past Lovers' was especially powerful. She and her new partner have done everything they need to do to meet on the physical plane."

(pause)

Higher Self: "There is true respect between them. Both are in full integrity. They will continue to have excellent communication with love and respect for one another."

(pause)

Higher Self: "Once they meet and she fully enters a romance with him she may become anxious or fearful at some point. That's when we want her to zip her lip. She has the self-control to do that. She can resolve any angst versus stuffing it, projecting or deflecting."

(pause)

Higher Self: "She has plenty of tools including repeating that twenty-one-day guided meditation I mentioned. She knows how to take care of herself well for the first time. She will be in this romance with an open heart."

← →

Hypnotherapist: "That's fantastic. What about her former husband and former boyfriend?"

Higher Self: "She's cleared the decks fully with both. The boyfriend was actively blocking her from being happy with someone new. We call this energy, 'wanting to have your cake and eat it too.' He rejected her due to not being able to address his own wounds but wanted to keep her in his life to feed his ego. His 'I love you but I'm not in love with you' declaration was truthful, but not workable energy for a healthy romance."

Hypnotherapist: "So what was the lesson?"

Higher Self: "She had to fully assert her power. She had to not only tell him but to show him in multiple states of consciousness he did not have a claim over her. She won't open the door to him again. It's complete."

(pause)

Higher Self: "Joe DiMaggio helped her take care of this in a humorous way during a dream. Her former boyfriend is highly telepathic and was muscling his way into her dreams. Joe not only had a man-to-man talk with him in the locker room – both were professional athletes – but moved him forcefully out through the door to the left. The left indicates the past; doors straight ahead are present day and doors to the right represent the future."

(pause)

Higher Self: "Joe then not only locked the door and swallowed the key quite comically in front of Wendy, but nailed the door shut and glue-gunned the edges to seal it. She woke up laughing. It was empowering."

(pause)

Higher Self: "She has no ill will toward her former boyfriend. But his pushing his way into her dreams to get her attention – which is energy – needed to stop. It was a form of psychic attack."

← →

Hypnotherapist: "Wonderful. Are you able to share an update on when she'll meet the new partner?"

Higher Self: "It should be soon. Literally just a few weeks or a month or two. We've been working on the best location. They were to meet at a dog rescue event she hosts, but he had to go out-of-town on business. There were flight delays due to the weather. He was not able to fly back in time to attend the event where they were to meet. He was stuck at an airport hotel overnight. She learned these details in a dream the night before the event to understand why he wasn't there."

(pause)

Higher Self: "She questioned was this wishful thinking on her part. I'd like to reassure her it is not. Her new partner moved here from out-of-state for two reasons: his new job and to be with Wendy."

261

(pause)
Higher Self: "We had someone at the dog rescue event mention the storm and flight delays to her. They validated her dream without her asking. We send her signs like this all the time as we do to everyone. We look forward to the day when more will heed their guidance from the Divine."

(pause)
Higher Self: "The question is who's paying attention and accepting the messages, signs and synchronicities? You need a balanced ego and discernment to be willing to explore this. You can simply express your open heart and your curiosity. 'I wonder if this is a sign?' allows us to then send more signs and synchronicities to you."

←→

Hypnotherapist: "What can you share about their relationship from a spiritual perspective?"
Higher Self: "They do not have a lot of shared past life energy together. Let's consider their new relationship a beautiful blank slate. They are not soul mates nor is there karma between them. They are not Twin-Flames or Twin-Rays."

(pause)
Higher Self: "He is simply a compatible life partner who's met her two or three times before. They have not been husband and wife or parent and child. They have enough connection, aligned energy and values and purpose to be compatible."

Hypnotherapist: "Is there anything that needs to happen to have them have a successful meeting and then a relationship over time?"
Higher Self: "He needs to do a little more heart-healing. She can place her hands over his heart right now and teach him how to do this for himself. She can do this for him as well as for herself, and vice versa both in the etheric at this moment, and later in the physical."

(pause)
Higher Self: "They are a beautiful white canvas – a beautiful blank slate to create their romance together."

←→

Hypnotherapist: "That sounds fabulous. Since it's Valentine's Day, would they like to do some painting and creating together right now to practice?"
Higher Self: "Yes. Both are saying yes! Let's paint and create."
Hypnotherapist: "Wonderful. Let's sit them side-by-side with their artist palettes and some fresh paint to create their future together. What happens?"
Higher Self: "She's released the rigid marriage and 'til death do we part' thinking. That was crucial as she may live hundreds of years or more in this one healthy body."

(pause)
Higher Self: "Meeting the primary soul mate she'd contracted to marry and discovering he was not capable of monogamy or commitment provided the opportunity to free up that overly rigid thinking. Bless him for his honesty with her as difficult as it was for them both."

←→

Hypnotherapist: "What's happening now?"
Higher Self: "They're having fun being silly and saying, 'Let's paint in France! Let's wear French berets and go out in the beautiful countryside with our baguette and cheeses and wine to paint.'"
(pause)
Higher Self: *(laughing)* "Honestly neither of them can paint – that makes it even more fun! They're laughing so hard as they realize it's about the process and the time together. It's not about the paintings."
(pause)
Higher Self: "They hear one another quite well. He can initiate communicate with her as can she with him. This is important as she didn't enjoy having to always initiate the telepathy with previous potential partners."
(pause)
Higher Self: "It felt like chasing to her. It didn't feel feminine. It made her tired and even sad over time."

←→

Hypnotherapist: "I understand. But this connection – this pairing is different, right? It feels healthy and fun and light for both parties?"
(pause)
Higher Self: "Yes. He has an excellent traditional career. It will be steadying for her, as she's been called to serve in a different manner. It will be a complementary relationship for both."
(pause)
Higher Self: "He hears her quite well and can not only initiate conversation and connection between them but can remote-view through her eyes, with her permission."
Hypnotherapist: "What types of things has she been choosing to show him?"
Higher Self: "Most often a dog rescue event. She knows to show him street signs and the address and microbrewery name. That's where they are most likely to meet. It won't be at his employer. That campus is huge. It won't be at her home. They need to be out and about to meet."

←→

Hypnotherapist: "Wonderful. How are her client sessions going?"
Higher Self: "They're A+ in quality. The only caveat we'd

263

like to share with her is to continue to plan well for each session and then be willing to throw out the plan. Be willing to toss it right out the window and follow her guidance during session as to how she can best help her client."
(pause)
Higher Self: "Some people are so blocked or lack knowledge of themselves that they can't allow their Higher Self or Guides to speak through them even with her facilitation. She should continue to try for thirty minutes and at least three different ways to help empower them."
(pause)
Higher Self: "At that point she should ask permission if she should share any impressions, but only one item at a time. Work to make it a natural ebb and flow conversation. Don't take over and turn it into a channeling or psychic reading. That is not the purpose of the type of past life regression healing sessions we ask her to facilitate."
(pause)
Higher Self: "All the ingredients are there for her to make the best possible soup with each client. She won't know exactly which recipe they're to create together until they have the session. Enjoy some mystery to life – expect it to be fun and enjoyable!"

←→

Hypnotherapist: "Very good. Speaking of channeling, how are her Magdalen channeled sessions going?"
Higher Self: "She needs to add more information to her website about them. Also get into the habit of reviewing and updating her website every three months. Then do a deeper dive every six months, and a comprehensive update annually."
(pause)
Hypnotherapist: "Why is this necessary – just to keep it current?"
Higher Self: "Yes, but at a deeper level it's to keep it reflecting her energy changes. As she raises her vibration, we want her to continue to attract ideal clients. When your website no longer reflects your current energy, you'll begin to attract clients that aren't aligned. That's a signal to update the website and other written materials."
Hypnotherapist: "Very good. I'm hearing it's both a good business practice and a good energy practice."
Higher Self: "Exactly."

←→

Hypnotherapist: "What is her best scheduling for writing? She states she loves it but finds it time-consuming. She'd like to improve her efficiency."
Higher Self: "The ideal writing and publishing work schedule is currently to block out a half day for four hours twice a week minimum, or one full eight-hour day."

(pause)
Higher Self: "But first she needs to get more flow to her work and to her life. The way to do this is to get up in the morning and to review her schedule for that day. She can then ask, 'Is this still my top priority to be in service?' That will allow more natural movement in her life – it won't be overly rigid."

(pause)
Higher Self: "Her daily task lists are too long. We need her to more *be* the natural healer and energy being she's meant to be, versus so much *do* energy. More being – more embodiment of the Divine - less doing. She's struggling with this concept. It feels lazy and unfocused to her after thirty plus years in industry."

(pause)

←→

Hypnotherapist: "Any suggestions how to accomplish that?"

Higher Self: "Yes. She needs to consciously remove some of the tasks from her list every day and trust the important things will get done. We her Higher Self and Guides breathe a sigh of relief when she deletes anything from her list! It allows new, more beneficial energy to find a place to land."

(pause)
Higher Self: "This new way to accomplish her writing will both provide a more expansive schedule. Simply work each day first on the things that have the most energy to them. What feels fun and exciting? Start there and use that momentum."

Hypnotherapist: "Thank you. Anything else on this topic?"

Higher Self: "Yes. Clearing your living spaces – your homes, offices, garages and cars – allows new beneficial energy to find space to land."

(pause)
Higher Self: "Giving things away you don't need and haven't touched in a year or more allows for upgrades to your life. That's why the Marie Kondo de-cluttering and purging system has been such a runaway hit. You need only keep and enjoy the items that are uniquely useful or sentimental for you."

←→

Hypnotherapist: "She mentioned struggling to find the right publishing attorney to help her with decisions to make about this book. Wendy has contacted six or seven attorneys but hasn't been able to find the right one. What's going on?"

Higher Self: "It's an issue of Divine Right Timing. We do want her to work with an attorney to dot her I's and cross her T's. She will find the ideal attorney soon via her friend

Karen or via the Washington State Bar Association. That consult will help her determine who the book is to be published by and a few other key decisions."

(pause)

Higher Self: "Joe DiMaggio would like to step forward now to speak as Wendy's Guide."

← →

Hypnotherapist: "Please do."

Joe: "The book is all in your hands now, Wendy, once you speak with the attorney. We are to complete my book together. Thank you for giving me a voice to tell my story. I'm helping you find the best publishing advice available as well as smoothing things out on the front-end energetically with all parties involved. I know you know what I mean."

(pause)

Wendy: "Yes, I do. Thank you, Joe. I'm so grateful."

Joe: "I'd like you to focus on healing my physical injuries you're carrying. Your right foot, your back, your right shoulder and elbow. I got put through the mill as does every professional athlete, but it's time for you to heal your body to accomplish your life purpose."

(pause)

Joe: "The books that were published under my name when I was alive were not technically written by me. The books were based on interviews with me and were written by a professional ghostwriter. I was a high school dropout and not much of a reader or writer, unlike Marilyn. She loved to read and to journal."

(pause)

Joe: "Those books were quite polished. This time we're writing my book together in a different way. We can continue to dialog back and forth, and you put the words on the page for me. This is a great system – just keep going! That's all you need to do."

(pause)

Joe: "Does she have other questions I can answer? The Higher Self says there are more on the list they wrote together for today's session."

← →

Hypnotherapist: "Yes. She's wondering if blogging is the best approach for her business. There's a specific strategy to blog one hundred two-thousand-word blogs to improve one's SEO (Search Engine Optimization) so more potential clients can find her? But this will be a tremendous time investment that takes away from her time writing, publishing and promoting her books. What's best for her? There are only so many hours in the day."

Joe: "We had her start this intensive blogging path to learn how to do it. More importantly it was to bring in a major healing for her. She had not comprehended that chronic physical pain is a symptom of not having forgiven oneself. The first blog brought this right up to the surface of her conscious mind."

(pause)

Joe: "The blog was really about forgiving herself to resolve chronic pain – not about 'improving my SEO.' Frankly, we don't like this exhausting solopreneur energy that is so often the case. Just have fun with your business! Go with the flow – notice what most lights up as your look at your planned day's activities as was mentioned earlier and do that. Be that – just be."

(pause)

Joe: "She has a powerful new altar for her business. She can add a mock-up of her book covers. She's learned it's best to have draft covers designed earlier in the process to help the book be birthed more quickly and easily. She can play it by ear on the blogs."

←→

Hypnotherapist: "Thank you. Is Wendy meant to request more radio and podcast speaking opportunities?"

Joe: "Heck yes! I will help her. I learned how and when to use my name and influence. I'd like her to sit and meditate and do a ritual first. She can then write a list of possible show hosts or show producers to contact."

(pause)

Joe: "I will help her craft the custom email messages to them. She can write them based on our conversations. I will explain the best approach or angle to her verbally. That's where I excel."

(pause)

Joe: "The bigger, more well-known shows will require an introduction from a friend who has been on that show or via an influencer. I'll help there, too. This will allow her to practice putting her energy where energy flows best."

(pause)

Joe: "There are new quality podcasts every day. There are radio guest opportunities for her. Her investment in traditional radio hosting was not wasted. It was valuable on multiple levels."

←→

Hypnotherapist: "Thank you. She's experiencing a significant block to getting the audio book version of her second book up for sale. Can you help her with this block? She's done the work to record and package it. It should be making money for her."

Joe: "Yes. Removing this block is like tearing down the Berlin Wall. We're tearing it down now from both sides. There are tons of people helping her on both sides."

(pause)

Joe: "There's only wiring left – the bricks and mortar are all gone. She's tried to move the audio files herself multiple times from where the Sound Engineer she recorded the book with stored them. She needs to try uploading them to where her audio books are sold from one more time herself."

(pause)

Joe: "If she can't complete this task due to a lack of technical knowledge, we'll send someone to help her with it. But first we had to address the energy block – the Berlin Wall."

Hypnotherapist: "So what caused this block or wall?"

←→

Joe: "Plimoth Plantation took five years to write as it had such a tremendous amount of energy to move. She was healing how to forgive a romantic partner who disappears without a word – who ghosts you, as the kids say nowadays."

(pause)

Joe: "She was mastering her own ghost energy and going more and more to the Light. She had to perfect forgiveness – no easy task. She was healing King Philip's War in which thousands of Colonials and even more Native Americans died. They lost their way of life after thousands of years due to the Europeans colonizing their land."

(pause)

Joe: "Wendy published the ebook and paperback versions with a happy sigh of relief. It was finally ready after five years. She then narrated and recorded the entire book in a single eight-hour day at a sound studio. This is unheard of. It's a super-power!"

(pause)

Joe: "The book's running time is almost seven hours. She was able to hold the energy and narrate the entire book with feeling in one sitting. Most professional narrators can only narrate for an hour or two at a time. This was a huge accomplishment that we don't want her to attempt again."

(pause)

Hypnotherapist: "What was the downside?"

Joe: "It depleted her energy too significantly. In the future she should only book a maximum of three to four hours in-studio. Most people book one or two. The energy then had to settle down from all that healing and movement and she couldn't upload it to make it available for sale as an audiobook. This won't be an issue again."

←→

Hypnotherapist: "Should she narrate more audiobooks in the future?"

Joe: "Absolutely. It's one of her super-powers and she

really enjoys it. Her narration will only get better."
(pause)
Joe: "She was guided to consider narrating a meditation book for another writer. But the pay was too low to cover the studio recording and editing time fixed costs let alone her time, energy and talents. It didn't pencil – she didn't pursue it."
(pause)
Joe: "Her first book has a running time of three hours and eight minutes which would normally take six hours for a professional narrator to voice."
(pause)
Joe: "She and a sportscaster friend voiced it in four hours as their first attempt. That was exceptional. It was that easy and fun because it was meant to be! This is flow – this is Spirit at work. Embrace it."
(pause)
Joe: "We'll decide later if she is to voice anyone else's work. As she becomes more well-known, she'll likely be offered more money to voice other people's work. We'll discuss if she is to do so or if it will dilute her brand."
(pause)
Joe: "It may be best she only narrates her own work. People receive healing simply from hearing her voice. This is a powerful ability and gift."
(pause)
Joe: "The Higher Self wants to explain this next piece. I'm giving up the floor. I just got benched!"
(Joe laughs)

←→

Higher Self: "Joe DiMaggio dropped his body in 1999. Clearly his soul – his spirit – lives on in a robust, tangible way. Joe was born into a large immigrant family that was quite poor, yet he died a wealthy man. A philanthropist. He's an excellent Guide and coach for Wendy in this area."
(pause)
Higher Self: "Wendy has been working with the Goddess Fortunata and Master Hilarion to improve her financial flow for many years. It hasn't worked."
(pause)
Higher Self: "I say to you when you give something your best effort for years and it doesn't work, isn't it time to change it up? Once again, she needs to learn what has flow – easy energetic flow to it. She needs to follow that energy as that's where she's most effective. This is true for other people, too – it's not specific to Wendy."

←→

Hypnotherapist: "That makes great sense. Thank you. Wendy has a question about trusting other people's readings for her? Normally she feels they're excellent, but she's had a few recent ones that felt off. What's the lesson?"

Higher Self: "She's remarkably good at working to get a 360-degree look at how she's performing. Because her life purpose is so expansive, we do send her for some carefully selected readings and healings. This also allows her to practice discernment without judgment or rancor as to her own truth."

(pause)

←→

Higher Self: "She's quite right we told her she had outgrown working with a specific Angel reader. The woman gave Wendy a jarring reading Wendy knew was incorrect. She told Wendy to stop offering client sessions. This was not correct information for Wendy. The reading reflected the other woman struggling with her own transitions in this area. She was projecting her path onto Wendy."

(pause)

Higher Self: "She gave Wendy several high-level, accurate readings in the past. Wendy will always think of her fondly and with gratitude as they also have past life history together, but she is not to work with her at this time. She discerned our message correctly and trusted her intuition. Job well-done."

←→

Higher Self: "She then experienced this again to become more skilled. Wendy was given a reading by a spiritual teacher who's highly proficient with past life energy. She speaks and lives well from the heart."

(pause)

Higher Self: "But she's not good with money. Her comments in this area weren't helpful for Wendy. Wendy knew to disregard them. It's crucial to learn to separate the wheat from the chaff – to discern your own truth. No one can or should do this for you."

(pause)

Higher Self: "That would be abdicating your free will. Your free will sovereignty is your most precious gift on this planet. It's why Earth is called the *Free Will Experiment* in the galaxy."

←→

Hypnotherapist: "Thank you for these specific examples. Did you say there was a third?"

Higher Self: "Yes. She recently attended an in-person meeting where there was a loving, skilled practitioner moving quickly from one person to the next in the room to offer healing. This sets Wendy's teeth on edge. Few can do that well. Wendy has learned the hard way she must always manage and protect her own energy – she and she alone is responsible for that."

(pause)

Higher Self: "She chose to allow the woman in her field but then immediately moved her out and put up her shields. Most people who don't know Wendy are surprised they can't read her. They do not have her permission. We don't want them in her energy field. It is not appropriate to feel into other people's energy without express permission."

(pause)

Higher Self: "She was told by the healer she had depression and dark energy that needed to be removed. This did not match how Wendy was feeling or what we told her was true."

Hypnotherapist: "What really happened?"

Higher Self: "The healer was not taking sufficient time to clear her energy between clients. She was projecting all the issues from the other clearings she'd done in the previous hour and dumping them at Wendy's doorstep."

(pause)

Higher Self: "Wendy appropriately blocked the planned healing and pushed the energy out of her field. The other healer then misinterpreted the dark and depressed energy as being Wendy's. By that point the practitioner was carrying a muddled soup of energy with her from a room full of people. It was not Wendy's."

←→

Hypnotherapist: "So this was a learning opportunity for her?"

Higher Self: "Yes. These three examples were to teach her to continue to up her discernment game. It's becoming well-honed. It's wonderful she picks up on these patterns and really works them to glean the true meaning. She knows we often send them to her in threes just a few days apart so she can easily recognize the pattern."

(pause)

Hypnotherapist: "Great. Anything else on this topic?"

Higher Self: "We'd like to encourage her to not feel guilty or question why she is to have a healing or a reading that we guide her to. We do encourage her to keep nurturing and investing in herself with paid sessions. They are appropriate and she's right on track."

(pause)

Higher Self: "Psychotherapists are required to be in psychotherapy themselves as a best practice – shouldn't spiritual teachers have a spiritual teacher of their own and a Past-Life Regressionist have their own sessions? This is how we grow as a Collective Consciousness. This is how mankind and the planet raise their vibration."

←→

Hypnotherapist: "Very good. She had a few relationship

questions. What's best with her mother? How is her cat doing? And is there anything we can ease with the estranged daughter?"

Higher Self: "She is to be patient and kind with her mother. Nothing else is expected."

(pause)

Higher Self: "Midnight her cat is communicating he does not need anything from her at this time. He doesn't want her to do too much intervention or over-manage the point when he chooses to drop his body. It's his choice how he will leave – support it."

(pause)

Higher Self: "This is a magnificent, highly experienced soul planning well for his new body. Love him and let him be. He'll ask for what he needs at the right time to cross over. She'll hear him accurately."

(pause)

Higher Self: "She should keep asking the daughter for forgiveness. The daughter is likely to writhe about on the planet and be messy until her mid-thirties as she's an experiential learner. That's the current trajectory - energy is always changing."

(pause)

Higher Self: "Wendy would do best to simply hold space for her daughter. Send her love from a distance until the daughter has her own child in her mid-thirties, which will lead to great growth for her, and allow for reconciliation with her own mother."

←→

Hypnotherapist: "Wise words. Is she meant to be pulling back from her dog rescue work that she really enjoys? It sounds like she's trying to figure out her best boundaries there, too."

Higher Self: "We've asked her to pull back as she was going overboard. The needs in this area are immense. They can be overwhelming without strong boundaries. It can lead to volunteer burnout or donor fatigue and more."

(pause)

Higher Self: "We recommend she ask Saint Francis and the Angels to clear any dog rescue event she will attend. To gently clear not only the dogs' energy with their permission, but the people attending. All will benefit."

(pause)

Higher Self: "We're recommending she cap her in-person attendance to three dog rescue events per month. Cross-training other hosts for the paid fundraising event she created would be ideal."

(pause)

Higher Self: "We don't recommend she do more airport

intake with the dogs or vet transport. Part of why we haven't healed her body fully before is she would have overused it doing dog rescue. She needs to be in the right role for the planet, and to balance that strong call to serve. Her soul contracts with both the rescue founder and the founder's husband are perfection."

(pause)

Higher Self: "She needs to focus on her writing and public speaking, with a focus on podcast and radio guesting."

←→

Hypnotherapist: "Is it time to start wrapping up? What else would you like her to know."

Higher Self: "Her new partner was one of the persecutors at Salem when she incarnated there to end the travesty of justice. He's had to clear up his karma in this area and to rise above being treated in an unfair and/ or nasty way. He's now helping clear the planet of the low vibrational Salem witchcraft energy."

(pause)

Higher Self: "We'd like her to stop questioning her prophetic dreams, psychic ability to simply know things, and guidance from Spirit. It's a waste of her energy and talent and ours. Finish the trust lesson!"

←→

Hypnotherapist: "Yes. Trust. She mentioned she'd love to help others raise their vibration to 5D – the fifth spiritual dimension of consciousness – and higher, but there doesn't seem to be any interest?"

Higher Self: "Let it come up naturally. There will be interest in this in the future. She should remember to inspire, not teach. She knows the difference. Inspiring allows people to find their own path, teaching can become too rote or dogmatic – too dry. It can be resented."

(pause)

Higher Self: "The Ashtar Command will help with the 5D work. We'd like her to stop poking at it. It's best to surrender it to the Divine. We know she's happy to work in that area. Now let it go so we can make it happen!"

(laughs)

Higher Self: "She's clear on her well-balanced contract with Ashtar and the Ashtar Command. You may think of them as the galactic Starfleet or police force for peace in the galaxy. Their contract is to be kept private. She understands it well."

(pause)

←→

Higher Self: "She'll be teaching how to youth – how to de-age. She hasn't realized this. That can be taught separately

273

as well as combined with the Saint Germaine plan to be able to live for hundreds of years in one healthy body if – I stress if – there is a life purpose of service that creates this need. This will become coveted information at the right time in the right place, and a joy to mentor others for."

(pause)

Higher Self: "She's now proficient with PowerPoint for presentation slides. She started this year with a bang with two big talks on January 2nd and January 3rd which took some hard work to plan for. Overall, she's doing great!"

←→

Hypnotherapist: "Will she be doing any travel?"

Higher Self: "Yes. She's to return to Glastonbury and to the UK. She's meant to see more of the United Kingdom. She's had approximately one hundred and fifty lives in the U.K. There's a lot more there to see and release and to celebrate. She's to travel to southern France. Also Sedona in Arizona. She knows where to go and the reasons."

(pause)

Higher Self: "The next trip will be easy and fun! She's to go with her new partner or a highly compatible girlfriend. We needed to build her confidence that she could travel solo internationally. On her next trip she can relax more and enjoy it with someone."

←→

Hypnotherapist: "Fantastic. What are the key takeaways for today?"

Higher Self: "First and foremost, to be versus to do. Her second priority is to go with the flow of energy and life day by day. Third, to accept and welcome Joe DiMaggio as her Guide. Wendy is Joe – Joe is Wendy – it's a merging of the soul at the Higher Self level. The lines are dissolving in an appropriate way."

(pause)

Higher Self: "She no longer cares that will sound ridiculous or impossible that she remembers being Joe DiMaggio, the Yankee Clipper. Keep a sense of humor about it. It sounds absurd to her, too, yet she knows she was Joe."

(pause)

Higher Self: "We'd like her to remember to laugh as often as possible every day. It keeps the energy moving and flowing in the best way as your vibration and frequency rise."

(pause)

Higher Self: "All her Guide and helpers are helping her create the platform for herself right now in 2020 that will take her through not only this year in the best possible way, but through all of her life."

(pause)

Higher Self: "She has a beautiful mind and can fulfill

not only the depth but the breadth of her life purpose."

←→

Our enlightening session was closed out. I expected to be doing a lot more in-person public speaking. I'd launched the year strong with not only the two talks on January second and third but with my first out-of-state trip to present at the prestigious IANDS (International Association of Near-Death Studies) group in Sacramento, California.

But magic is messy – the planet threw us all a gigantic curve ball. Two weeks after my Valentine's Day past-life regression, the first COVID-19 deaths were announced by the Washington State Department of Health on February 29th, 2020. The first corona virus deaths in the United States occurred at Evergreen Hospital in Kirkland, Washington a few miles from my home. Both my daughters were born at Evergreen, and I had loved working there for almost seven years. It was my hospital.

We bunkered down as my eighty-one-year-old mother was in the high-risk group. We adapted to the new normal the best we could. COVID was an immediate reality in my world as my former husband contracted it early as did my son-in-law's father, one of my friends and a former co-worker. Three of the four worked from home. Clearly COVID was highly contagious, and we didn't really know how it spread.

Two of the four had to be hospitalized. One came home on oxygen, but fortunately all four survived. That would not be the case for the more than 410,000 thousand people who would lose their lives in the United States as of January 22nd, 2021, and more than two million worldwide.

By the end of the year, I personally knew dozens of people who'd contracted COVID. One of my friends died, yet I was incredibly fortunate compared to many people.

I had to work hard to hold onto the energy of peace for the planet as peaceful protests for racial equality were usurped by organized rioters. My quiet affluent suburb moved briefly from 'stay at home' orders to a full lockdown due to the riots. I had to take special care to not listen or read the news programming as it had its own agenda, but to instead seek information as needed.

I looked for the silver linings despite the devastating health and financial impacts. I was thrilled by how quickly Earth began to heal herself with so much less driving and other human impacts. Many knew there would need to be a new normal. Some employers responded well by making the temporary emergency work-from-home allowances permanent. Yet week by week, more and more businesses failed faster than new businesses could be birthed.

My world became Zoom videoconferences as it did for

many people. I did my mother's weekly grocery shopping wearing a mask and did my best to limit contact. Fortunately, I'd been working with clients via first Skype and now Zoom for almost four years and had a great home office set-up, but many people were out of work or worried they would be.

With client volumes quieter than usual, I focused on completing this book. I began podcasting twice a month with Gregg Kirk as my co-host. "Waking Up Spiritually!" airs live monthly via our *Waking Up Spiritually* Facebook group and is archived on our website at https://wakingupspiritually.com; the YouTube channel, and the podcast apps.

The highlight of my year was my eldest daughter Tara and son-in-law Nathan's fairytale wedding at the historic Red Barn Farm in Eastern Washington. We missed the many family members who could not attend due to COVID.

Six months into the pandemic, I sensed it was time to get an assist to move to the next stage. I began a past-life regression therapy series with a hypnotherapist friend who was a fellow podcaster.

Chapter Thirteen – Joe Urges Emergency Preparedness

On August 20th, 2020, I began a series of past-life regression therapy session with a talented hypnotherapist in the United Kingdom. I was feeling significant burnout from the amount of care-taking my mother needed as we waited for her total hip replacement surgery and from financial challenges due to COVID's tremendous impact on the economy.

←→

(session in progress)
Hypnotherapist: "Would it be helpful to look for a life for inspiration to resolve the lack of consistent abundance?"

Higher Self: "Yes, it would. She doesn't need to explore any more problems with finances in past lives. That's been explored thoroughly."

(pause)
Higher Self: "We'd like her to explore what I can best describe as a 'rags to riches' lifetime. It's her most recent life. It was a parallel life for almost forty years. She not only did well financially, but there was fame in that lifetime. She's resistant to the fame now, which is blocking the intended financial flow."

Hypnotherapist: "Would it be appropriate to explore it to remove the blocks?"

(Wendy became tearful as she began releasing the energy)

←→

Higher Self: "Yes, it is. She's in a cycle of fully accepting the life. Then she becomes overly concerned 'what will people think?' This is a hallmark of a Life Path thirty-three in numerology. It's her life lesson to master – letting go of what other people think."

(pause)

Higher Self: "Let it go! What other people think truly does not matter. That does not concern us. We want her to focus on the end game."

Hypnotherapist: "What's the end game?"

Higher Self: "Achieving her life purpose. She can't do that until she masters letting go of what others think. It's time to do so today."

Hypnotherapist: "So how do we move forward in the best possible way?"

(Wendy experiences another round of tears with the next layer of emotional release)

←→

Higher Self: "I'm having Joe step forward. He's not only the most recent past/ parallel life, but he's become a Guide for Wendy. He's well-integrated with her Higher Self – her soul – as they are the same soul."

Hypnotherapist: "Joe, what was your life about?"

Joe: "My life was about the immigrant experience in the United States beginning in the early twentieth century. It was not a nice or easy 'melting pot.' "

(pause)

Joe: "The individual temporarily occupying the White House is stirring the pot hard. This is needed to show how much is deeply broken to allow the energy to up-level. It's not a bloodless process."

←→

Hypnotherapist: "What else can you tell us about your life? We're talking about Joe DiMaggio's life, correct?"

Joe: "Yes. My life as Joe DiMaggio. Wendy's life as me. I was fortunate to have talent, a strong work ethic, and incredibly good fortune to make a living playing the game of baseball that my brothers and I so loved. Three of us played professional baseball – three brothers all in the big league!"

(pause)

Joe: "I was privileged to continue to be able to earn a good living before sports endorsements and appearances paid more than the sport itself did like today."

Hypnotherapist: "Can you tell us more what that was like for you?"

Joe: "I was able to make select appearances and sign autographs to give that money to charities and to foundations. I was instrumental in the creation of the Joe DiMaggio Children's Hospital in Hollywood, Florida toward the end of my life."

(pause)

Joe: "This was truly satisfying for me. I didn't need to lead a lavish lifestyle. I loved kids and there was a big need."

Hypnotherapist: "Does this correlate to Wendy's life now?"

Joe: "It sure does! It's highly appealing to her to be able to do philanthropy again. She's done this before in a number of lives."

Hypnotherapist: "Can you tell us more about your life being a 'rags to riches' life you called it? Your parents were not wealthy?"

Joe: "No, they certainly were not. They immigrated from Sicily and had a large family. My father was a fisherman. My mother stayed home taking care of our whole family. That was a big job."

Hypnotherapist: "Does any of this energy continue to effect Wendy?"

Joe: "This has a mirror echo for Wendy in the sense her birth parents were not wealthy. Their early divorce when she was five or six compounded the financial issues. Her own divorce when her youngest was six did the same. That was another mirror echo."

←→

Hypnotherapist: "Thank you. I'd like to ask the Higher Self or you directly, Joe – are there qualities of yours that would benefit her that she can more embody now?"

Higher Self: "Yes. She would do well to fully take on Joe's peaceful confidence in himself. He was extremely comfortable with who he was, and where he came from. Coming from such a big family and being one of the youngest children made it prudent for him to learn how to get along well with others. His neighborhood did not have many people moving in or out. This encouraged both adults and the children to work things out peacefully."

Hypnotherapist: "Is Wendy able to be peaceful as well as confident in herself now?"

←→

Joe: "Yes, she can. She's evolved to become an innately kind and caring soul. She's had to work on her patience through a grinding contract with her mother. We are proud of them both as most would have thrown up their hands and walked away from that relationship."

(pause)

Joe: "The mother pulls on Wendy hard. Too hard. Ridiculously hard. Wendy has to speak up calmly for herself versus in anger. Her boundaries are better by the day."

Hypnotherapist: "That sounds important."

Joe: "It's more than important. Boundaries can become life or death for an Empath or a High-Sensitive. They can develop serious health problems and be jarred off their life path and purpose if they don't have the needed boundaries."

279

Hypnotherapist: "Yes. Did Joe have a natural talent for money?"

(The Higher Self began speaking in Joe's place)

Higher Self: "Yes, he did. This ability and experience didn't come from his parents. Their accomplishments were to cross the ocean for a better life, and to raise a large family with a lot of love and grounded practicality."

Hypnotherapist: "You mentioned Wendy has some blocks around fame. How did Joe handle his fame?"

Higher Self: "Fame wasn't heady for Joe. That fickle mistress never tricked him into getting a big ego – a big head! He had strong family roots and knew what mattered."

Hypnotherapist: "Good, so she's got a grounded foundation to pull from as well as positive experience. Are there new actions she can take now to help create wealth to meet that philanthropy goal?"

Higher Self: "Yes. It's time for her to be bolder and more decisive. For example, she's been over-analyzing the angelic guidance to temporarily move her long-term investments to a cash position. She needs to realize she creates her destiny. We all do. She's in charge of her life, but she's not consistently acting like it. She's the boss – time to own it."

(pause)

←→

Higher Self: "She's recently raised her vibration to 7D – the seventh spiritual dimension, or level of consciousness. She is functioning quite well there. Her ego is well-balanced. She's really doing her work at the soul level, or she wouldn't have been able to accomplish this move."

(pause)

Higher Self: "7D is home to the Angels. Not many people have accomplished this who began their earthly life at 3D We're still helping her repair her body and remove the last small blocks to fully live her purpose."

Hypnotherapist: "What's holding her back?"

Higher Self: "When she gets intuitive guidance and doesn't like the information, that doesn't make it wrong. She needs to simply validate the intuitive guidance and knows how to do so. She can muscle-test, meditate, auto write, lucid dream, or do a past-life regression."

(pause)

Higher Self: "We've nudged her to do an unusually high number of regressions the past few years as we were working to get her life fully on track with her purpose. But there's no point to someone having such a strong intuition if they're not going to act on it timely, including moving her investments temporarily to cash."

←→

Hypnotherapist: "Thank you. Is there anyone from her life as Joe DiMaggio back in her life now?"

Higher Self: "Yes. We've shown her the two major players. Her youngest daughter was her son Joe Junior – technically Joe DiMaggio the third. Joe Junior became estranged from his father including at the time of his father's death."

(pause)

Higher Self: "Her daughter doesn't understand this additional old estrangement energy between them. She doesn't wish to accept past lives as reality or accept anything metaphysical. The good news is both the mother, and the daughter are raising their vibration and will resolve the old estrangements this lifetime."

Hypnotherapist: "So it's hard for the current mother and daughter?"

Higher Self: "Yes. The daughter struggles daily as an ungrounded Empath. She overly associates her mother Wendy with her fears regarding energy and therefore rejects her. This will be resolved with time. Wendy just needs to ride it out. She needs to play the long game. She can do it."

←→

Hypnotherapist: "You mentioned a second person she recognized from her life as Joe?"

Higher Self: "Yes. The young woman who was the Marilyn Monroe married to this Joe DiMaggio – the Joe who's now Wendy. I'm making that distinction as there are other timelines with the same players. Everything's good there."

Hypnotherapist: "I see. Thank you."

←→

Hypnotherapist: "Are you ready to go to the last day of your lifetime?"

(pause)

Higher Self: "Just a moment. We need to have her sit up and take a few deep breaths. She died as Joe from lung cancer. The lungs are where we carry our grief. It can be from previous lifetimes."

(pause)

Higher Self: "This grief is mirroring worldwide right now in the form of COVID-19 as a disease of the lungs. It's grief that needs to be purged from the human collective."

Hypnotherapist: "Is she ready to go forward now to the last day of her lifetime as Joe? I want her to be comfortable."

Higher Self: "Yes, we're ready. She just had to sit up and blow her nose and take a few deep breaths."

(pause)

Higher Self: "Joe had a peaceful, easy death in his mid-

eighties. He was so happy to be back in his home after months in the hospital. He had an informal hospice of sorts at his residence. He had a surprisingly great time laughing and reminiscing with his closest family and friends. The exception was his son – his only child – was not present."
(Wendy sounded close to tears again)

←→

Hypnotherapist: "So there's emotion there to release. Let's do that now. May I ask why Joe's son was estranged?"
Higher Self: *(bluntly)* "Simple. He couldn't handle his father's fame. He struggled most of his adult life. He was a ne'er-do-well. Joe's son dropped his body shortly after his father died. He was only in his fifties."
Hypnotherapist: "Is there any problem with this playing out again with Wendy's daughter?"
Higher Self: "Good question. She's broken that mold from when she was Joe DiMaggio's son. In this incarnation she has a high IQ and is motivated and hard-working. She's completing her Engineering degree."

←→

Hypnotherapist: "Very good. May we move onto Joe DiMaggio Senior's afterlife – specifically his life review?"
Higher Self: "Absolutely. He surpassed his life purpose. He hit the ball out of the park! That incarnation merits an A++. A life well-lived. Much was learned and accomplished."
Hypnotherapist: "Are there other positives from Joe's life that could be embodied in the present lifetime now?"
Higher Self: "Yes. She would do well to fully incorporate that quiet self-confidence. It would help her stop over-thinking and getting caught up in her left brain. That can lead to getting too wrapped up in the ego. This is a common challenge for those of you with a high IQ. You do it too. I encourage you both to be in your bodies. Be in your hearts. Just place your hand over your heart and let the energy flow in the most beneficial way."

←→

Hypnotherapist: "Thank you. Was there anything else important in the life review?"
Higher Self: "Yes. Joe had a lot of drama and trauma with his romances – his two marriages. His other relationships were overall quite good, other than that difficult estrangement by his son's choice."
(pause)
Higher Self: "The two marriages were both difficult. Wendy then mirrored that with her marriage, which ended in divorce. That was energetically like Joe's first marriage. She then had the tumultuous relationship with the soul mate who woke her up that she had contracted to marry, like Joe with Marilyn."

(pause)
Higher Self: "She's worked through all that messiness and those challenges. Her future long-term relationship or marriage will be respectful, kind, and easy. It's what she's dreamed of for so long."

(pause)
Higher Self: "Her daughter not being an easy relationship is the daughter's choice – that mirroring from the DiMaggio father/ son life as I said earlier. It also has overtones to when Wendy's former husband was her son and became estranged by his choice as a teen."

(pause)
Higher Self: "The present-day daughter has some imprinting from her present-day father as he made that same choice long ago to become estranged from Wendy as a teen. Her daughter then did the same."

←→

Hypnotherapist: "Can we break the bonds to the negatives – leave them behind?"

Higher Self: "Yes! Brilliant request. We shall do so one by one."

(pause)
Higher Self: "Money negatives – resolved. Restoring good fortune, where appropriate, as Wendy will be an incredible financial steward."

(pause)
Higher Self: "Any allergies to fame – resolved. She'll never enjoy fame for fame's sake in this age of the Kardashians, but she'll learn well how to quietly use 'fame' – more often influence – where appropriate to benefit others, like Joe did."

(pause)
Higher Self: "Resolving any career roadblocks – check! That one's the easiest of the three."

←→

Hypnotherapist: "Fantastic! Are there more bonds to break?"

Higher Self: "Yes. She's leaving the energy of difficult marriages behind her, as well as decades alone, and the final marriage not occurring."

(pause)
Higher Self: "You may not be aware Joe chose to remain single for almost forty years after Marilyn's death. Her funeral took place on what was to be their second wedding day."

(pause)
Higher Self: "That mirrored in Wendy as heartbreak of the highest order with the soul mate boyfriend. It became clear that the man who woke her up and who she had

283

contracted to marry before incarnating was not - shall we say delicately - 'marriage material.' I'll leave it at that."

(pause)

Higher Self: "Joe had to help move him out of her field. That boyfriend was still trying to have her for himself, at some level, years after he broke up with her. It was remarkably selfish."

Hypnotherapist: "Yes, I understand. It sounds like that relationship was quite hard on her heart."

Higher Self: "Yes, it was. But the beauty of it – the opportunity for this soul – is she's lifted herself up! That deep sadness that Joe had – she's broken the bonds of that. She's broken the karmic cycle."

(pause)

Higher Self: "This is a big deal. She knows she will have a happy, fulfilling new romance. She's worked through the heavy emotional load of burying one's wife and dear friend of many years on one's intended wedding day. Kudos to her – she has processed that heavy spiritual load as a soul via several past-life regressions."

←→

Hypnotherapist: "That's amazing. Is there more healing work to do?"

Higher Self: "Yes. We're having her place her hands over her lower chakras to embody Joe's easy confidence. It's already within her now. She had it before. We are pulling it forward to the present day."

(pause)

Higher Self: "We are specifically healing her being willing to share this book publicly. It feels once again overly personal as did the first two books."

(pause)

Higher Self: "Getting this title complete, edited and published will allow her to move forward much more quickly with the twenty or more books she is meant to write this lifetime."

(pause)

Higher Self: "Two or three of them will be the biggest books for her. They are all important as they release energy not only for Wendy, but for mankind."

(pause)

Higher Self: "This title is likely to be the most popular. Things are now lining up well. Thank you for helping her."

Hypnotherapist: "My pleasure. Why has this life as Joe DiMaggio been hard for her to accept?"

←→

Higher Self: *(dryly)* "Beyond the obvious challenge of publicly stating you believe you were one of baseball's greatest players and one of the most famous figures of the twentieth

284

century?"

Hypnotherapist: "Yes. Is there more from an energy standpoint in addition to the 'let go of what other people think' lesson?"

Higher Self: "This life was also problematic for her because it was a parallel life. She was quite stubborn about accepting it. She had injuries as Wendy from that life as DiMaggio – most notably her right foot, lower back, and right elbow – that she wasn't meant to have in the current life."

Hypnotherapist: "Has she fully accepted the life now regardless if it's a literal past life or from the collective memories?"

Higher Self: "Accepted, yes. But does she find it easy to share this literal past life with others? No. Absolutely not! She struggles to talk about it publicly. That's what we're healing today."

(pause)

←→

Higher Self: "We pushed her on-stage to talk about her life as Joe a few years ago. That was hard for her to do even with a uniquely supportive audience at a group called Wisdom Soup."

(pause)

Higher Self: "We're not asking her to prove she lived the life of Joe DiMaggio. It's not possible to 'prove' past lives, depending on your definition of proof. We asked her to step to the plate, regardless – pun intended!"

(sound of laughter)

Higher Self: "Wendy likes Stuart Chase's quote, 'For those who believe, no proof is necessary. For those who don't believe, no proof is possible."

Hypnotherapist: "So she'll find a way to get it done – to have the self-confidence to come out publicly?"

Higher Self: "That is certainly the plan. She's being provided with all possible support to do so."

←→

Hypnotherapist: "May we move onto some of the questions she wrote for today's session?"

Higher Self: "Yes, you may. I'm going to step back and have Joe come forward to answer her questions. He can best guide her with those queries she's posed in writing for today."

Hypnotherapist: "Excellent. This new partner that she's going to meet – have they known each other in a past life or lives?"

Joe: "Yes, they've known each other in a minor role a few times. He is not a soul mate, by her choice. That energy can be an impediment to a rewarding romance. She's done the

285

soul mate grind with the present life former husband. He is more energetically aligned with their youngest daughter. They need one another. They both struggle with life and support one another in an appropriate way."

(pause)

Joe: "More to your point, she did such profound work with the soul mate in her first book, 'Regression Healing I' that it cleared the need for a soul mate relationship. She's graduated in that area! This doesn't happen often. She really did the work."

←→

Joe: "She then connected with her Twin-Flame – the other half of her soul. This is a specific type of soul mate. We only have one Twin-Flame, and not everyone has one. She spent three or four years telepathically working with him and healing him – working toward their meeting in the physical for a happy reunion and marriage."

(pause)

Joe: "Instead she discovered he could not sufficiently heal in this lifetime to withstand the intensity of the Twin-Flame burn. It's not for the faint of heart. Your Twin holds up the mirror of everything you have not healed in yourself."

(pause)

Joe: "Several of Wendy's spiritual teachers and healers worked to help him heal. She gave it her all. Yet he still dropped his body. He passed on early this year just before COVID began. He took an easier exit ramp than COVID – a massive heart attack."

Joe: "They only met in the physical for thirty seconds on the elevator at work years ago. She recognized him immediately when we began loudly singing an old 1960s hit to her, 'It Must Be Him!' "

(pause)

Joe: "He did not understand well enough what was happening. He got off on the third floor and she rode up to the fifth floor, which was symbolic of their vibrational levels at that time. They never met again although they certainly were meant to. She worked it hard."

←→

Joe: "The moment Wendy released the possibility of moving forward with the Twin-Flame partner she was immediately approached by her Twin-Ray. A Twin-Ray is the galactic off-planet version of a Twin-Flame."

(pause)

Joe: "They connected daily via telepathy for about six or nine months, and he then suddenly went quiet. She asked him how he was doing and learned he was no longer interested in a committed relationship."

(pause)
Joe: "He told her he now wanted to 'Just play the field and have a great time with lots of women.' She wished him well and ended their contract to meet. She thanked her Guides profusely for sparing her another player."

(pause)
Joe: "She'd completed that lesson so thoroughly with the soul mate in her first two books that she didn't need to repeat the experiences."

←→

Hypnotherapist: "Wow, that's a lot of work and energy. Years it sounds like. Can we focus on the new partner now that we've cut the bonds with the old energy?"

Joe: "That's the right request. She and her new partner have great energy on their own as well as together. He moved in from out-of-state to take a job at a Fortune 100 company in the town next to hers. He also came for the relationship with her."

(pause)
Joe: "Their paths will cross as soon as it can be arranged. They both knew where and when they were to meet. It was likely to be at the dog rescue event she hosts. He was meant to buy a ticket to her fundraiser. But then the pandemic put public events on hold, right when they were to meet. King County in Washington State hasn't been able to move beyond phase two of re-opening. She can't currently host the event."

(pause)
Joe: "We've been looking for a new way for them to meet organically, out in public, even in their masks. In a park – on a trail – at the farmer's market – in a grocery store? Restaurants are closed too, except for outdoor dining."

Hypnotherapist: "So that's all set. Are there any other lives negatively impacting her confidence in any way? Or her financial flow?"

←→

Joe: "The deeply satisfying romance meet is all set. I am flipping through her Akashic Records of her Earth lives as well as her galactic records to make sure there are no other bonds to break or cords to cut in those areas."

(long pause)
Joe: "Geez Louise, I'm not that much of a reader. This isn't an efficient way to look as she's had so many lives. Let's look instead for lives she can embrace where she had a natural easy confidence to be herself and to handle legacy money not only for herself and her loved ones, but for humanity and for the Earth and the animals."

(long pause – sound of Joe's laughter)
←→

Joe: "Found it! This is funny. The first life of that type for her to remember in detail and to model from is as me - as Joe DiMaggio! Also, her life as Queen Guinevere of Camelot in England and as Mary Magdalen."

Hypnotherapist: "Is she willing to do that?"

Joe: "She's squirming and hesitating a bit."

Hypnotherapist: "Why?"

Joe: "Because they're three famous, historical and Biblical past lives. There's her bugaboo − her resistance − her self-limiting belief."

(pause)

Joe: "That's exactly why we've chosen these for her to model from. This will complete her lesson to 'let go of what other people think.' Her soul mate she had so many lives with encouraged her to do that multiple times. When she frees up from that, she can hit the ball out of the park. It's time. The time is now."

Hypnotherapist: "So can she do it?"

← →

Joe: "It's up to her to decide if she can stomach this. To see if she can resolve her digestion and elimination problems. I had ulcers − she doesn't need to. Let's see if she can instead have fun with this! See the joy and the privilege in her present life. See the immense love that's available to her − to be at peace with it all."

(pause)

Joe: "We've given her all the tools needed to be confident to embrace such a large, unusual life purpose She chose it. Others have certainly succeeded with a large life purpose. She has too, in other lifetimes."

(pause)

Joe: "Batter up! She's on deck. I'll help her with her stance − her swing and her bat speed − her self-confidence."

← →

Hypnotherapist: "What's the best way for her to succeed with her life purpose?"

Joe: "To trust her intuition and to follow it at the right time It's important to understand Divine Right Timing. She understands it now although she had forgotten that concept until a few years ago."

(pause)

Joe: "My recommendation is to look at the COVID isolation as a time to slow down and really go within."

(pause)

Joe: "Work out your issues with your immediate family as many have been sequestered in tight quarters, trying to work or job-search from home and to home-school. She has it easy compared to many. Do the best you can to prep for what will likely be a challenging fall and early winter, at least in the United States."

Hypnotherapist: "Are we meant to talk about what may be coming?"

←→

Joe: *(smiling broadly)* "It's not a Zombie Apocalypse – let's have some sense of humor with this. But many will feel just as attacked. Life as we know it will change profoundly for some individuals."

(pause)

Joe: "These are necessary changes just like COVID was needed for Earth to heal herself to continue to be habitable."

Hypnotherapist: "Can you give an example?"

Joe: "Certainly. Here's an example – it is just an example. It may or may not come to pass. That is up to mankind to determine as your thoughts create your reality. I cannot fortune-tell this for you."

(pause)

Joe: "What if the stock market were not only to crash but to disappear? What is there were no more stocks and bonds to trade – what would that look like? Are there any changes you should make in preparation? This is a personal decision. Stay in your power."

(pause)

Joe: "Remember outcomes are based on the intent and the energy behind the decision. It is wise to make decisions from a place of love, not fear. Do not live in fear, as that is where you will build your home," as her friend Laurie says. You won't enjoy your life much from such a place of lack."

(pause)

Joe: "We've encouraged her to be more self-reliant from a food source and utilities perspective. Also, financially. Her thoughts truly create her reality. This is true for everyone. Penney's Pierce's book, 'Frequency: Power of Personal Vibration' explains this well."

(pause)

Joe: "This may sound selfish or like insider information, but it's not. This type of information has been broadcast to the 144,000 lightworkers and more for years with increasing specificity over the last few months. It's been widely shared."

(pause)

←→

Joe: "I'm saying prepare. Make sure your roof is well-sealed before it pours rain. Do your work you came to the planet to do. Go within – follow your own Divine guidance, not some spiritual guru's. That day is over."

(pause)

Joe: "Put your own oxygen mask on first and then take

care of your family and friends. Choose those who will be able to easily accept help and will help others in turn. Same with your neighbors. Understand it's a numbers game."

(pause)

Joe: "You may need to triage who you are to help. That may be immensely challenging. You will need to continually surrender to the Divine what we tell you that you cannot help with. This teaches humility and balance."

(pause)

Joe: "Do your best to be calm. Be the calm in the storm of what is likely to come. There may be civil unrest. Remember to breathe – take in a breath of life. Center yourself and believe that you're going to be alright!"

(pause)

Joe: "Remember that we incarnate to learn to experience human emotions while in a body. You must 'feel it to heal it.'

←→

Hypnotherapist: "Is there more?"

Joe: "Look for the helpers. Fred Rogers – Mister Rogers – said that. Look for the new opportunities. Find the silver linings. Look for the Heaven on Earth energy – the peace, the love, and the joy moments. Follow those trajectories and invest your energy there. Grow that energy."

(pause)

Joe: "Your power comes from your ability to shift your perspective even during a major re-set of the financial systems, the government, healthcare, politics, educations and more."

(pause)

Joe: "The COVID pandemic has been unsettling as we've had a challenging reminder that 'health is wealth.' We were close to destroying Earth through global warming and other issues."

(pause)

Joe: "COVID was engineered to stop Earth from being destroyed not only for humans but for the animals and all other living beings. You're not the only ones here."

(pause)

Joe: "Summer was a breather, and now it's time to prepare."

Hypnotherapist: "To prepare for what?"

←→

Joe: "To get your house in order. To prepare for what you have each created as 'Creator Gods.' That's not meant to sound ominous. Would you like some examples?"

Hypnotherapist: "Yes, please."

Joe: "Since the COVID changes began a lot of people have been working on their health, their homes, their relationships. Some are making excellent use of their time."

(pause)
Joe: "For example, the number of podcasts has doubled in the last four to five months as people are working to express themselves from their heart and to help others. All boats do rise with the tide."

(pause)
Joe: "The Collective Consciousness is rising as it needed to do, though that can be hard to see and to believe as more and more ugliness is brought to light. That's the key – it's being brought to the Light! That's what needs to happen."

(pause)
Joe: "Earth has healed herself remarkably quickly in so many ways with less people commuting to jobs many didn't enjoy. Employers are learning people really can work from home and be productive. There are more self-employed, yet it's a gigantic task to rebuild the world economy in sustainable ways."

←→

Hypnotherapist: "Thank you. Are there more examples?
Joe: "Yes. More people are willing to live communally, to try tiny homes or van life at least for a time. Less footprint. Many people are eating less meat, especially beef. More people are trying a vegetarian or vegan diet. The ranching necessary for beef is hard on the planet."

(pause)
Joe: "The number of books published is going to skyrocket from what's happening during the pandemic 'Great Pause.' The technology is now here for progress to come in leaps and bounds."

(pause)
Joe: "Yet I do caution against an over-reliance on technology. Don't forget your old school knowledge and abilities. Prepare for various scenarios you may not have wanted to think about before."

(pause)
Hypnotherapist: "Such as?"
Joe: "For example, what if the banks were closed for a few months during a financial re-set? Would you want to have some cash on hand in small bills or to access your safe deposit box first? Would you be wise to stock up on nonperishable foods and medicines or supplements, including pet supplies? Do you need a spare set of eyeglasses or keys made?"

(pause)
Joe: "What about water and gas? Do you need a generator or space heater or secondary source of heat or way to cook? Do you need to dig out your camping or travel gear and make sure it's in good shape? Do you have plenty of batteries, candles and propane for a propane stove or

barbeque? Have you considered buying or building a faraday cage to protect against solar flares? What about an EMP whole-house surge protector for your fuse box in case of a lightning strike or solar flare the grid can't handle?"

(pause)

Joe: "The North American ice storm of January 1998 was a big deal. More than four million people were without power in frigid weather for up to thirty days. The storm impacted multiple provinces and states so severely that some were without power, water and phone lines for a significant time, including Wendy's father and stepmother."

(pause)

Joe: "Emergency preparedness is never wasted as our grids can be surprisingly fragile. We take them for granted. Wikipedia has a good recap of that ice storm. I encourage people to read it as an example."

(pause)

Joe: "Is this a good time to take care of your medical, dental and vision visits and to go get a good haircut and massage before we bunker down again? Again, this is not meant to cause panic but rather preparedness. It is crucial to learn to meditate and go within and prepare yourself. Find a way to enjoy yourself every day – be in joy."

(pause)

Joe: "Love yourself first. Be confident in your own abilities, and then visualize hitting the ball out of the park each time you step to the plate. That's what I did. To visualize is to create!"

← →

Hypnotherapist: "Thank you for that detail. It was needed to understand your points. May I ask why does she suddenly have thyroid nodules? Is there an energetic component we can resolve so she can feel healthy?"

Joe: "Absolutely. Your energy reflects in your health in many ways. Get your energy in tip-top shape and you can live a healthy life perhaps for hundreds of years or more, if that's what you desire, as we discussed in previous sessions."

(pause)

Joe: "The reason she has thyroid nodules is Wendy has been reticent to speak about what she knows. It's taken six years to process the energy in this book – from one U.S. Presidential election cycle to the next and beyond."

(pause)

Joe: "That build-up of energy became too much for her body. It became thyroid nodules. They will resolve as she publishes and does the public speaking that we've asked her to do. If she can't speak at face-to-face gatherings, she can use Zoom. If the Internet is down, she knows how to broadcast telepathically including during the dream time.

No excuses – she needs to do her work. We're here to help every step of the way.

"That is all I need to share today. This session is now complete."

Hypnotherapist: "Thank you for all you've shared today."

← →

I felt a deep sense of peace and of gratitude after this past-life regression. It was now clear to me how I was to help anchor the "Heaven on Earth" energies of peace, love, and joy on the planet. I would not be taken out for my efforts to accomplish this as had happened numerous times previously.

I continued to do my best to hold the energy of peace for the United States and for the planet during the Presidential election in 2020. I was highly attuned to #PeaceNow energy and movement. I was incredibly grateful and relieved to learn in the fall of 2021 during an angel reading that the peace energy had been landed for the planet! The angels thanked me and told me to let it go.

I looked forward to my next past-life regression therapy session as well as to many other things in life. I was also fully enjoying each day as it came. I felt more peaceful than I'd ever felt. I felt gratitude for the first time to not only remember so much of my past life as Joe DiMaggio, but to have him as my Spirit Guide.

Chapter Fourteen – What Is Psychic Surgery?

I had an amazing dream the night of October seventeenth, 2020, that turned lucid. I was shown that Dr. Lorphan, an off-world psychic surgeon, had done extensive surgery to heal my digestion and elimination issues that had been problematic for the last few years. I was eager to learn more during my past-life regression the next day.

←→

(Session in progress)

Hypnotherapist: "Do you feel your Spirit Guides are here now?"

Wendy: "Yes, they are. They're giving me a funny visual. They've twisted the top of my head off quite gently – my crown chakra – like you'd twist the top off a bottle of water? They're pouring the answers – the resources – the help I need in through my crown chakra."

Hypnotherapist: "That's great. Let's go to a past life now..."

(A tunnel technique was used in combination with counting)

←→

Hypnotherapist: "Step out of the tunnel and be there now in that past life. What do you see?"

(pause)

Wendy: "I'm in Roman times. I'm a female slave."

Hypnotherapist: "How do you feel?"

Wendy: *(flatly, after a long pause)* "Horrible."

Hypnotherapist: "Have you seen this life before?"

Wendy: "No, but I've been hearing the word 'slave' multiple times during the last few weeks but didn't know why. It will be helpful to get answers today."

Hypnotherapist: "Is there anyone with you?"

Wendy: "I don't need to explore this in detail to release

it. My Guides are explaining this is a lifetime of abuse, of oppression, of fear, of starvation. It's a lot of the old Earth energies mankind really needs to outgrow."
(pause)
Wendy: "The pertinent point is 'That was then, and this is now!' I no longer need to energetically attract or accept abuse. No one does."
(pause)
Wendy: "There was some little chink in my armor – my energy body, my aura – where I was still attracting that energy. I'm going to switch now to my Higher Self to explain this from a higher plane."
Hypnotherapist: "Very good."

← →

Higher Self: "Her mother was the oppressor. Wendy was her slave. That's where some of this truly unpleasant energy between the two of them has originated. We can let it go – my goodness!"
Hypnotherapist: "Yes, that residual energy is no longer needed. You can let it go."
Higher Self: "Absolutely. We're going to heal this at a cellular level – let's completely wash this away. Let's turn this into a beautiful waterfall that is going to go all through her – through Wendy – through all space and time. I'm going to bring her back in, so she is empowered to do this for herself."
(pause)
Higher Self: "She's so well-integrated with her Higher Self and her Guides that we switch back and forth quite seamlessly. We'll keep you updated as to who is speaking so that things make sense for you."
(pause)

← →

Hypnotherapist: "Thank you."
Wendy: "I see myself going outside to the well repeatedly to carry the water in. It's a back-breaking task to bring the water in for the entire household for the whole day, every day."
(pause)
Wendy: "I'm changing those heavy jugs I had to use to haul the water into a beautiful waterfall – I'm pouring it over myself instead."
Hypnotherapist: "Yes."
Wendy: "I am setting myself free through all space and time. I'm forgiving the oppressors – I'm forgiving myself – I'm setting myself free!"
(pause)
Wendy: "We've obviously been on both sides of the equation.

Enough of this old nonsense – it's time to truly forgive."
(pause)
Wendy: "Let's get rid of these old scripts. It's time to build a nice fire and tear up these old scripts of mankind being so inhumane to one another because of skin color or gender or age or whatever arbitrary distinction there might be. They don't mean a damn thing! I'm burning up these old scripts – goodbye!"

← →

Hypnotherapist: "You can reframe it. You can change it from a bad thing to a good thing. It can become an opportunity."
Wendy: "Absolutely. These were just tough play runs we acted out – challenging experiences for growth. Tough schooling that we took on to have these experiences, and then put ourselves back together at the soul level when we were Home."
(pause)
Wendy: "And then to be willing to do it again? Wow, to do it again so many times – oh my goodness! So many lives. That takes a lot of courage and confidence in oneself and in the Divine."
Hypnotherapist: "You can keep reframing these experiences. As you said, turn those heavy jugs into a cleansing waterfall."
Wendy: "Yes."
Hypnotherapist: "Let it cleanse right through you."
Wendy: "Yes. It's cleaning right down to my DNA level – my RNA – my well cell. It's time to restore my full DNA so we're not just limited to what we have in present day. We can all begin restoring our full beautiful DNA that was stripped away because we couldn't handle it as a species."

← →

Hypnotherapist: "Do you feel you've released 100% of this energy?"
(The Higher Self stepped back in to answer)
Higher Self: "Let's assess. We're strengthening her lower chakras. She had an incredible healing for her digestion and elimination system last night from Dr. Lorphan during the dream time."
Hypnotherapist: "Who is Dr. Lorphan?"
Higher Self: "Dr. Lorphan is an off-planet psychic surgeon from the Great White Brotherhood. White refers to white magic only. It is nothing to do with race. Please disregard the old-fashioned name. It doesn't translate well nowadays. My apologies."
(pause)
Higher Self: "She also had a powerful healing for the same issue a week or two ago with her healer friend Gregg

Kirk. That healing opened the door for the surgery with Dr. Lorphan. We then woke her up from the dream so she could remember the experience and discuss it with you today."

Hypnotherapist: "That's amazing! Anything else for her to know?"

← →

Higher Self: "We want her to eliminate the remaining dairy she consumes. It's not good for her. Her body can't break it down. She needs to say goodbye to the last bit of dairy."
(pause)
Higher Self: "We're now doing some heart healing. One really expects better of one's mother than to be made a slave. It's just like Wendy's daughter hasn't been able to forgive her she became a human sacrifice. We're healing Wendy's heart from both experiences."
(pause)
Higher Self: "The heart healing will continue in the background."
Hypnotherapist: "Excellent. Can we move on from that life? Is that appropriate?"

← →

Higher Self: "Yes. There were some other Roman lives that were overlaid. She had trouble narrowing down to just one when we began speaking and you had her come out of the tunnel and go to one life. Two were presenting for healing."
Hypnotherapist: "What was the other Roman life to release?"
Higher Self: "She's letting go of the warring energy. She's a male dressed in a toga. It's gladiator stuff of old that has led to challenges for Wendy recently via a present-day attorney."
(pause)
Higher Self: "She's letting go of it. She has enough skill with past life energy that's all we have to say and show her. She'll take care of it. She's getting assistance to gently remove a painful arrow he jammed into her left kidney by hand during the gladiator life. He wanted it to be personal."
(pause)
Higher Self: "Yeshua and Mother Mary are doing this delicate work on her body. They are putting the attorney on notice he can no longer cause issues for her caused by that past life energy. She is free of him. You may continue."
Hypnotherapist: "Very good."

← →

Higher Self: "We want her back to that place where she's truly peaceful. That's our focus for today – having her be truly at peace."

(pause)

Higher Self: "We want her to hold the #PeaceNow vibration for mankind and the planet through the fall, especially through events that may occur on Remembrance Day and on the Winter Solstice. It may become a 'darkest before the dawn moment. Let's leave it at that."

Hypnotherapist: "Can we go to another life for more insights?"

←→

Higher Self: "Yes. We're assessing what would be most useful for her. We'd like to go to a lifetime where she was a prophet. She has had lifetimes where she was highly skilled as a seer, but she has some human conflict with these abilities now."

Hypnotherapist: "Oh? Why is that."

Higher Self: "There's some ego conflict. There's some small bit of fear left she's worked hard to conquer. That's why she always has so many questions and has such informative past life regression and healing sessions."

(pause)

Hypnotherapist: "What needs to be resolved?"

Higher Self: "She's had multiple lifetimes as a prophet where she was punished for her abilities. The answers flow to her easily this lifetime but then her ego questions, 'Is that right?' "

(pause)

Higher Self: "She jumps back from her own intuitive flow too much. We want her to get more comfortable that she does know the answers from within."

←→

Hypnotherapist: "So to be more confident?

Higher Self: "Both confident and comfortable. Self-assured. We want to look for a more positive life as a prophet or seer where it really was easy and where she was treated well."

(pause)

Higher Self: "No intuitive is one hundred percent accurate. You need to use your own discernment to find the truth within yourself. Even if someone is providing information to you, you must then discern your own truth."

(pause)

Higher Self: "What happened so often was the King – the wealthy person – whomever hired or supported her – had so much 'off with their head!' energy! When that the individual didn't like what she foretold or the energy changed, she was often harshly punished. Beaten, imprisoned, starved, tortured – killed. Or her loved ones were threatened or harmed, which is even worse for the psyche."

(pause)
Higher Self: "A psychic can only provide the best information they have at that moment in time. Things change. Energy isn't permanent. Nothing is permanent but change."

Hypnotherapist: "So that's what she's really releasing. Can you find a positive life of this type?"

(pause)

←→

Higher Self: "Yes, we've got it now. She was a Delphi Oracle. This was a lovely life. She saw a glimpse of this life before when she did a past life regression with one of the Newton hypnotherapists. They were oracles together. They recognized each other from Delphi. It was such a good life."

Hypnotherapist: "Was this in ancient Greece?"

Higher Self: "Yes. She was well-taken care of and well-respected."

(pause)
Higher Self: "We want her to feel well-taken care of right now and really tune into that energy. This is important because she has not been especially well-taken care of in this lifetime. She's more needed to be the caretaker. It's right in her astrology as well as in Joe DiMaggio's."

(pause)
Higher Self: "It's been a tough slog of overworking this lifetime. There wasn't sufficient financial or emotional support from the parents or from the former husband or boyfriends. We want to let go of that overworking. We want to bring in more ease and grace to her life now so she can fulfill her life mission. All will benefit."

(long pause)

←→

Hypnotherapist: "Are you connecting with that life in ancient Greece now?"

Higher Self: "Yes. I want to stress she was exceptionally well cared for. She could go for a lovely walk out in nature – her work was beautiful. It was important for her then as it is now to take a nice walk – to go enjoy a lovely meal. This kept her vibration and frequency high."

(pause)
Higher Self: "There was nice companionship. There was easy lovely shelter and food and clothing and jewelry. There were animals and music. There was perfect weather. Anything you could think of and desire, it was there. It was a Heaven on Earth lifetime. She's here to create that again now. She can show others how to do the same."

(pause)
Higher Self: "The job was to meditate and to pray and to then be able to speak the prophecies. You can consider it channeling."

(long pause)

←→

Hypnotherapist: "Yes?"
Higher Self: "I'm exploring did she use any tools or devices like tea leaves or cards?"
(pause)
Higher Self: "Yes, she did. She used tea leaves. She used some runes. I see her throwing the stones."
(pause)
Higher Self: "She's looking for the patterns – the signs and synchronicities. That's the common denominator between the two."
(pause)
Higher Self: "She could hear Spirit very well, just like now. That's another parallel to this life."

←→

Hypnotherapist: "So she was using her intuition?"
Higher Self: "It was more than her intuition. It was literally a voice in her left ear. Spirit spoke to her all day long just like now. She hears at the highest levels."
(pause)
Higher Self: "This is important. This is going to help resolve the left ear-ringing that she has now."
(pause)
Higher Self: "She has tremendous left ear-ringing. She's had it for about ten years. It's not easy to deal with. I'm going to do an assessment."
(pause)
Higher Self: "We see some physical component. Western medicine can't help her. She had it checked out years ago and we told her to stop."
(pause)
Higher Self: "She doesn't need hearing aids or a brain MRI. There's no tumor. Doctors can get overly excited. We need to adjust this energetically."
(pause)
Higher Self: "We want her to get more comfortable there is much quality information coming in from Spirit through her left ear. As her body continues to heal, as she more trusts her intuition and is willing to speak her truth versus jumping back from what she's hearing and shown, it will take care of both the ear-ringing and thyroid nodules."
(pause)
Higher Self: "She's simply being too heady now. The ear-ringing and the thyroid nodules are all up in or near the head. Just like as we heal the digestion and elimination challenges – as we heal the lower chakras, including the self-confidence, which is primarily in the solar plexus chakra – the ear-ringing will resolve."

Hypnotherapist: "Is the ringing in the ears possibly from a past life?"

Higher Self: "Yes. There's been lots of that. There was a tremendous explosion in World War II when she stepped on some sort of German flask bomb with the left foot. There were multiple war time and other incidents where there were physical explosions that would cause ringing in the ears."

(pause)

Higher Self: "But that would cause ringing in both ears. She only has it in her left ear. It's caused by so many Beings of Light being lined up to speak with and through her. There's so many of them!"

(pause)

Higher Self: "They are high vibrational in nature. They are appropriate to speak with her. She's tried working with her Guide to say, 'I can't hear when there's such a cacophony of sound. Are there too many talking at once?' "

(pause)

Higher Self: "She's asked her Guides to have them speak one at a time. She's asked Prince, her Guide who is to help with this to be the person who stands at the door and triages who gets in or who does not."

(pause)

Higher Self: "What's that called in English? I know. A bouncer! To be a spiritual bouncer for her. She needs to continue to work through that request with Prince. It hasn't yet been effective."

←→

Hypnotherapist: "Who specifically is trying to talk with her?"

Higher Self: "A lot of it is from off-planet. It's galactic in origin. It is benevolent and will assist mankind and the planet. We have the translator function working well. The messages are translated before they get to her, so they are in perfect English."

(pause)

Higher Self: "There are no translation errors or filtering problems. But we need to get the messages through the translator device without causing the ear-ringing that's jamming the signal."

(pause)

Higher Self: "She doesn't have to function like a psychic medium who's clairvoyant and has to slog through, 'I see this – what does that mean to you?' as they speak with their sitter or client."

(pause)

Higher Self: "It's straight up English by the time the

message gets to her. Her Master Teacher Prince is now laughing and saying, 'Thank you!' He's the translator – it's not a device, per se."

(pause)

←→

Higher Self: "She hears at the highest level in English and can communicate the messages beautifully. This is part of her life purpose."

(pause)

Higher Self: "Let's explore if there is too much volume. Is this appropriate there is this huge volume of information coming to her?"

(pause)

Higher Self: "No, it is not. Let's redistribute some of the people who have been shouting to her and standing in line for so long causing so much ear-ringing for years."

(pause)

Higher Self: "They need to go find other channels to speak with. There are more and more quality channels. More will begin channeling. We need to redistribute this line from Wendy to other channels."

Hypnotherapist: "How do we do that?"

(pause)

Higher Self: "I'm asking her to gently pull on her left earlobe and to massage her left ear a little bit. This will give a signal, 'I'm not listening to you.' "

(pause)

Higher Self: "We're asking her Guides – all her Guides, not just Prince – to point those away from her who do not need to speak with her specifically. We are asking that only the highest and the holiest connections come to her, and that they speak one at a time. She never thought to ask to reduce the number of requests before."

←→

Hypnotherapist: "With the volume being less will the communication be better?"

Higher Self: "Yes. She's had literally an estimated ten thousand Beings of Light trying to talk with her. Some shouting – some whispering. This is ridiculous. There are way too many."

(pause)

Higher Self: "She didn't have a good boundary. She's learned those in the last few months from her mother needing so much caregiving. This non-stop ear-ringing made it hard for her to speak and to channel. Which message to hear – which to share?"

(pause)

Higher Self: "Combine that with not being fully willing to speak due to all the punishments when a prophet and you can see the bolus of energy that became stuck as ear ringing."

(pause)

Higher Self: "Speaking in her case also includes writing her books. She is thrilled we have cleared her schedule so she can focus on writing and completing this book."

(pause)

Higher Self: "Another way of her communicating from the Divine is via podcasts. We will bring more radio and podcast guest opportunities to her and likely some video – TV – film."

←→

Hypnotherapist: "That's great. She had a question if she's setting up 'Magdalen's Book of Love' well as a future book?"

Higher Self: "Yes, she is. The breadcrumbs she's dropping toward it are quite energetically guided. She should keep going with them."

Hypnotherapist: "She has some questions about the details of self-publishing. Things like creating her covers and getting the books and short stories formatted. Can you comment?"

Higher Self: "She just needs to ask for energetic assistance in these areas first, and then surrender it to us. Be willing to not know the next step for a time. The ego needs to stay balanced and not move into fear. It takes time to align what's needed."

(pause)

Higher Self: "She can then return to the task when she's guided to do so, which may be as soon as the next day. This will help her not wear herself out so much. She'll be better synched up with the Divine from a practical task standpoint."

(pause)

Higher Self: "Things will go well from there, but there is a need to just get comfortable with the discomfort of not knowing what's next. Just try to keep your sense of humor. Don't be so serious! Her partner will help her with this."

Hypnotherapist: "Thank you. Is there another past life we should visit to help her?

←→

Higher Self: "What we'd like to suggest instead is to go through her full list of questions starting with the physical health. We'll take you to any past life that impedes or inspires what's needed."

Hypnotherapist: "Very good. Her first question was how to resolve the digestion and elimination challenges."

Higher Self: "There are no more past life issues presenting in this area. The comprehensive healing with Dr. Lorphan last night took care of it along with the other healing a few weeks ago."

←→

Hypnotherapist: "Wonderful. She has a question do the lower chakras need more support?"

Higher Self: "Yes, they did. Last night was a major healing. Her lower chakras were made larger and are moving more freely again. They are in good alignment with one another."

(pause)

Higher Self: "That was a major psychic surgery last night. Psychic surgery can frighten people, or they can disbelieve the efficacy – the effectiveness – so we chose to do it while she was asleep."

(pause)

Higher Self: "We knew we had her permission and request for aid. Resolving the digestion and elimination issues was the top item on her list for today. She fell asleep with her hands on her lower abdomen, working to heal it with Reiki healing energy."

(pause)

Higher Self: "Once that ninety-minute psychic surgery was complete, we assessed can she handle conscious knowledge of this healing? Can she be not only accepting but excited and in gratitude? Can she talk about it and explain it in a coherent, grounded way? When those answers were all yes, we awakened her, so she'd remember her 'dream.' "

Hypnotherapist: "Do these types of surgeries happen often?"

←→

Higher Self: "People are offered these opportunities for healing. You may be asleep, or you may be woken up. Or they come up in meditation or when fully conscious."

(pause)

Higher Self: "Because Dr. Lorphan is an off-planet surgeon – not of this world – it can really frighten 'humans' to have an 'alien' perform surgery on you. So many of you have forgotten your Star seed origins and your galactic families."

Hypnotherapist: "Is it done in the astral plane?"

Higher Self: "Yes and no. Depends on your definition of the astral plane. She was sound asleep at home in her body. She was not astral traveling. We met her half-way. We asked her to raise her vibration. We brought ours down."

(pause)

Higher Self: "Specifically they met in 7D in this instance. The seventh spiritual dimension or level of consciousness, which then has layers upon layers within. We discussed doing the surgery in 12D but chose to do it in 7D. This will allow her to hold the healing more easily in her human form as she recently moved up to 7D."

←→

Hypnotherapist: "So what happened then?"
Higher Self: "We woke her up and asked her can you remember your dream? She replied, 'Yes – I was having an unpleasant dream. I was out running errands in several stores and needed to use the restroom. But I couldn't find one or the line was too long, or the stalls were full or too filthy to use.' "
(pause)
    Higher Self: "She knew this dream was about elimination – letting go of what no longer serves her. She's had the dream numerous times before. She was aware of those dreams. After a three plus year struggle to heal her digestion and elimination, we took care of it for her. She was ready!"
(pause)
    Higher Self: "It was a profound surgery and clearing for her kidneys – her liver – her bladder – her urethra – her colon. It was a major surgery. Quite profound – a ninety-minute psychic surgery."

←→

    Hypnotherapist: "That's amazing. Can you overview the past lives impacting the issues she's been having with being dehydrated despite drinking plenty of water?"
    Higher Self: "Yes, I can. But you need to remember we're working with someone who's incarnated approximately 2,600 times into a body of some type – and only approximately half of them human."
(pause)
    Higher Self: "There have been lots of experiences where there wasn't enough clean drinking water. Water couldn't be found or was contaminated, or it was withheld."
(pause)
    Higher Self: "'Water is Life' is much more than a Lakota Native American belief. It's certainly more than a slogan. Your bodies are what – seventy percent or more water?"
    Hypnotherapist: "Yes. That's true. And that's a lot of lifetimes to process."
    Higher Self: "Yes. That's why we appreciate you following our lead of working from her list and then looking for the lifetime to resolve the issue or challenge. Working both the releases, the celebrations and excellent outcomes is quite brilliant. She'll be able to resolve it now."
(pause)
    Higher Self: "The human ego can too often be drawn to the sob stories. The drama and the trauma. We don't want her to get stuck in that place. We want to lighten up her seriousness. We need to look for the fun and joy for her! This is a fantastic way to keep your vibration high."

Hypnotherapist: "Thank you. Can we move onto wealth and career?"

Higher Self: "Yes, please."

Hypnotherapist: "She'd like to verify if her Emotion Code work with the practitioner she's working with is effective?"

Higher Self: "It is ahead of schedule. It is fantastic. Releasing these old emotions via this technique is finally going to resolve the root issue of the financial abundance lack she's been stuck in."

(pause)

Higher Self: "There is a beautiful contract between these two ladies. That practitioner owed Wendy several favors and is repaying it fully in this lifetime. She will help Wendy resolve her financial flow and to meet her partner. It's ahead of schedule – it's brilliant – it's going to change everything!"

← →

Hypnotherapist: "Thank you. Can we move onto relationships and past lives? Are there any more to release or learn from with her mother?"

Higher Self: "That was well-covered via the slave past life that came through earlier. She also knows about the two challenging caregiver lives with her."

Hypnotherapist: "Is she now establishing pristine boundaries?"

Higher Self: "Yes, she is – for the first time ever. The mother really was the litmus case as she was the hardest person to do this with. Let's thank her for being such an excellent teacher. This hasn't been easy for either of them."

(pause)

Higher Self: "She now has healthy boundaries with her mother in every arena – physically, emotionally, mentally, and spiritually. This takes care of her boundary issues with everyone else. No one else will test her this hard."

← →

Hypnotherapist: "Is she resolving her trust issues?"

Higher Self: "Trusting herself fully is the final stage. It's the proverbial chicken and the egg."

(pause)

Higher Self: "Physically healing her body and allowing it to be healed is finally possible because of her enhanced self-confidence, self-love, and self-respect. That allows the body to heal. And she has more self-confidence because her body is healed. One feeds the other."

(pause)

Higher Self: "So yes, trust is being restored from the serious issues she had with the Universe and with God since being present at the crucifixion."

Hypnotherapist: "I'd like to thank her Guides. Can Wendy return to the room now and come out of the hypnotic state?"

Higher Self: "Please state the present date in full for her. She could use a little help reorienting to the current day and time. She's eight months short of today's date."

(Hypnotherapist helped Wendy orient to the present day)

← →

Wendy: *(laughing)* "That's much better – I was still in February 2020. I was having trouble getting back to October. Thank you - this was so helpful! I didn't know about the arrow that we removed from my left kidney and the strong encouragement to more follow my intuition. Also, to keep working with the positive lives. I've done so much to release the challenging energy from past lives, but I haven't worked much with the most positive ones. This was amazing. Thank you!"

Chapter Fifteen – The Blue Mermaid & the Temple of Isis

On November 14th, 2020, I had my next past life regression therapy session in the series. I'd submitted my questions for my Higher Self and Guides ahead via email. My hypnotherapist helped me relax via several techniques as we began our session via Zoom.

←→

(Session in progress)
Hypnotherapist: "Step out of the tunnel into the Light. What are you sensing? Be there now."
(no reply)
Hypnotherapist: "Where are you now?"
Wendy's Higher Self: *(dreamily)* "I'm in a beautiful Temple. It's a Temple of Isis in Egypt. The river is flowing by. The Nile is so clean. The temple is so gracious. The space is quite open. It's so beautiful!"
Hypnotherapist: "What else do you notice about this temple?"
Higher Self: "There are flowers and other things carved into the pillars and into the temple building itself. The weather is wonderful most of the time. There are open cut-outs for windows. You can smell the flowers and different scents. I want to say incense. But it's not acrid or harsh. It's more like an essential oil scent. I'm just very happy to be back in the temple."

←→

Hypnotherapist: "What do you do there?"
Higher Self: "I'm in training as a Priestess. We do a wide variety of things to honor the Divine and to assist mankind and the planet."
(pause)

Higher Self: "The main reason I'm returning here now is to remember how to powerfully meditate in a natural and benevolent way to benefit mankind. We would meditate together to focus on a particular issue."
(pause)
Higher Self: "If we were getting visions of a volcano that was about to erupt, we knew better than to interfere. We knew the wisdom of Mother Earth in planning that sort of event, but we would meditate to ask for ease and grace. We would send love to that upcoming event. We'd work to have it be as graceful and beneficial as possible. We would not ask to prevent it as that's ego."

←→

Hypnotherapist: "Are there people there you have a close relationship with?"
Higher Self: "Yes, Mary does. Most of us are here for a lifetime. Our fellow priestesses become our family."
(pause)
Higher Self: "I want to clarify we're not required to stay here in the temple. There is no lifetime vow like for a nunnery."
(pause)
Higher Self: "There could occasionally be a good reason to leave. That cause would be accepted and discussed, and a plan formulated so your position could be filled."
Hypnotherapist: "Do you get the feeling the people at the temple incarnate with you in other lives?"
Higher Self: "That's a good question. Let me look."

←→

Higher Self: "I have had the good fortune to know Isis in many lifetimes. Let me examine the energy more deeply."
(pause)
Higher Self: "Who else? Is there anyone else in Wendy's life now that studied with her at the Temple of Isis?"
(long pause)
Higher Self: "No, Isis is the only common denominator. Mother Mary brought me here originally as Mary Magdalen when I was a young girl, but she only visits from time to time. She doesn't stay."
Hypnotherapist: "If you page through that life in its entirety, is there a particular event that stands out as a great learning moment?"
Higher Self: "Yes. The great learning is what I just stated. It's the power of that carefully aligned group meditation energy and the way that may – I stress may – play out in Wendy's life. The future is always changing."
(pause)
Higher Self: "She doesn't need to be in-person with people

or on Zoom or the phone to mediate in this powerful manner. She can simply reach out to people energetically to join their intentions together using this Mystery School technique."

←→

Higher Self: *(laughing)* "The Mystery School skills don't need to be a mystery anymore! Earth and mankind have raised their vibration enough there are no issues now with sharing these memories and abilities."
(pause)
Higher Self: "If there is a power outage and people get upset by that – or if there are various challenges that come up like the example of the volcano, which can lead to tsunamis and other quote 'natural disasters,' she knows she can simply meditate to reach people to help calm them with her heart and mind. She can also do it during the dream time. She's a Dream Weaver. She uses that ability only in a benevolent way."
(pause)
Higher Self: "It doesn't have to be all 3D like, 'I'm going to schedule a Zoom call!' Your infrastructure is likely to be going down for a time to allow for an energetic re-set. It's good to be as relaxed as possible about the upcoming storms whether they be metaphoric or literal. She'll just tap back into those skills in a calm and confident way."

←→

Hypnotherapist: "Okay, this is fascinating stuff. May we ask your Spirit Guides some questions?"
Higher Self: "Yes, they've all been here since before we started this morning."
Hypnotherapist: "Okay. What's the best way to address the continuing health challenges?"
Higher Self: "She needs to surrender those to the Overlighting Deva of her health. She's still working too hard to heal her own health. She's still being too independent. We would like to strengthen her relationship with the Overlighting Deva of her health."
(pause)
Higher Self: "She called in a new one recently, which was appropriate. Let's have that lovely being stand in front of her and the two of them get better acquainted. When she feels there might be a health issue or there is a struggle going on, she just needs to surrender it to that being – that's what she's for!"

←→

Hypnotherapist: "What does she look like?"
Higher Self: "She's beautiful. Stunning. She's appearing in human form, but she's all green. Green skin, green hair – green everything. She doesn't look 'alien' in any way – she's

310

part of the Earth. The Overlighting Deva of her health is coming up from the Earth."

(pause)

Higher Self: "She's giving Wendy a big hug and saying thank you for giving me my job back!"

Overlighting Deva: *(sounding tearful)* "You've been trying too hard to do my job for me. Trust me – give it over to me."

(pause)

Higher Self: "Wendy is doing that. Wendy is hugging her back – she is releasing the tension that she's still been feeling around her health."

Hypnotherapist: "Excellent. Are we ready to move on?"

Higher Self: "Yes, that will continue in the background. Wendy's Higher Self and the Over lighting Deva of her health will have tea and get better acquainted. You can ask the next question."

←→

Hypnotherapist: "How can she balance up the water and fire in her body? She's still dehydrated despite drinking lots of water and knows she needs more fire. We worked on this last time."

Higher Self: "Yes, let's address that right now. A fun, helpful way to do that is to bring in her fire dragon and her water dragon and allow them to become best friends!"

(pause)

Higher Self: "Then her fire dragon can get her metabolism working well. He can help rev up her engine – her metabolism. The water dragon will make sure it's balanced – it's not too much – so she's not struggling with dehydration."

(pause)

Higher Self: "We again turn this over to the Over lighting Deva of her health. That's who can best get her metabolism right, her liver, her kidneys, her adrenals all to be happy."

(pause)

Higher Self: "She had that powerful healing and surgery with Dr. Lorphan the night before her last session with you. Her stomach and digestion and elimination system doesn't need more surgery or even any energy tweaks. It just needs more time to get balanced up."

Hypnotherapist: "Very good."

←→

Higher Self: "Let's watch those dragons sashay in! They're very sensuous. Picture it being like Chinese New Year. Have you seen those outdoor parades with the big colorful costumes?"

Hypnotherapist: "Yes."

Higher Self: "They look like they're going to potentially

311

fight, but it's a playful dance. We want to invite those fire and water dragons back in for her. Her Earth and Air elements are finally well-balanced. We just need this bit of work today to address the fire and water balance."

(pause)

Higher Self: "She can just picture those dragons dancing together. It's beautifully choreographed and balanced. It's a dance for the ages! She can meditate for five minutes and have fun like at a Chinese New Year parade she's seen in Chinatown and on television. Find a YouTube."

←→

Hypnotherapist: "Great. What's the best way for her to energetically clear her home and property?"

Higher Self: "Her ritual has become stale so she's resisting doing it. It's perfect to do it on the Full Moon and the New Moon, but she should not beat herself up if she can't do it right on that day. Do it a day or two before or after is fine, too."

(pause)

Higher Self: "She just needs to take five to ten minutes to do a powerful clearing and balancing of the home and property preferably twice a month. The way she's using her pow-wow rattle – her intention – the way she's opening and closing her doors and windows is just right."

(pause)

Higher Self: "She just needs to spark it up – to keep it fun and easy. She can bring the dragons with her. She can invite Isis."

←→

Higher Self: "We would like her to connect more with Isis. That's why we opened today with returning to the Mary Magdalen life. Mary was in the Temple of Isis that life for ten years from ages nine to nineteen."

(pause)

Higher Self: "We want her to look at the privilege of this. Oh, my goodness, Isis is offering to help you clear your home! She can call in a specific Archangel – call in a certain past life. Again, she's been doing this work on her own for a long time so it's gotten a bit stale and boring."

(pause)

Higher Self: "She can wake up on the Full Moon Day – wake up on the New Moon Day – and ask, 'Who's going to help me clear my home and property today?' And then just have fun with it!"

←→

Hypnotherapist: "Okay. How is she doing with the new healthy boundaries with her mother?"

Higher Self: "Exceptionally well. She's remembering to take a breath before she interacts with her mother. Her mother is now respecting her boundaries ninety-five percent of the time. This is totally new for them. This is a tremendous accomplishment these two souls have not accomplished before in this lifetime."

(pause)

Higher Self: "To look at an eighty-one-year-old and her adult daughter and to see that they are finally being respectful adults with one another is fantastic!"

←→

Hypnotherapist: "Okay – the last question Wendy wrote is whether she's well prepared to hold the energy of peace for the planet even if there is a possible earth rift volcanic explosion and solar flares? She believes those may be coming to allow Earth to cool."

Higher Self: "Yes, she is. That's a perfect question to end with and we can then free form if there's time left."

(pause)

Higher Self: "This question is also why she went back to the Egyptian Temple of Isis at Philae when we started. It's now an island. It was rebuilt when the Nile was rerouted as the temple would have been under water."

(pause)

Higher Self: "The energy is still there at the rebuilt temple from when she was there two thousand years ago. She just needs to remember that lifetime and the experiences from when she lived and trained there as Magdalen."

(pause)

Higher Self: "We recommend she re-read her book draft about that lifetime in the temple. The purpose is not to edit it, but to reread it as it will open even more memories and doorways for her."

(pause)

Higher Self: "There may be significant time when she's possibly without electrical power and running on a generator. She doesn't run her computer or television then. She can print out the pages ahead to read by lantern light. She can read and charge her Kindle and cell phone from wall outlets that work when the generator's running. She has a secondary heat source and ways to cook. She'll be fine."

←→

Hypnotherapist: "Wonderful. I have one more question."

Higher Self: "Please proceed."

Hypnotherapist: "If we have a choice to pick our body, why this specific one?"

Higher Self: "She chose a challenging body to teach her how to be a healer. She is a marvelous healer from first-hand experience. She is not only doing past-life regression

313

healing during her sessions, but much more."

(pause)

Higher Self: "Past-life regression is a fantastic modality all on its own. Even if the practitioner has no other knowledge to contribute, they can facilitate healing assuming they step out of the way of the Higher Self and Guides, they can facilitate healing. That can be powerful."

(pause)

Higher Self: "Wendy is different because she has had so many health issues that she can truly feel the emotions her clients have. The health challenges were also how we were able to nudge her to get so much formal training – not only the Reiki Master, Certified Spiritual Teacher, and hypnotherapy training, but the formal channeling. She didn't plan any of that when she earned her MBA degree. It didn't present for almost thirty more years."

←→

Higher Self: "This doesn't really show when she's facilitating a Between-Lives session like she did with you because there she more needs to follow the script. It's a powerful script. The version she trained with is almost seventy-five pages."

(pause)

Higher Self: "That's a lot for most practitioners to work their way through live with a client while still following their intuition to best serve them. It's why not many are trained for Between-Lives work or for the Newton Institute trademarked Life-Between-Lives sessions. And the practitioner needs to be able to hold high vibration energy for not only the client, but for themselves, for four or more hours. Not everyone can do that. Some are more suited to the one-hour sessions like you facilitate."

(pause)

Higher Self: "Her two-and-a-half hour and four-hour past-life regressions she facilitates are truly Regression Healing sessions. She named them correctly from the beginning. They're more than a standard past-life regression. She teaches people how to heal in a temple and to connect with their Guides."

Hypnotherapist: "Excellent. Is it appropriate to move on?"

←→

Higher Self: "Yes. Let's have her go be a mermaid. It's so relaxing. She has lots of mermaid and merman past lives both in Atlantis and other lifetimes. Let's go to a true past life where Wendy was a mermaid."

Hypnotherapist: "Why a mermaid?"

Higher Self: "Because of the freedom of movement. So much of the Earth is water. It proves to Wendy she can breathe underwater and above water and survive anything

she chooses to. Not only survive but thrive."
(pause)
Higher Self: "That's why we're bringing this up. There may be some poor air quality coming up and that tends to make her uncomfortable. We want her to remember her magical mermaid lungs!"
(pause)
Higher Self: "COVID is a lung disease. You can feel the pressure of that where she lives in Washington State because there are currently over two thousand new cases a day."
(pause)
Higher Self: "We want her to stop watching and listening to the small bit of news she's succumbing to. She's falling too deeply into the news regarding the COVID volume spiking."
(pause)
Higher Self: "We knew it would. We warned her there's another flu season to get through with COVID. Flu season is technically September through June which matches the traditional school year. But flu of course spikes November through March or April. Since school isn't in session in some locations it won't be as marked this September to June."
(pause)
Higher Self: "Let's return to the mermaid life. We see her as a mermaid. She's very blue. There's lots of blue with her long blue hair, her pale blue skin, and scales."
(pause)
Higher Self: "We want her to feel that freedom of movement and know that her lungs are fantastic no matter what is going on."

←→

Higher Self: "This brings us back to her Shapeshifter energy when we explore being a mermaid. We want her to let go of any negative associations with shapeshifting. She's been punished several times for it."
(pause)
Higher Self: "She's a master shapeshifter. That's part of what caused the severe scoliosis this lifetime – having felt smacked for shapeshifting. It's a wonderful ability and skill to shapeshift. It's not evil. She'll know when to use it at the right time for the right reasons."
(pause)
Higher Self: "Let's let go of any punitive experiences that she's had around witchcraft, too. She only uses her white witchcraft. There are no issues there. She's in full integrity and making good choices."

←→

Higher Self: "We'd like her to let go of any restrictions being told she can't perform telekinesis – time travel – shapeshift – be whatever she wants to be. This leads back to the confidence we talked about in earlier sessions."

(pause)

Higher Self: "We're having her put her hands over her solar plexus chakra to be whatever she needs to be – is meant to be – wants to be. We're having her let go of what other people think and have punished her for because the punishments always related to being fully in her power!"

(pause)

Higher Self: "She has not connected these dots before. That's why the challenging contract with her former boyfriend. He was to 'Break her heart repeatedly, until she stood in her power fully, without abusing it.'"

(pause)

Higher Self: "It can perturb people that she knows how to work with time when time slows down and turns elastic, and she's told to get ready to help. It can concern some that she knows how to shapeshift and to jump timelines."

(pause)

Higher Self: "I'm not talking astral travel as a soul – I'm talking about time travel with your body. She knows the vibrational level of the planet is not quite aligned to do so again. She'll know when it's time to perform these sacred practices once more. She'll be guided to them."

(pause)

Higher Self: "This use of her power won't come from an egoic place – or a scarcity or lack mindset. It will be divinely guided and in divine right time. She'll know when to share these skills, and when to work with others who want to remember and relearn their skills and abilities, too."

Hypnotherapist: "Okay."

Higher Self: "This is why the mermaid energy is so freeing for her. It's quite magical. She can be fully in her power and trust herself."

←→

Hypnotherapist: "I can imagine. To me it brings the energy of that white sand and palm trees – the beautiful blue water and swimming."

Higher Self: "Absolutely. There's so much clear beautiful water element here. We're bringing in that fun fire dragon for her as there's so much water in her system. We need to keep it balanced for her."

(pause)

Higher Self: "Oh, that's interesting. The fire dragon is presenting as male and the water dragon as a female. That makes perfect sense as what those properties are."

(pause)

Higher Self: "She's had too few males in her present life.

She's now bringing in that fire dragon well. He's going to build campfires for her. He's going to clear the brush for her. The two dragons can make a home there."

(pause)

Higher Self: "These are all the constructive aspects to fire – the warmth – the companionship – the enjoyment of that to balance all that water mermaid energy."

Hypnotherapist: "May we move forward and end?"

Higher Self: "Yes."

←→

Hypnotherapist: "I'd like Wendy to come forward in time to the present day. Let's thank her Spirit Guides and integrate this into her daily life. She can be more present in the now.

(pause)

Hypnotherapist: "How are you feeling?"

Wendy: "I'm doing great! I'm hearing to commend you for this session via Zoom. It was divinely guided. There's no difference in the results between in-person and over Zoom."

Hypnotherapist: "Exactly. We're complete for today."

Wendy: "Thank you."

←→

As always, I looked forward to listening to the recording of our session as I couldn't remember much detail. We'd have one more session in the series to close out the year and likely the book.

Chapter Sixteen – Joe Bats Clean-Up!

I sent my questions ahead for my December 12th, 2020, session. I hadn't realized it would be a Full Moon when we scheduled the date. The Full Moon is a powerful time to release energy that doesn't serve us. The New Moon is equally powerful with helping us attract beneficial new energy.

I told my hypnotherapist I was having trouble grounding. I hadn't been able to lie down on my bed as I vibrated right up out of my body. I was sitting on the floor of my bedroom with the cold winter air coming in from a window as we began. I had all my grounding crystals around me. My top priority was to get grounded.

←→

(Session in progress)

Hypnotherapist: "You can now step out of the tunnel into the light when I reach the count of zero. Where are you – what are you sensing?"

Joe (DiMaggio): "She's been doing so much ascension work that your suggestion she take the staircase down into the earth to the healing garden really helped. She normally naturally goes up a staircase to the Light to a healing garden, but she's too ungrounded today."

(pause)

Joe: "We did a lot of grounding work with her this morning to be able to have this session. She's experiencing vertigo which is a classic sign of not being grounded in the body and with the planet."

(pause)

Joe: "What we'd like to suggest to help her ground is that she spend five minutes outside each day walking around her

own yard and property, preferably in the morning."
(pause)
Joe: "Or she can wait until after lunch and see if there's any sun to enjoy and warm it up a bit since it's winter. She can walk around in her own yard and get more grounded. That's our first suggestion. This will really help her."

←→

Joe: "She heard us well she shouldn't just ground to Earth each day. She needs to ground to the planets she most relates to. Venus, the Purple Planet and into the Pleiades. She should definitely ground to Sirius – the dog star."
(pause)
Joe: "Grounding to those places will give her the shape of a square – that will be quite stable for her versus just grounding to the magnetic core of Earth."
(pause)
Joe: "No – just a moment. We're showing her to ground first to Earth and then to the other three locations around her as a triangle. She'll be grounded in four spots, but it's not a square."
(pause)
Joe: "When she feels nice and grounded again, she can return to that process of asking Prince to bring through one clear message from one of those planets. That will bring the ear-ringing under control."
(pause)
Joe: "In the interim, speaking aloud with us is good practice for channeling messages from the Divine. She doesn't need changes – just more time. It's good she asked this question as she hadn't seen any progress but that's because she's been doing some rapid ascension again."

←→

Hypnotherapist: "Fantastic. She'd like to know is she working well with the new Overlighting Deva of her Health – with Midge?"
Joe: "Yes, that was the fun little name they agreed on yesterday. It's too long and formal to always call her in as 'the Overlighting Deva of my Health.' We suggested she just call her Midge."
(pause)
Joe: "Yes, they are working together well. They are developing their relationship. It is quite beneficial and will continue to blossom. It's just what she needs. No adjustments are needed – just a round of applause for them both!"

←→

Hypnotherapist: "Fantastic. Okay - what about the fire and water dragons. Are we increasing the metabolism?"

319

Joe: "Yes. There's been lots of progress. It's a balanced healing. Her work with Raven ManyVoices including with the dragons has been extremely helpful. They should continue to work together."

(pause)

Joe: "She's been surprised she can't find her dragon statue but has been accepting it's wherever it needs to be. She's not being thoughtless or irresponsible. Her spiritual tools like her crystals move where they need to be."

(long pause)

Joe: *(smiling)* "She now knows where her dragon is! We just told her it's inside her dining room cabinet. It's inside the antique vitrine she has again now from her 1800s past life as Eliza Ann Webber, the Sea Captain's wife up in Halifax."

(pause)

Joe: "She consciously brings up that fire and metabolism every day. She's asking Midge to do the work with ease and grace. This is an important health issue for her."

←→

Hypnotherapist: "Have I had positive past lives with my mother – is there positive energy to bring forward?"

Joe: "This is an excellent question. We're so glad she learned this technique with you."

(pause)

Joe: "I'm looking for positive past lives with Elizabeth. Plimoth Plantation was the best. There have been several positive past lives where Wendy was Elizabeth's mother. Wendy sensed that history when they had reversed roles, but it annoys her mother. The energy came across to her mother as a know-it-all child. She didn't have the wisdom at that time to celebrate a wise, sensitive child."

(pause)

Joe: "Wendy celebrates this energy in her daughters – particularly her youngest. There are no more useful past lives with her mother to explore or to celebrate. Her best stance is to just do her best to be kind – to be patient with the mother. Their boundaries are remarkably better. There's a marked improvement between them. Everything is good as is. No changes needed."

(pause)

Joe: "I'd like to add she should do the astrology reading with the gal in the United Kingdom who looks at the client's time in the womb from an astrological viewpoint. There may be a bit more gold for Wendy to mine there. She should have that reading with Debbie Buss."

←→

Hypnotherapist: "Has she had any positive lives with her younger daughter besides Plimoth?"

Joe: "I'm seeing multiple positive off-planet lives. They're in the Pleaides – mainly on the Dog Planet."

(Joe laughs heartily)

Joe: "This is a play on words. She and her daughter had a high point in their relationship when the young lady began college. They volunteered together for dog rescue work. It was meant to remind them of their dog star past lives together."

(pause)

Joe: "That was the best energy for them in a shared past life. When Wendy wants to tune into positive energy with her youngest, she needs to look off-planet. Her daughter simply doesn't like Earth."

←→

Joe: "Wendy had a dream a few nights ago she was trying to bicycle to visit her youngest at college. She realized she's had the same dream before. She just couldn't get there. There were all types of ridiculous impediments."

(pause)

Joe: "It wasn't going well. She turned the dream lucid and asked us, 'Why have I been guided to say the Ho'oponopono forgiveness prayer daily to my daughter for an entire year, yet I still can't connect with her? Has it not been long enough, or has it not been effective?' "

(pause)

Joe: "We told her don't try and bicycle to your daughter's college anymore – take an Uber! She asked us, 'Why would I take an Uber versus driving myself? What's the difference energetically? She got it immediately."

(pause)

Joe: "The difference is there'd be a driver. An Uber driver. Anyone in a dream with a title – a hotel clerk, an Uber driver – is a Guide. That meant she should ask one of her daughter's Guides to help mend this bridge between them."

(pause)

Joe: "Archangel Gabriel stepped forward immediately and told Wendy, 'I work with your youngest regularly, like I do with your mother. You are wise to choose to work with one of her Guides as your daughter is struggling, whereas you are doing great.' "

(pause)

Joe: "She now knows to look for positive lives off-planet and to work with her daughter's Guide."

←→

Hypnotherapist: "Excellent. How is her homing beacon looking – how does it attract one's partner?"

Joe: "The homing beacon is only present in women. It's located in the lower right abdomen. It's not a physical organ.

It's not like a surgeon can say look, there's the homing beacon."

(Joe laughs)

Joe: "When the energy of the homing beacon is healthy it signals a wonderful mate or life partner. It works somewhat like a lighthouse. It's a beacon that can be both seen and heard. Hers is looking great! It was a tiny little pinprick a few years ago. Then at one point it got out-of-whack and was exuding energy that attracted the wrong partner. He fell in love with her and proposed, but she knew he wasn't the right man for her."

(pause)

Joe: "We then turned off her homing beacon to reset it. It's now a beautiful Coleman lantern flame about six to eight inches in height. It's burning bright!"

(pause)

Joe: "Her new partner will feel comfortable with her from the start. It will be like coming home for them both. There's no better feeling."

(pause)

Joe: "That's what a homing beacon is. It's how a woman attracts the right man when she's feeling happy and healthy herself."

← →

Hypnotherapist: "Thank you. Do Wendy and her new partner have any energy to clear from Salem? Did they have a shared past life there during the Witchcraft Trials?"

Joe: *(sighing)* "Yes, they were both there at the same time for that drama and trauma. Salem, Massachusetts was a nasty travesty of justice. It was just a tiny blip compared to what happened in Europe with all the witchcraft accusation injustices for centuries. We know you had a life like that you explored during your past-life regression with Wendy."

(pause)

Joe: "Salem was the U.S. version. Less than a hundred people were put to death. Some died of starvation or exposure being unfairly imprisoned. It's not exactly balmy in Massachusetts in the winter as the early Colonials found out."

(pause)

Joe: "So let's move from history to specifics. Her new partner was one of the persecutors during the Salem Witchcraft Trials. He's done a bang-up job cleaning up this old energy. He's now incredibly fair – extremely patient. He's almost too patient, but he has backbone and will stand up for what's right."

(pause)

Joe: "He's scrupulous now – he cares about what's fair, what's right, what's just. He's cleaned up his energy from being an unfair accuser and is cleaning that up for the planet. He feels like he might be an attorney now?"

(pause)

Joe: "She stood up to testify to end the Salem Witchcraft Trials. This was terrifying to do as a female teenager in that time and place. She stood up to end the travesty of justice. She still has that backbone and courage now."

(pause)

Joe: "Those unnecessary deaths – those ridiculous trials were terrible. They've both cleaned up that energy well. They're both on the side of what's right not only for themselves as individuals, but for humanity."

(pause)

Joe: "It's important to know there won't be any problems with past life energy between them when they meet. He's not going to consciously recall that life. He'd probably burst out laughing if she asks his permission to share an impression of it with him. It would be an interesting conversation. She should initiate it at the right time if he's game."

(pause)

Joe: "They're going to have great fun together! I'm also seeing a powerful melding of her #PeaceNow energy with his #JusticeNow energy. She's been looking for that type of energetic match as has he. That energy will up-level for the planet with their help."

←→

Hypnotherapist: "She wants to be certain she should be publishing what she's tangentially written about her family. Has she appropriately protected their privacy?"

Joe: "Yes, she's been struggling with that. When she shares something publicly that includes other people, she's been using the bar of 'Is it kind, is it true, is it necessary?' as her starting point."

(pause)

Joe: "We're checking if she's settled down in her heart hearing this from me. It's not wise to publish when you have push-pull energy like this. These issues should be energetically cleared first."

(pause)

Joe: "We're bringing in her parents Higher Selves. Both are saying 'Yes, daughter, go ahead with your book. It's appropriate in the way written – move forward.'"

←→

Joe: "Let's look at her daughter now. She's concerned there are quite a few comments in Wendy's sessions about her daughter's struggles. Should that be changed? She purposefully never uses her daughter's name to provide her privacy and dignity."

(long pause)

Joe: "Wendy needs to be truthful and in integrity. It would be a big takeaway to remove all that information – all that progress. It would unweave what those two souls have accomplished to now exclude it."

(pause)

Joe: "Her daughter's Higher Self is here. She's saying, 'Mom, just go ahead and include it. You're overthinking. I don't care. It won't bother me. You need to do what you need to do. It's not going to be a further divide between us. It's written from a place of caring – it's from a higher perspective – it's from the Light. You're not betraying anything I've told you. It's from your soul perspective. Go for it.' "

(pause)

Joe: "That makes her feel so much better. Her energy is calming down."

←→

Hypnotherapist: "That was the last question. Is it appropriate to wrap up?"

Joe: "Do you have any suggestions for her to continue to move forward? If you don't have questions for Wendy, there are about one hundred angels and Ascended Masters gathered for you both."

(pause)

Hypnotherapist: "What are the most important things for Wendy to consider right now?"

Joe: "For Wendy to consider in her life?"

Hypnotherapist: "Yes."

Joe: "To be true to herself. To continue to move forward in feeling joy every day. To really enjoy the freedom that she now has and has not had before."

(pause)

Joe: "We are adjusting the financial freedom. She will have that for the first time. We are adjusting she is finally healthy. We are bringing in the freedom and joy from having a happy romance for the first time. The career and service work has never been an issue for her. She excels there easily like she does with energy."

←→

Hypnotherapist: "Very good. Anything else?"

Joe: "I'd like to address why so many good speaking opportunities that she worked hard to get and did an excellent job with didn't convert to clients? Here's why. It's because the self-confidence and self-respect had not yet been healed. They are now. The boundaries weren't there. They are now. This is what our work together during this past life regression therapy series really boils down to. That's the bottom line."

(pause)

Joe: "We want her to be confident she's included the right content in this book. She is on the best path for her next publications. She is moving into a three year numerologically with a lot of writing, her new partner, and a few wonderful select clients. She is not meant to have twelve or more clients a week. It's not her path. She's to have a few ideal clients for the long sessions – those that are a terrific fit with her vibrationally."

←→

Joe: "She needs to update her website. We know she doesn't love that task as it's clunky and fiddly. We'll help her. She should ask me to sit with her as her career guide for the first time. We'll have fun with it! I wasn't using websites when I passed on in 1999 but am certainly not stuck in a time-warp. I've learned and grown so much since then and will do more so as I partner with Wendy. I've been learning and learning! Let's put it to the test."

(pause)

Joe: "She should call in Mary Ann, the avatar for her ideal clients at the same time for the website review. The three of us will work together on some quick but meaningful and effective website updates. Mary Ann is to help with the specific language to attract the right clients. She will help with the key words. Wendy can call her website provider or hire someone if needed to help her better organize all her interviews on the website, for example, but needs to put the time in to get the energy right first."

←→

Joe: "You may now move forward and end today's session. Please help her ground again and orient to the current day and time. Remember, she's a gifted time traveler so we need to bring her back to the current day and time. Help her ground again via that garden down the staircase into the Earth."

(pause)

Joe: "Wait – I have an idea. I'm adjusting her homing beacon to always bring her back to her current life, to the present day and time. It can serve that purpose as well as attracting the partner. This will help her relax she can never get lost. The abilities are all within her. Home is within herself wherever she is. She's not going to go through the terrifying time travel misadventures that make good TV and film content!"

(Joe laughs heartily)

←→

Hypnotherapist: "Great. It's time to come back to your present life as Wendy. You're feeling great – you've learned so much today. Let's thank your Guides and Higher Self and

Super Conscious and all that helped us today. I ask that they help you integrate into your daily life – that you be more present in the now – more grounded – lighter. Let's go back to that garden – get comfortable there – connect from it to Earth – you can feel more peaceful, more connected to Earth – connect with Mother Nature – be more present in the now."

(long pause)

←→

Joe: "That helps. Her Guides are bringing in the fairies and nature spirits. It's like a scene from David and Goliath. She's sitting on the ground like she is in her room right now and they're weaving things over her feet and legs. They're helping her get fully back on the planet."

(pause)

Joe: "It's wonderful she's moved up to 7D but that's created a challenge to be in the now here on the planet as she's so up with the angels. Now she'll be more down with the fairies, too. She also knows to ground to the other planets I listed. She can balance better now."

Hypnotherapist: "I'm going to count you up to five – you're feeling good, relaxed and grounded."

(long pause)

←→

Wendy: "Okay, I'm back. I know it's Saturday, December twelfth, 2020 – 1212 – 2020. I didn't realize when we scheduled that today is a Full Moon. I'm here now on the planet, oriented to the right day and time. I'm grounded – phew."

Hypnotherapist: "Yes. That's some strong numerology with 1212 and 2020."

Wendy: "There's some remarkable astrology, too. Things that haven't happened in hundreds of years are coming to pass in the next few weeks. I've been careful to not do spiritual bypass and to stay in the now as I've been feeling myself so away with the angels."

(pause)

Wendy: "I've had a lot of vertigo the last few weeks and knew that meant I wasn't grounded. I did a session with Gregg Kirk on Monday, and we redid my grounding protocols. I know that may sound odd to people who don't have to think about grounding their energy. For example, I find that athletes – especially runners and joggers – don't have to even think about grounding. They just naturally are well-grounded in their energy."

(pause)

Wendy: "I was recently gifted some home gym equipment and my Guides asked me to put it out on my back porch. I was so surprised as I was planning to put it upstairs in my guest room. Having it outside on the covered porch helps me ground while I exercise."

(pause)

Wendy: "Thank you so much for today's session. This was incredibly helpful!"

Hypnotherapist: "You're so welcome. This was great."

Our session was complete.

← →

I'd been hearing "Your life is already written in the stars!" from my Spirit Guides for years but had never fully grasped what that meant.

In December of 2020 I had the womb astrology reading with Debbie Buss that Joe had recommended. It was amazing! I was thrilled to know I'd healed my Chiron wound and had also moved through my second Saturn Return.

In January of 2021 Debbie studied Joe DiMaggio's and my natal or birth charts as well as our numerology. Both Joe and I have a life path six in numerology when you add up the digits in our dates of birth and keep adding until you reach a single digit. Life path six is about service, balance and responsibility and is often called "The Caretaker."

We both had our Chiron in Pisces at a connection of five degrees. Chiron is the dwarf planet named for the wounded Greek centaur and is commonly known as the "Wounded Healer." Chiron represents our deepest wound and what we need to overcome in life. Its location in our birth chart is quite symbolic.

There are twelve houses in astrology. It's important to understand which house each of the major planets is located, based on the date, time, and location of your birth. Chiron was in Joe's first house – the House of Self.

Chiron is in my twelfth House of the Subconscious. I see the twelfth house as being a place of transformation where we can work with our shadow, our past, and determine our best future. The twelfth house is also known as the House of Sacrifice.

The moment Debbie described our Chiron placements to me verbally, I saw Joe hand his bat over to me. It felt like a scene from "Field of Dreams." I could see the twelve houses like the face of a clock. I felt like my soul had run around the bases from the first house where Joe had his Chiron to the twelfth house where my Chiron is located.

I felt a tremendous sense of happiness my soul had completed the hard work to heal that pattern of deep wounding. I'd done the hardest part of healing my Chiron wound in my relationship with the soul mate who woke me up spiritually in 2010. Chiron often correlates to painful romantic relationships.

Joe's Transit North Node at his death was in the sign of Leo. This lined up with my Natal North Node. My North Node is in Leo based on the time of my birth. The North Node indicates our destiny and ultimate life lessons. This felt like another symbolic passing of the torch.

Joe DiMaggio and I also share the same three key numbers as an additional synchronicity. I find it amazing that could all be read from our birth charts and based on our numerology. Our life truly is "written in the stars" in many ways.

Debbie Buss can be reached at debbiebuss1@gmail.com or via her Facebook page at https://www.facebook.com/debbie.buss2

←→

I finally felt fully at peace including with my historic, Biblical, and famous past lives. I felt protected and guided for the next big adventures with the Angels, and with additional youthing, shape-shifting and time travel adventures which I now saw had a connection.

When I had a challenging day I could always meditate and go be a dragon, a mermaid, or anything else I needed to be. It was time to be 'fully in my power, without abusing it' and 'to let go of what other people think' to live my life purpose. Freedom!

Book Discussion Questions

1. What role do you feel Joe DiMaggio was meant to play in Marilyn Monroe's life?

2. What do you believe was Joe and Marilyn's primary soul contract together?

3. Do you feel there was an element of destiny in how their relationship played out over time?

4. If so, how did destiny balance with the free will choices both made?

5. How important do you think mastering forgiveness was for Marilyn and Joe's souls to progress?

6. Is there an area where you need to 'let go of what other people think?'

7. Do you feel connected with your own Higher Self or soul wisdom? What about your Spirit Guides?

8. Do you feel on track with your life purpose?

9. Do you feel you've been successful in balancing your ego and resolving unnecessary fear?

10. Have you been able to discover any of your past lives? If yes, how did this most benefit you?

11. What would you most like to resolve or enhance in your life with a past-life regression healing?

Author's Note

As a Past Life Energy Healer, Wendy helps adults from around the world release pain, anxiety, and depression. Wendy leads clients through a healing process through the techniques she has learned working with some of the world's most renowned hypnotherapy experts including Dr. Brian Weiss,. People can finally start living this life with joy and purpose when they release the energy that does not serve them.

Register for a complimentary group energy healing with Q & A or workshop with Wendy via her website: *https://www.wendyrosewilliams.com/*
Or google her full name, *Wendy Rose Williams*.

You can also listen to a selection of Wendy's radio and podcast interviews from her website

Join Wendy's mail list to be the first to learn about new publications, programs, and specials:
https://www.wendyrosewilliams.com/contact
Your email address will not be shared or sold.

Additional Books by
Wendy Rose Williams

- *Regression Healing I: The Huntsman, the Lord High Mayor and the World War II Solider*

- *The Flow I: Plimoth Plantation (the prequel)*

- *The War Dog* – a short story in the multi-author collaboration *Heaven Sent: True Stories of Pets That Have Touched Our Hearts in Miraculous Way* (Proceeds benefit veteran and animal charities)

"Waking Up Spiritually!" Podcast

Join Wendy LIVE once a month for the "Waking Up Spiritually!" podcast
https://www.facebook.com/groups/wakingupspiritually
The podcast is recorded and archived on the Waking Up Spiritually website as well as on YouTube and on your favorite podcast apps:
https://wakingupspiritually.com/broadcasts/

Contact Info & Social Media Links

Website:
https://www.wendyrosewilliams.com/

Email:
Wendy@WendyRoseWilliams.com

YouTube:
@WendyRoseWilliams

Facebook:
https://www.facebook.com/gwendolyn.rose.79

Instagram:
@WilliamsWendyRose

Amazon Author Page:
https://www.amazon.com/Wendy-Rose-Williams/e/
B07N5WZNDK